Fieldwork, Participation and Practice

Fieldwork, Participation and Practice

Ethics and Dilemmas in Qualitative Research

Marlene de Laine

SAGE Publications
London • Thousand Oaks • New Delhi

SAGE Publications Ltd
6 Bonhill Street
London EC2A 4PU

SAGE Publications Inc.
2455 Teller Road
Thousand Oaks, California 91320

SAGE Publications India Pvt Ltd
32, M-Block Market
Greater Kailash – I
New Delhi 110 048

British Library Cataloguing in Publication data

A catalogue record for this book is available from the British Library

ISBN 0 7619 5486 4
ISBN 0 7619 5487 2 (pbk)

Library of Congress catalog record available

Typeset by Photoprint, Torquay, Devon
Printed in Great Britain by Redwood Books, Trowbridge, Wiltshire

To Lisa, Thompson and Georgie

Contents

CHAPTER 1

Introduction

Now that the richness and power of ethnography and other kinds of qualitative research are confirmed in social science, practitioners work through the complications of fieldwork looking for less harmful possibilities for making sense of people's lives. The free exploration of intriguing ideas was tempered in anthropology over the last half of the twentieth century by the importance given to other values, including human rights. The individual has the right to determine for him or herself what others might do with their ideas and attitudes. A great deal of soul searching has taken place; terms like deception and informed consent have emerged to inform of a concern by anthropologists and sociologists for the rights of the individual and those studied.

The emergence of new forms of social research, especially critical participatory and applied research, has meant fieldworkers must make their research goals explicit and seek permission from and respect the privacy of the people (Barrett, 1996). Knowledge for its own sake was no longer acceptable among some segments of the academic audience, who argue for a critical perspective on social life. The issues emerging in qualitative research in contemporary times importantly include what we consider constitutes ethics, and an explication and extension of traditional ethical models to deal with the new activism (Lincoln, 1995).

With the 'crisis of representation' the emphasis has largely been concentrated on textual matters but there are a number of fieldworkers who would prefer to see more attention paid to grass-roots level actual fieldwork practice (Fabian, 1991). The conditions of fieldwork (paradoxes, ambiguities and dilemmas) that require researchers engage in face-to-face contact with subjects, rather than assume an impersonal detached approach of positivism and quantitative research, are considered inherently problematic. The production of knowledge puts fieldworkers in close contact with subjects and this closeness creates problems with the management of anonymity and confidentiality (Lincoln, 1995). Ethical problems and dilemmas are a necessary part of fieldwork. They cannot be adequately anticipated and usually emerge *ex post factum* (Fabian, 1991).

In contemporary fieldwork the trend is for more participation and less observation. Detachment of the subject from the researcher and the research is rejected. The gap between researcher and subject has to be closed and there is to be communion with methods, analysis, interpretation and 'writing-it-up', and with social relationships. The new 'activism' calls for social relationships that are intimate and close and requires researchers to demonstrate more authenticity, sensitivity, maturity and integrity than in previous moments of social science (Lincoln, 1995).

Fieldwork becomes especially problematic when researchers cross boundaries of conventional and sensitive topics, public and private space, overt and covert methods, field notes to texts, and overlap roles and relationships. Multiple roles and relationships in the field are a feature of some feminist participatory and activist approaches. The researcher who demonstrates empathy and care and engages on an emotional level with subjects can enter the ground of the therapist, but without the same training and back-up support in sociology and anthropology needed for debriefing or counselling services and sessions. Overlapping or multiple roles and relationships present researchers with a range of complex and unavoidable ethical and practical dilemmas.

Friendships that facilitate access to confidences and physical regions that are private and secret can make problematic disclosure and publication of personal information. Research goals can become complicated when ethical and professional obligations to disclose and publish clash with moral and personal obligations to subjects to ensure secrets be kept private, confidentiality maintained and trust not betrayed. When various parties with different interests and expectations clash there can arise an ethical and practical dilemma for which there is no satisfactory solution, but only a compromising experience that must be lived through and lived with.

The 'ethics of relationships' that is established in the field between the researcher and subject carries over into the text. The author must accord the subject the same respect in print as would be conveyed in the face-to-face situation; one must not say in print what would not be said to someone's face (Hornstein, 1996). Professional and research standards of a discipline do not favour concealing information and 'gatekeepers' may exert a powerful moral pressure on the researcher to meet their demands of disclosure. Managing the conflicting expectations of gatekeepers, sponsors and subjects can put pressure on the researcher to conform, but one party (usually the subject) may be compromised, along with the researcher.

Ethical dilemmas

Ethical and moral dilemmas are an unavoidable consequence, or an occupational hazard of fieldwork. Dilemmas and ambivalences do not always reveal themselves clearly and are virtually impossible to plan for in advance (Punch, 1986: 33). An ethical dilemma arises when the researcher experiences conflict, especially conflict that cannot clearly be addressed by one's own moral principles, or the establishment of ethical codes (Hill, Glaser and Harden, 1995).

An ethical dilemma may be described as a problem for which no course of action seems satisfactory; it exists because there are 'good' but contradictory ethical reasons to take conflicting and incompatible courses of action. Ethical dilemmas are situations in which there is no 'right' decision, 'only a decision that is thoughtfully made and perhaps "more right" than the alternatives' (Hill, Glaser and Harden, 1995: 19).

When confronted with an ethical dilemma, the researcher needs more than a code of ethics for guidance (Hill, Glaser and Harden, 1995). The researcher needs some understanding of how to use the code together with other resources to make a decision that is more 'right'. The individual's intentions, motivations and ways of cognitively structuring the ethically sensitive situation are equally important to ethical and moral practice as are conforming to or violating an ethical code. Ethical decision making includes being consciously aware of one's values, principles and allegiance to ethical codes, intuition and feelings, within a context that is characterized by professional and power relationships.

Sieber suggests a number of ways in which ethical dilemmas may arise in research on human behaviour and social life (Sieber, 1996: 15–16). Students may be attuned to ethical issues in research but still find themselves enmeshed in dilemmas because they had not foreseen how research may impact on the participant's privacy, or adequately anticipated the risk of harm arising from research for participants and for the self. On the other hand, an ethical problem may be foreseen but there may be no apparent way to avoid the problem (Sieber, 1996). The researcher may 'assume' disclosure of information will cause participants to consider they have been 'wronged' and this may lead to attempts to reduce harm through partial self-censorship (Lee, 1993). The researcher may foresee a problem but be unsure of what to do because the consequences of subsequent action are unclear (Sieber, 1996). The student's current moral outlook may simply be inadequate to the task of envisaging ethical implications arising from use of non-verbal communication.

The literature about the ethical decision-making process describes ethical codes in various forms, notably absolutist and relativistic, and the general moral principles underlying codes (do not betray confidence and trust; do no 'harm' to others). From the perspective of ethical codes and guidelines, dilemmas are almost exclusively looked at objectively and from an intellectual distance (Hill, Glaser and Harden, 1995: 23). In actual fieldwork, researchers experience ethical dilemmas with an immediacy and personal involvement that draws on intuition and empathy, feelings and emotion. These dimensions cannot be separated out from decision making in a complex power structure. In a feminist approach, one's personal experience and involvement are 'legitimate' and necessary factors to take into account when making ethical decisions.

Situational and contextual elements cannot be adequately handled by drawing on ethical codes because other elements (moral values, ideals, personal and professional standards, empathy or intuition), a necessary aspect of feminist analysis, are missing. Ethical codes are general and absolute. They are intellectualized, objective contructions that make no allowance for cultural, social, personal and emotional variations. The personalized relationships that are currently recommended in some segments of the academic audience underpin one of the emerging issues for discussion in qualitative research today: the extension and recon-figuration of what researchers consider ethics in research is about (Lincoln, 1995). The tradition in ethics committees has been to see ethics in terms of what we do to subjects, rather than the wider moral and social responsibilities of simply *being a researcher* (Kellehear, 1993: 14). The traditional impersonal and objective ethical model assumed the separation of researcher and researched, but the new fieldwork being practised suggests less distance or detachment between researchers and researched; and a new ethic or moral imperative that is not yet codified.

Ethical dilemmas that admit of no comfortable outcome but must be lived are experiences that researchers need to know about. The researcher without a satisfactory solution to an ethical problem may have to reconcile the self to compromise. Contingencies or controversies of fieldwork, however, need not be seen only as obstructions to data collection; they can be experienced as opportunities for celebration since they force self-awareness and give promise of change. A moment in fieldwork may be created to implement a more 'open' attitude toward what subjects expect of the researcher and how they experience the fieldworker. This could contribute to the establishment of fieldwork that is more moral (Liberman, 1999).

The aims of this text are:

1. To promote an understanding of the harmful possibilities of fieldwork.
2. To foster ways to deal with ethical and practical dilemmas.

In each of the chapters, attempts are made to describe the pitfalls and dangers likely to confront the fieldworker; to provide examples of ethical and moral dilemmas, how they were created and how the fieldworker solved or lived with the problem; and what, if anything, could have been done to avoid them.

In Chapter 2 consideration is given to the issue of moral choice. Students are advised to adopt a new form of research that is more moral and less morally objectionable (Schwandt, 1995). The concept 'moral career' provides a useful conceptual frame for investigating the moral dimensions of the interpretivist inquirer, especially her or his conceptualization of their fieldwork practice and conceptualization of self (Schwandt, 1995). The term 'career' has usually been reserved for those who expect to enjoy pathways leading to a rise in status within respectable professions. Goffman (1961a) used the concept to trace the *moral* aspects of mental patients, whose passageway through the institution involved the internalization of a fair amount of *moral* transformation. The concept moral career facilitates a dual focus and makes possible a stereoscopic look at internal matters (felt-identity), and external public matters of official position in society (self-image) (1961a).

In Chapter 2 Schwandt's (1995) hypothesis is explained. He offers no comprehensive examination of the moral career of the interpretive enquirer, only a few observations about one specific passage in fieldwork that allows for two ways of problem solving. Fieldwork requires the inquirer confront controversies; these controversies constitute a moral passage, defined as wrestling with 'problems of self-identity and relationship' (Schwandt, 1995: 133). Controversies, as problems of identity and researcher–respondent relationships in actual fieldwork, for a truly moral outcome, require 'organization of the connections between self, other and world, and reflection on what is right to do and good to be as a social inquirer' (Schwandt, 1995: 134). Fieldwork problems demand the union of intellect and passion to constitute a moral passage, an emphasis only on the intellectualizing aspect of research means something of the human quality is missing.

Ditton's (1977a) work is drawn on to show how the conceptual tool 'moral career' has been used in social science to identify different contingent moral steps or decisions that facilitate a fair degree of *moral* transformation. The example focuses on salesmen at a bakery who are inducted and acclimatized to normative practices for the situation, and how they attempt to neutralize *moral* consequences to ensure they do not contaminate the production of a total social 'me' (to use interactionist terminology). The normative experience for salesmen is assumed as Ditton's lived experience, since participant-observation was carried out in the bakery. Engaging with 'situational honesty' may not be that uncommon for fieldworkers, burdened by 'guilty knowledge' that could adversely impact on self-image and felt-identity.

The practical side of the ethical problem is made understandable by a focus on a variety of neutralization techniques that provide a sociological perspective on co-workers processes of adjustment to activities that affect identity (Ditton, 1974). There is a need to ensure that the subsidiary and minor deviant role assumed by salesmen does not assume a controlling and master status and contaminate the production of a total social 'me'. To this end a variety of excuses and justifications are employed, an overview of which is provided in this chapter.

The traditional ethical model, in both perspectives (absolutist and relativist), is examined and compared with an alternative ethical model proposed by Denzin (1997). He calls the 'postpragmatic' or postmodern alternative to the 'traditional impersonal positivist ethical model', into which students have been socialized during undergraduate years and against which postgraduates continue to justify fieldwork, characterized by *looking at*, rather than *being with* the other, the 'feminist communitarian ethical model'. Other ethical issues to be considered in Chapter 2 include covert research and the issue of 'passing' (concealing discrediting information that could damage identity).

Chapter 3 features the issue of access, mainly in terms of access to a conceptual framework for staging appearances and performances; but access is also looked at in relation to entry into back regions of social establishments as well as back regions of the mind. In fieldwork, uncovering the member's intersubjectivity is central to one's capacity to portray emotional and motivational attunement to a group's moral order and to perform activities appropriate for an audience the fieldworker confronts. Access to 'insider' information is crucial to 'impression management' and precedes the major research task, that of data collection. Staging the self appropriately, with appearance and performances, is shown importantly to require access to codes, 'recipes' or scripts (terminology depending on methodological or philosophical perspectives).

Access to 'experts' in the field, who assume the role of trainer and facilitate the researcher's socialization to a subculture, and observation of degradation ceremonies, that bring together previously implied scattered pieces of information, are shown to facilitate access to a moral order and provide a shared understanding of appropriate acts for staging subsequent appearances and performances. 'Status degradation ceremonies' relate to any communicative work that results in the transformation of another's identity to that of subordinate figure (Garfinkel, 1956: 420). Status degradation ceremonies usually feature a number of witnesses who share a common definition of the situation of a rule breaker, and who are sufficiently inspired to moral indignation to promote public denunciation. Such denunciation ceremonies or confrontations between a marginal person and agents of control serve to communicate the values and norms of the social group. They can illuminate the source of ethical and moral dilemmas that confront the researcher and co-workers in a specific socio-political situation.

The concept 'moral community' is explored to highlight the ambiguous and anomalous situation that can be the context in which the researcher is lodged, and required to perform activities in an appropriate way, in advance of knowing what 'appropriate' means in social, motivational and emotional ways for that situation; projecting a definition of the situation for 'normals' is made questionable. In situations where rules and roles are not clearly formed or are ambiguous, the stage is set for making mistakes. Time is needed to learn the script. One not able to recognize and generate acceptable behaviour display for the situation may risk being caught 'out of face' or in 'wrong face', and is confronted with the task of having to 'save face'. A critique of Goffman's earlier work (1959, 1967) is included in this chapter, since Goffman assumed performing roles would be unproblematic for 'normals'; his earlier work is critiqued on such grounds in this chapter. During the preliminary phase of fieldwork, when the researcher is learning implicit roles and rules, the cues to correct for discrepancies may be inadvertently ignored. This may evoke the antagonism of others towards her or him and cause the researcher to experience personal stress.

Informed consent is considered in terms of access to multiple roles and relationships. From a dramaturgical perspective, the manipulation that is implied in human social life is carried over into research practice with the suggestion of a continuum where research is more or less overt. This type of argument raises the issue 'when is manipulation not considered ethical?' (Hunt and Benford, 1997). The concept 'passing' once again captures matters of 'impression management', with management of undisclosed discrediting information about 'the self', when the actor is in the damage-control mode (Goffman, 1963: 58).

The dramaturgical approach to social phenomena acknowledges that the staging of the self or 'impression management' is problematic. With dramaturgy, life proceeds like a drama, with each person as actor, director, audience and critic of herself and her relations to others, who are seen as having the same qualities (Lyman and Scott, 1975: 107). Concepts borrowed from the theatre (actors, roles, scripts, performances and audiences) are terms used in this and other chapters, in relation to techniques used and the principal problems with impression management in the field and in the text. Appearance is shown to set the scene for social interaction and reference is made to the work of Stone, who claims 'through appearance identities are placed, values appraised, moods appreciated, and attitudes anticipated' (Stone, 1962: 101).

Chapter 4 directs a focus on back regions and sensitive methods, and problems with deception and betrayal of trust. Privacy is linked with back regions and relates to a person or group's interest in separating self from others. Fieldworkers have traditionally explored activities in physical locations that are generally not frequented by the public. In ethnographies there is sometimes a distinction made between two vantage points, 'front stage' and 'back stage', and associated interactional modes. According to Goffman (1959: 110), when we examine the order that is maintained in a given region we find two kinds of demands – 'moral and instrumental': the former refers to rules regarding respect for people and places. Instrumental demands refer to duties such as an employer might demand of an employee to whom they pay a wage (care of property, maintenance of work levels, and so on).

In the front region of establishment actors express appropriate conduct for the sphere of activity in progress with characteristically formal behaviour, composure, involvement and social interaction to capture respect for the activity in progress. Appropriate behavioural displays are aimed to convince an audience of what actors purport to be and what they purport to be doing. A back-stage vantage point may provide the researcher with access to interpersonal conflict, private family problems and attitudes and behaviours that deviate from the ideal or official policy (Hansen, 1976). A back-stage vantage point may require the researcher engage in some mild form of deviance or deviation from the official or normative behaviour for the situation. Back regions allow informal social practices to flourish in relatively non-threatening circumstances. Back-stage language consists of 'reciprocal first-naming, co-operative decision-making . . . playful aggressivity and kidding' (Goffman, 1959: 129).

How social interaction and information are managed in back regions constitutes the interpersonal dimension of privacy. Interacting in such areas and reporting on such matters is crucially linked with ethics. Privacy rights may be threatened where uninvited observations of behaviour that diverts from the ideal, the official or 'legitimate' are made. Researchers who focus on such situations can anticipate finding themselves faced with problems of disclosure that relate to protection of privacy and from harm. Observation of back-stage activities carries a responsibility to respect a person or group's interest in having information managed appropriately.

One who intrudes into back regions may pose the threat of risk to others who fear exposure; formal approaches for access may be refused. Those who study back region sites and back-stage activities may be drawn to the use of dubious methods for infiltration of 'fronts'. Researchers have gained access to back regions without consent. Deception, betrayal and clandestine observation, aspects of the 'darker side' of fieldwork (Wolcott, 1995), conjure in the minds a picture of back-region activities that are not strictly 'legitimate'.

Addressed in this chapter also are complicity and probing, strategies used to gain access to back regions like corridors and women's powder rooms, and to back regions of the mind. Informed consent is shown to be no guarantee that research will be ethical and moral. A focus on some of the early interactionist studies show that a number of Chicago School ethnographers performed fieldwork in back regions and used dubious methods. At the time they may not have been overly concerned by the ethics of fieldwork, but later some were burdened by 'guilty knowledge'.

Researchers had not anticipated they would be socialized into performing activities defined 'sensitive' by virtue of choice of topics, which have lodged them in back regions. As a consequence, they may have internalized a fair amount of moral transformation and been required to use strategies of neutralization to protect identity. In this chapter a number of strategies are explored. These include researcher-based and ethical relativist-oriented rationales, the 'indeterminacy repertoire' and excuses and justifications. Students are advised to be cautious with choice of fieldwork topic, setting and methods since associating with sensitive phenomena has the potential to contaminate. An example is provided that shows how the researcher's moral career was perceived by an outspoken other, at a time when attempts were being made to use past fieldwork experiences to make a theoretical point, in a class instigated for the purpose of learning about qualitative research.

Chapter 5 focuses on the difficulty with directing the role-playing self into and through roles and relationships in the field. A consideration is given to personal qualities as prerequisites of role and the various types of roles that may constitute being a researcher (peripheral, active and complete membership, insider/outsider, complete observer/complete participants), and the strengths and weaknesses of different modes of involvement. Multiple roles and overlapping relations are addressed with a focus on the researcher as therapist, and the associated ethical and practical problems discussed. Friendships and 'friend-like' relationships are addressed, whether friendship is different in fieldwork and the 'closeness/distance dilemma' that can have ethical ramifications for the researcher.

Feminist approaches to overlapping roles and relations are explored and close friendships formed in the field are considered in relation to 'exploitation'. One may become detached from role, cease to consider the academic group as the prime and dominant reference group and 'go native'. The tendency to 'go native' may be abetted by 'prolonged engagement' (Lincoln and Guba, 1985). The researcher who is in the process of becoming detached from the profession may subsequently struggle with role conflict (Adler and Adler, 1987). These matters are also discussed in Chapter 5.

Multiple roles are shown to set up 'a conflict of interests' or of consciousness and create ethical and practical dilemmas. The dual roles of friend and researcher create the possibility of collecting information willingly shared, as well as unwittingly conveyed (Hansen, 1976: 132). The ethnographer may use confidences passed between friends as data. A paradox of the communicative process is that the more relaxed the participants are in the company of the researcher, the less likely the transfer of personal and secret information will be inhibited, and the more likely betrayal and trust could occur with disclosure. The individual's rights of privacy may be best protected by ensuring subjects are aware the friend is also a researcher, and by careful consideration of materials that should be kept 'off the record'. Dual roles are shown to create ethical implications with disclosure and publication.

Chapter 6 directs a focus on audience segregation and juggling with the interests and agendas of various parties linked together in the research enterprise, (gatekeepers and sponsors, the academic community, comprised of supervisors, other staff members and postgraduates, assessors and publishers, the subjects and, importantly, the self). Ethical dilemmas emerge from disparities between the rights of various parties to the research enterprise and the clash of expectations and demands made by powerful parties. The rights and responsibilities owed various parties are addressed: the subjects' right to privacy and protection from harm; the wider community to knowledge that holds promise of benefit to the community; the profession to original knowledge for the discipline; and the ethnographer's right to protect the self from the harmful possibilities of fieldwork and disclosure. When disclosing information to a wider audience, the researchers are shown to be vulnerable. They must take into consideration the receptivity of the wider audience, mainly constituted by academics, and the participating audience's interpretation of the author's representation and position on disclosing information (Hunt and Benford, 1997: 116). The latter obligation is shown sometimes to clash with the former and cause ethical and moral dilemma.

Postgraduate students rely on their supervisor/s to advise them on matters of ethical significance. Postgraduate students are not in a particularly strong position to question the advice offered by a supervisor and most postgraduates would feel uncomfortable about disagreeing with superiors, especially over the most important feature of a researcher's work life – the alibility to do research. They would avoid conflict with supervisors. Academics are unlikely to support a student who disagrees with a colleague or opposes the bureaucratic system on moral and ethical grounds. The structure of the researcher–supervisor relationship can blunt the student's sense of ethical and moral sensitivity and the bureaucratic structure can work against researchers assuming a high moral and ethical stance.

The hierarchical system of academic departments can encourage the neophyte researcher to believe responsibility can be transferred to another person. The postgraduates' sensitivity toward their own ethical obligations are shown to be adversely affected by a number of forces operating outside the researcher's control, including the impersonal bureaucratic structure which gives an impression that matters of ethical importance can be dealt with at another level. The researcher–supervisor relationship may become strained where 'assumed' rather than 'actual' responses of subjects to textual representations create a pressure for partial self-censorship and the profession demands disclosure. Possible ways of dealing with such circumstances are provided in this chapter.

Fieldwork may trap the researcher in a web of cross-cutting ties that run counter to one's moral values, ideals, personal loyalties and allegiances, intuition and feelings, and require major compromise of self. Case studies are provided to highlight the ways that different parties might seek to have agendas implemented and what the consequences are in moral and ethical terms for the researcher, the subjects and the research. Most settings of ethnographic interest are complex and stratified, with differing and shifting allegiances and loyalties that have the potential to set up a 'conflicts of interest' (Fabian, 1991). Physical separation of audiences may facilitate information control and protect identities to some extent, but ultimately the researcher must address the matter of conflicting loyalties, obligations and expectations.

Chapter 7 looks at field notes, ethics and the emotional self. Contemporary researchers are paying more attention to the ethnographer's emotional experience, as a valuable way of interpreting findings, as well as understanding the ethnographer's fieldwork experience (Jackson, 1990). Without description and analysis of the emotional dynamics of interpersonal relations a valuable piece of the framework or context necessary to interpret findings and understand the research experience is lost (Berg, 1988; Jackson, 1990).

During fieldwork the ethnographer must work out her or his relationships in the field to other participants, to various parties with an interest in the research and to their emotions (Jackson, 1990: 29). The process by which the researcher moves from writing field notes to a final written account is by no means obvious, but we know some researchers have sought solace in an impersonal, detached approach toward fieldwork and field notes. The traditional approach towards emotions has tended to be superficial; a 'cognitive bias' in sociology and anthropology has meant neglect of the affective and subjective dimensions of experiences in the field.

The norm of traditional or modern ethnography, that downplayed the emotional dynamics of interpersonal relations in the field, and emotions generated within the researcher as they conduct their work in the field, may have clouded the researcher's perceptiveness of what counts as data. Researchers have responded in various ways to the suggestion that they record in field notes such information as emotional states and feelings. Reference is made in this chapter to the fusions of thinking and feeling that are evident in the traditional representation of fieldwork experience in field notes, with consideration given to field notes that depict epiphanies (Johnson, 1975; Lehnerer, 1996).

Field notes provide a glimpse behind the scenes, a look at impression management, as it was taken for granted among fieldworkers at different moments in the historical unfolding of qualitative research in the social sciences. Textbooks on fieldwork almost exclusively focus on gaining entry, establishing rapport, building trust and so on, but critics have identified the step-by-step plan or process as far too simplistic, since fieldwork appears as a series of resolvable problems when in fact this is not the reality. Each step in fieldwork is affected by the development of interpersonal contingencies in the setting. Being in the subject's world means being surrounded by the real life contingencies, as an enduring problematic of fieldwork (Gumbrium and Holstein, 1997: 68–69). Contingencies make the researcher vulnerable and may cause personal stress.

I discuss in this chapter the place of emotions in traditional fieldwork and in contemporary feminist scholarship. An overview is provided of the social constructionist view of emotions, with an emphasis on Hoschild's 'emotion work' (1979, 1983). Young and Lee's (1996) analysis of Young's field note account is explored. I take into consideration degradation ceremonies and epiphanies that have functioned to high-light the highly personal and emotional aspects of fieldwork experiences. Epiphanies are shown to be 'turning point experiences', moments when people redefine themselves and their life projects (Denzin, 1992a: 82). Such interactional moments 'leave marks on people's lives (and) have the potential for creating transformative experiences for the person' (1992a: 15). 'Role detachment' may constitute an epiphany or 'turning-point event', or the death of a family member or near death experience of a research subject, or a point in the moral career of the interpretive inquirer, when there is realization that all 'honesty exits' are closed and they must live with the consequences, or when the lived experi-ence of fieldwork forces a realization that the methods section of a dissertation proposal is more appropriately the topic of the doctoral thesis (Lehnerer, 1996).

The liminal properties of field notes are explored in this chapter, with reference to betwixt and between words, betwixt and between selves and betwixt and between worlds (Jackson, 1990). Supporting evidence of crossing boundaries between worlds and selves is found in the work of McGettigan (1997) and in the field notes provided by Lehnerer (1996). A discussion of field notes and ethics covers auditing the content and form of notes and cultural scenarios reflected within them that provide a commentary on the emotional displays of research respondents to researchers in the role of moral entrepreneur. Field notes are shown to reflect on patterns of 'involvement', 'comfort' and 'identifying', as collective experiences of fieldworkers of various theoretical and philosophical persuasions, published in ethnographies of mainstream sociological literature, that ideally are templates for learning; but which can become problematic for the management of 'emotion work' when there is lack of fit with actual fieldwork practice (Young and Lee, 1996).

Chapter 8 looks at 'textual management' of self and others. Academic writing has undergone considerable change during the last few decades, particularly since the ground breaking text *Writing culture: the poetics and politics of ethnography* (Clifford and Marcus, 1986), the companion volume *Anthropology as cultural critique* (Marcus and Fischer, 1986) and Van Maanen's *Tales of the Field* (1988) ushered in the 'writing culture' debate in the mid-1980s. A brief historical overview is presented of the 'crisis of representation' debate.

Prior to the postmodern turn, anthropology and sociology have not been overly concerned with communicative contexts (dialogue, social relationships, voice, intuition and feelings). The position of the third-person omniscient author in realist texts, which spoke on behalf of others with an authority based on having 'been there', was not questioned. The main critique of 'ethnographic realism' is shown to have come from within the discipline of anthropology. Ethnographer critics, broadly sympathetic to ethnography and themselves with considerable experience in the use of the ethnographic method, questioned their own practice, reporting styles and procedures, and accused others of not being reflexive enough and for failing to adopt a critical attitude (Brewer, 1994). In questioning their own practice, ethnographers have also drawn attention to the problematic nature of the author, the playing out of power and ethical relations through 'voice'.

In this chapter emphasis is on the alternative contemporary approach to textual representation, emphasizing in particular the issue of author and the concept of voice in its multiple dimensions, and political and ethical implications. How to present the author's self in text, while simultaneously writing in the subject's accounts and representing their selves, is the main focus of the chapter. The contemporary focus on voice is shown not to be exclusively around the theme of power, but rather on ethics or the moral relationship of the observer and observed. The feminist ideals of equality and solidarity between the researcher and researched that underpins the two-pronged crisis set in motion broadly within the academic audience with the 'writing culture' debate calls for the emancipation of voices.

Biographies, autobiographies, confessional tales, confessional and dramatic ethnography, such new forms of writing in disciplines like anthropology and sociology, are explored in relation to socio-political, ethical, moral and personal concerns. The focus on dramatic sequences captures the presentational style of new experimental ethnographies; the stories or narratives experienced by the ethnographer in the field are dramatic events with transformative potentiality (McGettigan, 1997). Some say writers have turned cultural objects, including themselves, into subjects. 'Dramatic ethnography' is shown to focus on a particular event or sequence of events of obvious significance to the cultural members studied (Van Maanen, 1995).

The 'ethics of relationships' is shown to surface in the text in the way authors demonstrate the same respect in print to those with whom they have formed close relationships in the field. One is being advised not to say in print what they would not express to others in the face-to-face social situation (Hornstein, 1996). The 'textual management of self' requires the author give attention to the public's right to know and the subject's right to privacy. Emphasis is given to the author's need to be accountable to relationships they write about, but to balance these with ethical and moral imperatives (there is the public's right to know that needs consideration). The decision to write the self into the text in sociologically relevant ways, in case studies, life histories and auto-biographies, is recommended, but with recognition that such practices produce a sufficient amount of descriptive material to make a deductive disclosure. Links could be made between the researcher and subjects and information divulged that they would prefer others did not know about.

The greater freedom to experiment with texts is recognized as not automatically a guarantee of a better product. New styles of writing are shown to require new criteria to evaluate the quality of qualitative inquiry. In particular, reference is made to verisimilitude, aesthetics and ethics. When moving from fieldwork to 'writing it up', decisions have to be made on how best to present information to persuade an audience of the text's credibility (or verisimilitude) and for promoting appropriate moral and ethical tone.

In this chapter, disclosure and publication are portrayed as events that make the ethnographer-author vulnerable to critics from the two main audiences (academic and subject), and a successful performance is linked with partial 'self-censorship' (Lee, 1993) and 'ethical proofreading' of manuscripts (Johnson, 1982). Harms from fieldwork are generally thought to occur with publishing and disclosure (Lee, 1993). The problem posed by secrecy moves beyond 'how to get it' to include 'what to do with it' (Fabian, 1991). Data themselves are not necessarily sensitive or particularly harmful, but the possibilities of causing harm accrue from the uses to which data are put. The new ethnographer or postgraduate needs adequately to anticipate problems of disclosure and publication and be mindful of potential ethical and moral implications.

When deciding what to include in the text and how to include it, the author goes beyond reporting what actually happened to interpreting how an audience will respond. The social, emotional, political and ethical implications of fieldwork may all feature in the author's perceptions of audience receptivity. Anticipatory strategies of 'writing it up' enable the author more adequately to deal with identity, loyalties, obligations and interpretations. Strategies of 'self-censorship' are dealt with. Some authors are shown to omit materials from published reports in consideration of self, professional associates, the research institution and research participants (Lee, 1993: 187). Others decide not to publish at all. Some intentionally delay publication so as to promote good personal relations, protect individuals and groups from harm and avoid becoming entangled in embroilment of various kinds.

Moral and ethical problems may arise where individuals or members of a group are not appropriately acknowledged, or acknowledged in a manner they deem to be less than appropriate, given their status, past experience or role performance in a given team project that is being written about. To be appropriately presented requires attention be paid to protocols. Included in this chapter is a discussion of acknowledgements, referencing and the ethical and practical issues associated with co-authorship.

Ethnographers who enter another culture (as well as those who do fieldwork at home and enter subcultures) must be personally and pro-

fessionally responsible for the problems they choose to study, their conduct in the field and the use to which their findings are put (Partridge,
1979). Each of these aspects of fieldwork constitutes a moral dilemma.
New ethnographers and postgraduate students cannot adequately foresee the ethical and moral consequences of fieldwork. This book covers
sensitive topics, back-region study, dubious methods, multiple and overlapping roles and various role relationships (power, intimate and social),
the necessary negotiations between the researcher and others in professional and power contexts. The conditions of fieldwork (the paradoxes, ambiguities, indeterminacies and dilemmas connected with these
dimensions), in a type of research that requires the researcher be in
contact with subjects, rather than the impersonal detached stance of
positivist quantitative research, means ethical and moral problems are an
inherent part of fieldwork (Fabian, 1991).

Controversies and contingencies of fieldwork, however, are not to be
viewed merely as obstructions to observation and cause for avoidance of
fieldwork. The controversies and contingencies may be regarded as
opportunism for celebration, since they carry the potential to make
the researcher less immune to what others expect and experience the
researcher as, and thus force self-awareness. There is the promise of
development of moral researchers and moral fieldwork in the future.

CHAPTER 2

The moral career of the qualitative fieldworker

A number of external forces have been recognized as influential to the rise of ethics in research: the rise of feminism and feminist scholarship; consciousness with the rights of the individual; the emergence of critical and participatory approaches in social science research; and the establishment of ethics committees within various disciplines, university departments and research institutions (Punch, 1994). Within the various social science disciplines, notably anthropology and sociology, and feminist scholarship there has been more emphasis in recent times given to ethical and moral dilemmas of fieldwork, and concern with the traditional ethical model (comprised of both absolutist and relativist perspectives), as being too impersonal, objective and rational to handle the practice of fieldwork that has moved towards a more personal, interactive and moral form.

The conditions of fieldwork (paradoxes, ambiguities and dilemmas) that is qualitative, by way of contrast to quantitative research inquiry (positivistic-oriented and impersonal), that put the researcher in direct contact with people to form various types of relationships (power, personal and social), make fieldwork inherently problematic (Fabian, 1991). Ethical and moral dilemmas are an occupational work hazard of fieldwork that the researcher cannot plan for, but nonetheless must be addressed on the spot, by drawing on values, ideals, ethical codes, moral and professional standards, intuition and emotions.

A significant moral issue at the heart of fieldwork practice in social science is the call for more participation and less observation, of *being with* and *for* the other, not *looking at*. The alternative to the traditional detached aloof observer, distanced from subjects to foster analysis and interpretation, is the researcher in the 'round'; is the thinking, feeling human being who is caring, sharing and genuinely interested in friendship and the needs of others. The new form of fieldwork being suggested not only puts people in contact with others in more sensitive ways than in past moments in social science, but also calls for more maturity, greater sensitivity, authenticity and integrity. It also creates difficulties with the management of *anonymity* and *confidentiality* (Lincoln, 1995, 1998). The traditional absolutist ethical model that favours impersonal relations and objective, rational, intellectualizing of problems seems less able to address the actualities of fieldwork in social science than ever before.

The priorities of ethics committees tend to centre on the potentially harmful interventions of researchers in the lives of people, the issue of informed consent, and with ensuring the confidentiality of data on study participants (Daly and McDonald, 1996). The generalized and narrow focus tends to give the false impression that ethics in research is about 'what we do to others', and tends to neglect the wider moral and social responsibilities of *simply being a researcher* (Kellehear, 1993: 14). Many ethical problems and dilemmas of fieldwork arise from unanticipated consequences, not outcomes from a researcher intent to deceive and betray the trust of others. There is an implied assumption with the traditional ethical model that once the objective, rational and impersonal dictates of codes are met, so too are the researcher's obligations to research subjects; but in the climate of new forms of research emerging this clearly is not the case.

Ethical codes and guidelines are by necessity generalizations and therefore lack the complexity and specificity of any given ethical or moral dilemma. Ethical dilemmas, from the perspective of ethical codes and guidelines, are looked at objectively and from intellectual distance (Hill, Glaser and Harden, 1995: 23). Ethical dilemmas in fieldwork seem less to do with informed consent and more to do with overlapping roles, relationships and the interests, expectations, allegiances and loyalties of parties concerned. In the immediacy of personal involvement in a par-ticular ethical dilemma, situational or contextual, personal elements come into play (values, ideals, moral, professional and personal standards, intuition and feelings). These elements cannot be completely separated from ethical decision making in the actual practice of qualitative field-workers, particularly with feminist scholars.

In this chapter students are being advised that there is a moral choice to be made which differentiates between being a disinterested, aloof and essentially traditional or modern researcher, or one who wants to be *with* rather than *look at* the other. The new form of fieldwork practice that is proposed requires a new ethic or a new moral imperative to replace the objective, impersonal traditional ethical model (comprised of two per-spectives, absolutist and relativist) that assumes distance between the researcher and the researched. One of the emerging issues in the social sciences as we enter the twenty-first century is the extension and reconfiguration of what we consider to be ethics in qualitative research (Lincoln, 1995). What is proposed is a replacement of the impersonal, objective traditional ethical model with 'the feminist ethic of care' or 'the feminist communitarian ethical model' (Denzin, 1997), to govern the more human and moral approach to fieldwork.

This is a scene-setting chapter insomuch as there is consideration given to two possible ways of being a researcher (an objective neutral observer and a morally involved researcher). These are two extremes, since being a neutral observer is virtually impossible in long-term fieldwork; there are degrees to which one is involved during fieldwork in social, ethical and emotional terms. The utterly detached observer, who stands aloof and is 'dispassionate', would seem to be unable to blend a range of cognitive, emotional and ethical capabilities together and unite the analytical with the moral. We know, however, that the researcher takes to the field a repertoire of roles and face-saving practices; that multiple roles include 'learner', 'friend' and 'collaborator'; and that such roles unite the researcher and other people in bonds of friendship, rather than isolate and detach them (Rosaldo, 1994: 183). Long-term immersion in the field is a total experience that demands all of the researcher's resources – intellectual, emotional, political, intuitive and moral. The fieldwork experience makes problematic any notion of the identity being compartmentalized into, on the one hand, an 'analytic psyche' and, on the other, a feeling human being with likes and dislikes, fears and concerns.

One may equate the covert researcher, who conceals identity, deceives others and betrays trust, as a morally neutral and 'dispassionate' observer, in some ways akin to the positivistic-oriented 'scientists' who remain detached from people they observe in the field, but the comparison is too simplistic. The self of the covert researcher may be experienced variously, as not 'dispassionate' and uncaring but sympathetic toward the feelings and concerns of subjects, and yet also seemingly an unfeeling and morally neutral observer for whom relationships and people are not personally meaningful (Mitchell, 1991). To stand 'dispassionately' aside at crucial moments is to be an 'outsider' in external appearance, but internally the identity is by no means detached or concealed. There are no 'dispassionate observers, only researchers who are represented and experienced' (Mitchell, 1991). Such ideas are explored in this chapter with a focus on the moral career of the covert researcher.

Choices available to the researcher

A case in question

Schwandt (1995) has some thoughts on the moral career of the interpretive inquirer and what it means to *be* a social inquirer, not so much in methodological or pragmatic terms but in a moral sense. He found students struggling with two very different ethical choices during the process of becoming and being an interpretive inquirer, each entailing a different conceptualization of the kind of researcher they were expected to be. In his paper 'Thoughts on the moral career of the interpretive inquirer' (1995), Schwandt draws on Goffman's concept moral career to explore the moral dimensions of the interpretive inquirer. The concept of career identifies 'the regular sequence of changes . . . in the person's self and his framework of imagery for judging himself and others' (Goffman, 1961a). The concept or frame directs a focus on self, in internal and external aspects (for example, an image perceived and felt by the actor, and an image portrayed for the public through role and status).

Schwandt's (1995) working hypothesis is that during fieldwork the interpretivist inquirer confronts a 'moral passage' that leads to one of two different 'career paths'. For simplicity sake he calls these career 'A' and career 'B'. With the former career, the researcher finds solutions to the controversies of fieldwork by turning to an impersonal, universalistic ethical model. With the latter, confronting controversies in fieldwork constitutes a 'moral passage' that may involve wrestling with problems of self-identity and relationship. Problems are not conceptualized as having solutions so much as being lived; they draw on the intellectual faculties and the passions. The mind, emotions and feelings come together in the thinking person when organizing connections between self, other and the world and when reflecting on what it is 'right' to do, and 'good' to be as a social inquirer (Schwandt, 1995: 134). The moral passage traversed by the interpretive inquirer involves addressing technical, methodological, ethical and political strategies and techniques.

Prior to entry to the field postgraduates are preoccupied with developing a focus for the study, concentrating on finding a problem, selecting methods and a methodology. At this stage a set of techniques shapes the image of the self-as-researcher. Establishing rapport and trust may be considered necessary skills required to gain access and need learning about. Participant observation may be understood as a technique that leads to the formation of relationships for designated ends. Participant-observation provides access to data that may otherwise not be possible using methods like structured interviewing or questionnaires (Bernard, 1994). The student draws information about fieldwork from textbooks on qualitative methods, or by reading and rereading modern and post-modern ethnographies to familiarize one with themes as background to understanding ethnography and participating in the dialogue of one's discipline, whether this be anthropology, sociology, education, and so on.

As fieldwork unfolds the student grapples with a series of methodological and ethical–political issues, perhaps not previously read about in textbooks on qualitative research methods and journal articles and only vicariously experienced through the words of others (Schwandt, 1995). Eventually controversies come to be lived realities as the novice ethnographer interacts with respondents and informants and confronts experiences that others have previously spoken about. They may begin to worry about the moral implications of cultivating friendships in the pursuit of ethnographic goals, or about the need to be sympathetic toward observations that have real and negative impact on participants. The act of confronting controversies marks the interpretive inquirer's entry to a moral passage or turning point event in a moral career (Schwandt, 1995). When problems emerge the interpretive inquirer's response may be blunted by circumstances beyond her or his control. Other problems may reveal themselves most dramatically as contingencies, or turning-point events in a moral passage, and may cause considerable shock. Some contingencies of a moral career may stand in stark relief against the routine everyday practices in the field and literally force self-awareness upon the researcher, compelling her or him to attempt to understand what others expected of and how they experienced the researcher.

From the perspective of an impersonal, universalistic ethical model there is an assumption that a rational and intellectualized solution will be found to a problem. The researcher is required to adopt the appropriate strategy or technique. A solution may be found by selecting for a contingency of fieldwork in this way but this does not have the potential for promoting moral transformation in the researcher, since the impersonal ethical model deals with objective, rational and intellectualized matters mainly and not intuitive, emotional, moral issues. On the other hand, the interpretivist inquirer may be challenged in a passage or contingent step in fieldwork by problems that do not wholly admit of solution, such as ethical and moral dilemmas. The interpretive inquirer may experience moral transformation of self as a result of being 'open' to the expectations and experiences of others and not immune. Problems of identity and relationship in career 'B' are not to be solved so much as lived with passion.

A feature in the socialization of postgraduate students in the social sciences has been identifying with two main paradigms or worldviews (positivist and interpretive), and with recognizing sets of ideas about the nature of the world, of ways of being in the world, what it means to do research that is 'scientific', and appropriate methods. Metaphors of the positivist paradigm like objectivity, control and utility have filtered into other paradigms (interpretive and critical), to inform and guide postgraduate students in ways of being in the world and *looking* at human behaviour rather than *being with* people. What needs importantly to be recognized, along with methodological, technical or pragmatic issues of fieldwork, is what it means to be a fieldworker in moral terms; how selves of interpretive inquirers take shape in moral careers, to create and uphold the model way Schwandt says we should be as inquirers (1995).

When formulating a response to the question 'How shall I *be* toward these people?' a universalistic/scientific frame for knowing about others may guide the interpretive inquirer. They may import impersonal and utilitarian ways of being in the world with the other into the setting. From this perspective, people are perceived as means to an end. Schwandt (1995) argues there is moral choice to be made; there is an alternative set of moral norms and expectations (norms of caring, sharing, nurturing, empathy, of being a morally involved observer) which the new researcher may demonstrate by being-in-the-world *with the other*. A contingent moral step in the career of the researcher, where a decision needs to be made about identity, constitutes a 'moral passage', or turning point event, a contingency if you like. Vital contingencies of fieldwork 'are not to be viewed only as obstacles to one's inquiries but as opportunities to learn which inquiries are the one's that really matter' (Liberman, 1999: 49). Characteristics of 'vital' contingencies, they force self-awareness upon the researcher to be open to others and not immune to their interpretations; at the same time they make the researcher vulnerable.

The 'moral career' of the worker

Scholars of interactionist persuasion have seen the benefits of drawing on Erving Goffman's earlier work for tracing the moral career of a category of persons. Jason Ditton (1977a) used the concept 'moral career' to analyse moral transformation of male bakery staff working at an establishment he called Wellbread Bakery. The term 'career' has generally been reserved to those who expect to enjoy pathways leading to a rise in status within respectable professions. Goffman used the concept career to focus on what he calls 'an exercise in the institutional approach to the study of self'. He focused on 'making out' in the underlife of a mental hospital (1961a: 119).

One of Ditton's (1977a) concerns is with ways of conceiving of selves, importantly one's own, against a code of moral conduct that had evolved over time, as a frame of reference against which socialized bread salesmen patterned routine daily work practices. Ditton's work provides a useful way to explore some of the concepts of Schwandt's (1995) hypothesis.

The workers at Wellbread fiddled prices; this was the norm for the situation and a case of 'situational honesty'. The novice was advised to 'put a penny on here, and a halfpenny on there' and was warned by supervisors 'not to overdo it' (Ditton, 1974: 535). The money fiddled went into company coffers, but in Ditton's view this was the worker's means of gaining some control over the sales situation, and hence the accounting system for which he was responsible (1974: 535). Further to this, long and unsociable hours, low salary and the unstable commission management backed by the traditional commercial threats of 'contract' (that is the deductions of money can be drawn from the worker's pay packet) and 'bond' (which underlines the unlikelihood of management giving references for those who resign) were incentives to the promotion of the fiddle (1974: 535).

Induction and acclimatization at the establishment had a potential to shape a subsequent moral career of the salesman. The same may apply to the novice researcher, who is cast in the role of 'naïve sympathiser', to be trained, indoctrinated and taught gradually to assume intragroup responsibilities, both formal and informal, and take their place as a group member in a subculture (Mitchell, 1991). The salesman did not have previous experience but learnt on the job. The novice salesmen underwent a three-week training period: in the first week his full concentration was on techniques required on the job. So intent was he on absorbing his instructions (read fieldworker) that he failed fully to appreciate the part played by superiors in creating 'a pseudo-legal bond' by introducing him to practices that were morally questionable (Ditton, 1974: 536).

At the end of the second week there is a gradual awareness that mistakes he has been trying to avoid are not only inevitable but will occur when he has full responsibility for the salesman job. The parallels that can be made with the fieldworker relate to a period of time spent in the field that is reserved for 'becoming' a researcher, prior to being what a fieldworker is supposed to be. The trainee salesman is alerted to the fact that his job security requires that he be innovative and creative and play with rules, his job security depended on it. He had to 'put a penny on here and a penny on there'. The realization that the 'honesty exit' was closed is a crucial career turning point and generally shocks most trainees (Ditton, 1974: 536).

It is not unusual to find in the social science literature reference to researchers who are burdened with 'guilty knowledge' because as trainee fieldworkers they were inducted to the 'full membership role' (Adler and Adler, 1987) and became acclimatized to group norms to which they were expected to conform. For the fieldworker, the shock may come with realization of the ethical implications of disclosure and publication for 'images of self' – the publicly accessible impressions of an actor from which a measure of adjustment may be gauged – and 'self-identity' – the private and personal facets accessible to the actor (Goffman, 1961a: 119).

A contingency in the moral career of the bread salesman involved ensuring the partial fiddling self did not undermine the production of a total social 'me' (to use the terminology of symbolic interactionism). Were the bread salesman to be exposed as 'fiddler' by a disgruntled customer, the part-time fiddling self may be publicly translated into a full identity or master status. Excuses and justifications were used to neutralize blame and protect identity. The end of the training period may be seen as 'vital contingency' when actors were made self-aware and vulnerable. The question for Ditton was not 'Why do they do it?' but 'How do they do it?' How do bread salesmen (as a group) rationalize how they will *be* toward customers? How do they manage to preserve integrity and self-respect knowing they are part-time fiddlers?

Ditton draws on Scott and Lyman's work on accounts (1968) and Matza and Sykes's techniques of 'neutralization' (1957) to analyse the responses of the workers. He notes, on the one hand, the salesman might admit the act in question was wrong, bad or inappropriate, but they deny responsibility (Scott and Lyman, 1968: 47). Traditional researchers have attempted to neutralize their acts of intrusion into the lives of other people as something other than wrong in the light of past historical circumstances. The underdevelopment of anthropological ethics in the past is one excuse with dubious neutralizing impact on questionable past ethical fieldwork practices (Rynkiewich, 1976). Another neutralization technique is what Matza and Sykes call 'denial of the victim' (1957). The worker might offer accounts in which one accepts responsibility for the act in question but denies the pejorative quality that is associated with it. Any moral indignation an actor may have about the self and research practice may be negated by denial of a victim (no one was hurt). Where no actual harm has come to the subject, it may be said that there is no case to answer.

Two ethical models

The traditional ethical model

Denzin (1997) discusses two ethical models in relation to research in social science; the traditional ethical model (underpinned by positivism); and an alternative 'feminist communitarian ethical model'. The two models represent moral choice available to ethnographers. They inform and guide fieldwork practice and textual representation in different ways.

With respect to the traditional ethical model, principles have been developed and devised into a professional code of conduct for research practice. Universal principles established for science have assumed prominence within many professional ethics committees that have pro-liferated within universities and other research bodies in more recent years. The bio-medical model is accepted as the standard for all research (quantitative and qualitative) in some committees. Many committees that watch over research work with professional codes restrict the focus on ethics to areas of informed consent, confidentiality and restriction of covert or deceptive research (Daly and McDonald, 1996: xvii).

Ethical absolutism and ethical relativism

The traditional ethical model allows for two ethical perspectives or rationales for fieldwork practice and textual representation: ethical absolutism and ethical relativism (Minichiello et al., 1997). Ethno-graphers have long debated the issue of a fixed code and prefer a set of guidelines to inform fieldwork ethics. Many adherents of codes, with distinctive liberated and individualistic attitudes, prefer various forms of ethical relativism. They reject ethical absolutist ideas on grounds that there can be no absolute principles and no absolute guidelines. The individual must confront moral and ethical issues on a personal basis and make ethical decisions based on individual conscience. From the relativist's point of view no method of sociological research is considered intrinsically any more ethical than any other.

The absolutist perspective of the traditional model or system of ethics assumes participants will be informed prior to fieldwork of role and purpose, and that consent will be free and informed. All individuals qualifying for inclusion do so in accordance with impersonal criteria established by the researcher/s. All participants are thought to have equal rights to privacy and protection from psychological or physical harm, and confidentiality is assumed. An absolutist attitude reflects uniform and impersonal ways of being in the world, and scientific assumptions about human behaviour that accord with the natural sciences. The impersonal, absolutist ethical model mirrors the positivist paradigmatic view of the world and ways of being in it and interacting with others, and the use of research methods. A fully competent researcher is presumed to be ethically conscientious and will conform to scientific protocols, which include *looking at* participants rather than being *with* them in spirit and purpose. The 'ideal' subject, from the traditional ethical model perspective, is one who is informed (Denzin, 1997).

Ethical relativism reflects alternative sets of ideas about ethics, the world and research methods embedded in both the interpretive and critical paradigms. The assumption is the world is socially created and open for interpretation by those actively involved in reproducing it. With the critical perspective, there is the assumption that powerful groups in society have an interest in ensuring communication of knowledge will be distorted. With the relativist perspective, actors are granted the liberty to exercise individual conscience in ethical matters, including importantly the issue of consent. Critical relativists may recognize covert inquiry as justifiable on political and moral grounds, since it may open windows on the exploitation by elites and powerful groups, which an absolutist approach to consent may impede. Informed consent may be seen as an obstruction to access gatekeepers can use to protect their interests. In response relativists may recognize that something less than full disclosure or lying is necessary to combat 'exploitation' and for promotion of the greater good of the group.

Ethnographers from disciplines like anthropology have made ethical codes for qualitative fieldwork questionable, especially the absolutist approach to consent, because it is not considered fine-grained enough to address the actualities of fieldwork (Wax, 1980). Consent, the one-off, single event contractual arrangement prior to research, has been overlooked in preference to a more processual and negotiated agreement before and during fieldwork. Ongoing negotiation may serve to remind people who have built relationships with the researcher during the research process that their friend is also a researcher, and that what they say to them may be taken down and used as data.

Denzin (1997) is critical of the traditional ethical model (in both its absolutist and relativist forms) for turning human beings into objects, promoting scientists to positions of power over subjects, and for according 'scientific knowledge' a privileged status. The impersonal, universalistic ethical model assumes solutions can be made for ethical problems and dilemmas on rational, objective grounds; emotionality and intuition is relegated to a secondary position in the ethical decision-making process (1997: 273). The researcher who addresses wholeheartedly positivism's research norms (valid research design, competent researcher, minimizes risks, and informed consent) is assumed to be ethically responsible but, as emphasized by Schwandt (1995), there is more to interpretive social science than methodological and pragmatic issues. There is the matter of the whole person to consider and the 'moral career' of the interpretive inquirer.

An impersonal/universalistic ethic

An impersonal, universalistic ethical framework informs and guides modern interpretive researchers, which is reflective of positivist paradigm or worldview, embodying sets of ideas about reality, what constitutes 'science', ways of being with others and research methods (Ellen, 1984). With the positivist paradigm there is an assumption that human social life can be studied in the same way as the natural sciences, with methods borrowed from the natural sciences to yield findings that may be comparable, replicable and generalizable. Many interpretive researchers in social science have rejected the absolutist perspective on research and ethics. Symbolic interactionists assume social life is not determined by internal forces (instincts or impulses), or by external forces (cultural norms, rules and regulations), but is the product of people interacting together and responding to interpretations they place on social phenomena, rather than responding to some stimuli – external or internal (Jacob, 1987).

Interpretive ethnographers of various theoretical persuasions assume that a measure of distance between the self and the subject assists with developing a shared understanding, which is the goal of ethnography. Distancing facilitates analysis and interpretation and avoids bias and distortion. One of the paradoxes of fieldwork is that the researcher is required to engage in face-to-face contact with subjects and establish rapport and trust; yet there is a need for critical distance to prevent one from 'going native'. Marginality and the temptation to 'go native' (the researcher accepts the subject's reference group as their own) capture something of the ambiguity that is characteristic of participant-observation. Modern ethnographers struggled to balance closeness with distance, whereas more recently one finds suggestions that the participant-observer should 'participate' more and 'observe' less (Wolcott, 1995). For others, participating in 'close' ways is potentially morally problematic since it could create problems with the management of *anonymity* and *confidentiality* (Lincoln, 1995). Some would say that in general terms modern interpretivist researchers have not moved totally away from the notion of the other as something to be *looked at* rather than be *with* (as in a genuine caring and sharing relationship).

Remnants of ideas encapsulated within the positivist paradigm tend to surface in the practice of the modern interpretive inquirer during first observations. The researcher is advised to question their taken-for-granted understanding of everyday life, as technique for enhancing theoretical sensitivity and for fostering a capacity to think theoretically about others rather than in lay terms (Strauss and Corbin, 1990). What is called 'epoche' in some forms of phenomenology captures the notion of the distance that is preferred in some forms of qualitative social inquiry. Analysis in ethnography and other kinds of qualitative research remains clouded in mystery. At base the exploration of indigenous under-standings of reality derives from social interaction with participants in face-to-face contact, yet these people can virtually disappear from a text that is devoted to the comparison between sociocultural systems grounded on the observer's theoretical criteria. An impersonal, ration-alized analytic distance is deemed necessary and understandable with the production of knowledge *about* the other.

With modern interpretive inquiry, the various kinds of information, the subject's indigenous understandings and the ethnographer's cultural beliefs and theoretical knowledge are synthesized in the analytical and interpretive process. Subjects with lay understanding have not generally been included as collaborators in analysis and interpretation. Adopting a critical and participatory action approach, however, is no guarantee either that distance will be closed between the researcher and subjects and that social interaction will be seen as something other than a means to an end and not a case of 'exploitation'. With analysis, the researcher might draw on heavy sociological or academic theories that subjects would not comprehend. This has been a concern acknowledged with action research in more recent times. Those who have prioritized critical theories over ideas from the everyday world and clarified their allegiance with institutionalized, theoretically heavy academic disciplines may inhibit rather than encourage ongoing collaboration. They could con-tribute to the people's loss of interest with continuing exploration of their social world once the researcher leaves the field and to 'data decay' (Jordan and Yeomans, 1995). It seems that social interaction is also regarded as means to an end in some forms of action research. In some forms of research knowledge *about* the world includes knowing *about* the other, as distinct from knowing *with* the other (Schwandt, 1995: 136).

An impersonal, scientific approach favours disengagement from the obligations of friendship, of listening, taking and sharing confidences, and engaging in activities that mean temporary departing from the research agenda. The positivist notion that distance be maintained between the inquirer and research participants implies a reluctance to be distracted temporarily from the research agenda. The tendency to depersonalize individuals and groups is implied with a consideration that anything personal is something less than 'scientific', 'theoretical' and 'professional' (Behar, 1995). In modern ethnographic research the personal is customarily relegated to footnotes and appendices, hidden from view in field notes and not included in the body of the text. The modern ethnographer was expected to report fully and frankly her findings and any moral dilemmas that might emerge in the field were not openly discussed; they were presumably handled the best way possible without comment.

Challenge to the traditional ethical model

A distinctive ethics in feminist research acknowledges the primary purpose of research is to empower women and eliminate oppression (Barrett, 1996: 164). Political activism and support of women's goals is one and the same thing in feminist scholarship. An ethical mandate embraces collaborative, nurturing principles 'more akin to the mother–child relationship' than the patriarchal relations of conventional male-dominated social science (1996: 171). Feminist scholars have been explicit in their commitment as researchers to help redress 'systematic injustice' and empower disempowered individuals and groups for the purpose of reorganizing society (Lincoln, 1995: 47). Criticalists have tended to reject or be highly critical of research that is not applied or focused on the promotion of change to real life circumstances, or with a potential to produce knowledge that has positive effects for people other than the researcher.

Feminist-oriented researchers seek ways to avoid ethical problems and dilemmas, and provide a critique of past dubious actions and interactions of modern interpretive researchers who have shown a predisposition towards dismissing the moral consequences of their actions. Emerging issues in qualitative research include extension and reconfiguration of what we consider ethics to be. The new activism implies the need for a new ethics or moral imperative to be devised and formulated. We might see Denzin's (1997) 'feminist communitarian ethical model' as a contribution to the emerging issue of establishing a moral imperative in social science.

A relational or care-based ethic

Denzin (1997) proposes a 'feminist communitarian ethical model' to take qualitative research forward in the twenty-first century and he summarizes the differences between this model and the traditional ethical model that has informed both qualitative and quantitative researchers in the past. The feminist-inspired ethic is set apart from the tradional model essentially in terms of rejecting the rationalized, objective norms required by ethical committees norms (valid research designs, competency as a researcher, minimization of risks, informed consent, and so on).

What is assumed is essentially a personally involved, politically committed ethnographer, not the morally neutral observer of positivism. Researchers require sensitivity, authenticity, integrity and maturity, perhaps more than in previous moments of social science, because people are put in contact with people in more intimate and close ways (Lincoln, 1995). The ideal researcher informed by this ethic is a morally involved, self-aware, self-reflexive and interacting individual who holds the self personally responsible for the political and ethical consequences of their actions (Denzin, 1997: 277). Researchers may be encouraged to make decisions that draw on values, ethical codes, moral and professional standards, intuition and feelings, and to ask the self 'Is this the "right" and "good" thing to do, does it feel "right" and would I want others to do this to me?' They are expected to build collaborative, reciprocal, trusting and friendly relations with those studied and value the connectedness that forms between them and others.

The relational way of interacting is to be affective rather than intellectual. Emotional bonds are to bind people together in friendship, love, nurturance and understanding to base on a shared emotional experience. The ethic of caring 'celebrates personal expressiveness, emotionality, and empathy' (Denzin, 1997: 276). Moral decisions are to be based on justifications derived from moral terms ('solidarity', 'community', 'love', 'mutuality', 'moral identities' 'subject as co-participant', 'empowerment', and so on) (1997: 275).

In this framework every moral act is a contingent accomplishment measured against the ideals of a feminist, interactive and universal moral respect for every individual. Research should ratify the dignity of self and the values of human life; research should promote human justice and the empowerment of groups. The alternative moral choice, elaborated for critical interpretivist researchers, constitutes an alternative moral epistemology to the traditional, impersonal ethical model. There is attunement with a particular people's histories and social contexts and with emotional possibilities.

When fieldworkers have established networks of reciprocity with subjects who are equal and treated as total human beings in the round (with feelings, aspirations, idiosyncrasies, and so on), and relationships are established on shared emotions, certain standards of morality apply rather than purely rationalized and intellectualized norms. Where reciprocal relationships have developed between friends who enjoy 'close' bonds and shared emotions, confidences and activities, the quality of relationship has progressed far beyond the requirements of 'informed consent' (Wax, 1982: 46). Participants who aspire and adhere to moral norms (solidarity, care, empathy, reciprocity, and so on) have embarked on a moral career different from that of modern interpretive inquirer, informed by the traditional ethical model, in either of its perspectives (Schwandt, 1995).

Ethical dilemmas of interpretive fieldwork

The difficulties with operating under the guidance of the absolutist ethical model in qualitative fieldwork might be explored by focusing on ethical, moral and practical dilemmas. Abstract ideas about the morality of fieldwork may be made more understandable by locating them in concrete field practices and examples. The overlapping of roles and relationships presents researchers and other professionals with a range of complex ethical and moral dilemmas for which there is no satisfactory solution. Multiple roles (friend/therapist/researcher) and dual relationships (friend/researcher) have a propensity to create 'conflicts of interests'. Where the central concern in research is to explain the micro processes of human interaction, and understanding of subtle dynamics of behaviour is grounded on the establishment of friendships, ethical dilemmas become critical (Hansen, 1976).

One's obligations to a discipline may need to be balanced with one's moral and professional standards, feelings and intuitions. One's personal, even ethical obligations to the people they study may stand *in conflict* with one's ethical obligations to one's discipline (Liberman, 1999: 62). The demands of the discipline, that favours objective analysis of data, and of human beings, that gave adequate documentation, may need to be balanced with a responsible concern for the personal rights and well-being of the people. The ethical standards of research can be met only if the rights of subject's privacy are not neglected and the integrity of fellow human beings is upheld.

The equality one might think is created with friendships formed in the field is complicated by the different histories interactants bring to their many relationships. The researcher may have expert knowledge and experience with reading subtle clues which people inadvertently express. The researcher is in a position to take advantage of the other and accumulate vast amounts of information by virtue of being a friend. Not being fully detached in some situations may be seen as failure in the role of objective analyst (Hansen, 1976: 131). People can feel they have been exploited when they are able to identify themselves in the text, despite the use of pseudonyms and other masking strategies.

The desire for rapport and the obligation adequately to protect the subject's right to privacy can create ethical dilemma. Even though the researcher may think subjects identify him or her as a researcher, subjects can forget. It may be difficult for the researcher adequately to ensure that the role of researcher is *visible* where fieldwork is done in the urban setting, perhaps in one's own workplace, or where strong friendships have been established between the researcher and subjects. It may be difficult to know if people tolerate probing because they recognize the research aims or because they do not want to alienate the researcher whose friendship they value, or because they are politically useful to them (Chrisman, 1976: 141). Multiple roles and identities (researcher/full member) create problems with protection of information.

When the researcher is party to secret information the impact of personal obligations and relationships on research might be pronounced; the researcher may be forced to balance research aims with rules of secrecy (Chrisman, 1976: 146). The continual acceptance of members of a secret society may be contingent on trust. Continued participation may provide some assurance to be confident with the ethical position, but with disclosure some compromising of bonds of trust and good faith may occur. Moral obligations to subjects need to be very carefully considered with the proposition of a 'greater good' if the ethical standards of the profession are to be met (Hansen, 1976: 134).

One's ethical stance is heavily influenced by events and feelings experienced in the field where personal participation and commitment are concerned. One may be obligated to be as open as possible to the need to balance ethical codes, professional standards and personal feelings with obligations from the process of engaging with others in secret and private activities. The process of research can be such that the significance given to the various mix of elements may change at different points in the research process (the subject's interests and expectations may have priority during data collection, but the discipline could be more significant with disclosure). Objective, rational, intellectualized ethical codes are not context specific and amenable to decision making that draws on intuition, feelings and the researcher's moral values.

Friendships in the field make available much information that might be categorized as 'off the record'. Research goals are aimed towards disclosure and publication, not concealing information. With disclosure the researcher might experience powerful moral pressure from a clash of interests and expectations when one party demands loyalty and allegiance and conflicts with another. The researchers may be torn between doing what they feel is 'right' by the subjects, based on intuition and empathy and what should be done, consciously aware of the need to uphold ethical norms and do no harm, and the obligation to the discipline to provide an interpretation of a people and their practices (uncensored and complete) that would contravene the moral imperatives.

The paradox of fieldwork is that one can pursue research for the 'right' reasons, with consent gained for the promotion of understanding of a people and their practices for the purpose of devising ways to assist them with individual or group problems, but find the self wanting to act in professional and moral ways, yet willing to turn a blind eye to certain immoral acts because to do otherwise would run counter to the research agenda. Taylor (1991) was morally offended by the conditions of the ward he studied and attendants' poor treatment of the residents under their charge. He did not report his observations or leave the field until he got the information he wanted. He continued to interact with attendants whom he liked and who had opened up to him, and the continued observation without condemnation was tantamount to condoning and supporting abuse of mentally disabled people (1991: 246). Taylor should have left the field sooner, but instead allowed his personal preferences to override professional, ethical and moral imperatives.

A contingency in the moral career

The traditional interpretive inquirer may experience a way of being in the world *with* the other in some interactional sequences more so than others, and in a way that is consistent with a feminist 'ethic of care' (Denzin, 1997). While for many activities involvement may be more characteristic of positivistic-inspired research, with the gender blind, autonomous and relatively neutral observer engaged in a utilitarian exercise to gather data, there may be encounters where the actor is not *looking* but standing alongside and *with* the other. Some interactional sequences of fieldwork may provide examples of behaviour that feature decision making between the morally involved observer and subject or co-participant, where covenant, mutuality, solidarity and care are moral terms that aptly describe moral practice.

Fieldwork for my doctorate featured participant-observation of a number of second-hand clothing stores run by two separate groups in the Adelaide metropolitan area. Such shops operate as trade outlets for the sale-donated second-hand garments. Second-hand garments are sold to a paying clientele to raise profit and to subsidize the government allowance, needed to provide welfare to the needy. Many volunteer women were clustered into various shops to work a day or two each week. I worked for two such organizations over 24 months. The majority of my time was spent in one store where I was inducted and indoctrinated to take my place as a full group member with a number of intragroup responsibilities. Names of people, groups and places are not provided for obvious reasons.

Price negotiation

I turn to the paired arrangement in which my Wednesday morning companion and I negotiated the value of our purchases each week. Women who engaged in this type of interchange were doing much more than merely effecting a change in prices. In the face-to-face interaction they also shared their private selves for they communicated their notions of what was fair, right and proper conduct in this situation. They also indicated a desire that another would seal the legitimacy they bestowed upon activities by expressing their approval. There was an element of risk in such sequences for one was placing one's reputation on the line.

In the situation of the charity store certain standards of propriety were relative and situational rather than absolute. Indeed, there was no standard on concessions, which entirely covered the population congregated within various stores which the association ran. What was considered 'legitimate' or otherwise varied inside the same store and between stores run by the same group. Either the shop manageress gave women a price that newcomers were advised not to question because 'it is her way of saying thankyou for your help', or small work parties negotiated prices among themselves. Sometimes women paired off to negotiate the value of their purchases. Having said this, no moral system is entirely relative and contextual; a moral code evolved by women over time eventually stood as a framework alongside the policy rule of 'no concessions'.

My entry into these activities occurred sometime after I joined the store as a volunteer. Increasingly my co-worker and other workers encouraged me to buy things for myself and I obliged. This action signalled her assurance that I would approve of her doing likewise and give her my support. Each week our negotiation commenced after the worker's shift was completed. She would bring to my attention the 'returns' that needed to be recorded and anything she wanted to lay by was duly entered in the lay-by book. Once these tasks were out of the way we engaged in the delicate process of negotiating prices – one so personal as to raise questions about poverty and a lack of concern for pride.

She would hold up each garment for me to see before stating the price she wanted to pay. A favourable response (nod) was an indication I knew that she knew the value of the goods, that she had acted appropriately in terms of the quoted price and had my support. I was acutely aware of my desire and need to support her claim and not act in any way that could cause her to be caught 'out of face' or with 'wrong face', which would require 'face-work' (Goffman, 1967). This would have undoubtedly disrupted the flow of the performance we were jointly engaged in promoting. You might say I was acting in a calculating manner, since I was expressing myself in a given way to evoke a response I was concerned to obtain. We both fluctuated between behaving in a wholly calculating manner and being calculating but relatively unaware of it (Goffman, 1959: 17). I knew the women with whom I worked had awareness that they were entitled to some privilege for having donated their time and energy to the organization, since comments surfaced in discussions about entitlement on the odd occasion.

The researcher had a genuine concern to convey to the worker confidence in her designating a price to reflect her utmost integrity. She was concerned to be seen doing the right thing and did not want to compromise her integrity, but she also wanted a good price. Each act reflected a measure of calculating behaviour. We were privately engaged in a treacherous task of self-presentation and one inappropriate act could weaken the façade. The risk of threat of exposing the private self was felt most intensely on one occasion when she said, 'You're not spying on me, are you?'

Non-verbal symbolism was an in-built mechanism in price negotiation for policing excesses and exerting control. Circumspection was paramount. Both parties to the encounter watched eye and facial movements carefully. Moments of silence provided a glimpse of what might be in the other's mind. A moment of silence, a raised eyebrow or a grimace could register my reservation and she would retract her bid and follow quickly with another, which was usually lower and hopefully would be received more favourably.

Much of the communication work was expressed at the non-verbal level. I was virtually unable to look up and observe garments my co-worker held out for perusal because of sensitivity. As each item was held up, the state of disrepair was described, with words like 'torn', 'worn' and 'faded'. The customary practice in the store was to reduce prices for goods purchased by customers that were damaged or soiled. Sometimes I feigned an attitude of total disinterest in the items held out on display. When my gaze turned toward the items she would sometimes say, in empathy, 'isn't it embarrassing, isn't it terrible', but despite the protestations we knew we would be doing the same the following week.

Revisiting field notes and reflecting on past experience in view of the current issues of identifying *with*, rather than detachment, the evidence would suggest there are no completely detached researchers, only researchers that are presented and experienced (Mitchell, 1991). There were moments when being in the world *with* the other was an intense and personally moving experience that involved genuine care, personal expressivity, emotionality and empathy. Roles of 'trainee', 'friend' and 'collaborator' variously linked the researcher with other women in shared activities, confidences and emotional experiences.

At times the self was experienced as the 'dispassionate' objective and morally neutral observer. At times the researcher could be excused for thinking she was not hiding very much from others, since it was not uncommon for co-workers to say, 'There she goes again, day-dreaming, life passes her by', and 'It's time you got more involved.' During the more vital contingencies, however, particularly degradation ceremonies, where one witnessed the ritual devaluation of a rule breaker who had inspired moral indignations and public denunciation, it was virtually impossible to stand outside the communication work and be a morally neutral observer (Garfinkel, 1956).

Covert research

Informed consent – 'divulging one's identity and research purpose to all and sundry' – is a central issue of professional ethical codes and guidelines (Punch, 1986: 36). The issue of ethics in some committees is concentrated on the traditional areas of informed consent and the restriction of covert or deceptive research (Daly and McDonald, 1996). Researchers have sought access to back regions behind 'fronts' by using covert methods, and have deceived subjects. They have not told them about the research role or purpose of research. Deliberately to embark upon a research project using covert methods is likened to skating on thin ice (Punch, 1986). There are few exchanges in the literature that suggest the researcher did not seek consent prior to fieldwork.

Justifications

With variations to absolutist standards there will be excuses and justifications to rationalize outcomes. The dramaturgical approach towards impression management sees research on a continuum of being more or less overt, and this makes problematic the establishment of any attempt to establish a cut-off point at which research may be said to be unethical (Hunt and Benford, 1997: 117). Impression management is part of human social life and the notion of people wearing masks is not hard to apply to covert research. 'Fronts' are not always easy to penetrate and some ethnographers have resorted to covert measures to explore behind the scenes. Interestingly, the first generation of symbolic interactionists has been linked with most infractions of this nature and their successors have been among the most ethically conscious ethnographers in debate about ethics in research (Adler and Adler, 1994; Chrisman, 1976; Denzin, 1997; Hansen, 1976).

Ethical relativism has been linked with symbolic interactionism and covert methods used by first generation ethnographers. Many of the earlier interactionists debunked absolutist claims, presumably because the perspective on ethics failed to recognize the interpretive inquirer's constructionist view of the world and the place of individual conscience in determining action (Denzin, 1968). A distinctive liberal and relativist attitude mirrors the interactionists' worldview and assumptions about human behaviour. Ethics may be seen as part of the socially created world and subject to interpretation and enactment according to the individual's conscience. Erving Goffman saw life as a masquerade that was comprised of actors wearing many masks. Perhaps covert research was perceived in terms of wearing yet another mask and the covert role yet another to be taken from the repertoire of roles and face-saving strategies for 'passing' in establishments where 'normals' are frequently found.

In the debate about covert research, some ethnographers argue strongly against the approach: because the practice runs against the principle of 'informed consent' (people agreeing to take part in the research on the basis of knowledge of what it is really about); invades privacy; contaminates private spheres of life and involves deception

(Woods, 1992: 378). According to Woods (1992: 379) some 'seek to justify covert research they have conducted (Humphreys, 1975) and others see some as unavoidable (Denzin, 1968)'. Woods elaborates upon the fact that ' "Consent" is not a straightforward business . . . there is a "hierarchy of consent", senior personnel acting as "gatekeepers" and subordinates possibly being forced to participate. Also, one encounters so many people during a typical study, often casually, that it is imposs-ible to secure the consent of all' (1992). It is commonly recognized that ethnographers rarely tell all the people they study everything about research. Informed consent is not straightforward and nor is it easily achievable.

Ethical codes and guidelines provide models for conduct but there will be many individual adaptations and variations in response to the indeterminacies of the field. Nothing remains the same in the field. The research design changes, fieldwork sites and hosts change, relationships and even the social world changes, and fieldworkers themselves are changed by the experience. The indeterminacies of fieldwork underpin the rationale for a more processual and negotiative approach to informed consent among modern ethnographers (Wax, 1982).

The moral career of the covert, interpretive inquirer

The notion of moral career (Goffman, 1961a), as a conceptual frame for investigating the moral dimension of mental patients in the asylum, has implications for some thoughts on the moral career of the covert inter-pretive inquirer. Goffman's inmates in the asylum engaged in a system of 'secondary adjustments', or 'practices that do not directly challenge staff but allow inmates to obtain forbidden satisfactions' (1961a: 56). The actor, who is socialized to the underlife of the institution, has intern-alized a fair amount of moral transformation. Length of stay in the asylum and position achieved in an informal hierarchy is expressed through extensive right over the distribution of privilege or 'secondary adjustments'.

Goffman writes: 'To engage in a particular activity in the prescribed spirit is to accept being a particular kind of person who dwells in a particular world' (1961a: 170). 'To forgo prescribed activities or to engage in them in unprescribed ways or for unprescribed purposes is to with-draw from the official self' (1961a). The appropriate spirit prescribed for the social inquirer nowadays is a critical spirit that values collaborative research with subjects who are co-participants working towards em-powerment, emancipation and dialogical presence in the text (Denzin, 1997). To forego prescribed activities may mean withdrawing from the official researcher role and being faced with a self that is deceptive, deceitful or 'sneaky'; or by securing informed consent but acting as an impersonal, objective rational being who is immune to the expectations of subjects and their experiences of the researcher.

Passing

Passing is linked with information control and personal identity and in particular with the 'management of undisclosed information about the self' (Goffman, 1963: 58). When an individual passes she or he runs the risk of being discredited through information about the self being brought forward that effects identity and control. The individual's social identity may be threatened by the exposure of pretensions through some incident in the field. If there is something discreditable about an individual's past or present, 'negotiation of self' can become a precarious mission indeed.

The problems with deviant behaviour in research are to do with managing self. For example, Ditton (1974) asks of bread salesmen 'How do they do it?' meaning how do they ensure their part-time fiddling self does not contaminate the production of a total social 'me'. The posturing self of the covert, interpretive inquirer may be a self that is under constant scrutiny from the self and from others in the field. Additional monitoring and filtering responses towards the 'me' may be required. The covert researcher may resist asking subjects questions to elicit responses that directly linked with the research goal, a stance that may be motivated, ironically, on moral grounds. Interviewing is considered a central component of the participant-observation technique; not interviewing subjects constitutes a flaw in the application of the theoretically informed fieldwork technique. Engaging in activities in unprescribed ways, or ways not prescribed by ethical codes, may be more apparent in some phases of fieldwork than others.

Exit from the field marks a boundary crossing, the movement from field notes to text. Disclosure and publication are contingencies, or steps in the moral career pathway, when the researcher is made most vulnerable to the interests and expectations of various parties and the exertion of a powerful moral pressure to perform in ways they may find unethical.

Conclusion

Dilemmas and ambivalences are an inevitable part of fieldwork and virtually impossible to resolve in advance (Punch, 1986). Becoming an interpretive inquirer means having to deal with the question 'How will I be toward these people?' Methods of research are notorious for causing dilemma and may even result in 'dangerous encounters' (Alty and Rodham, 1998). With every step of ethnographic research there are unforeseeable ethical and moral problems. Each type of problem requires a different approach and some problems and dilemmas are without solutions. The general advice given to the fieldworker is to 'proceed with caution' rather than avoid sensitive topics that make disclosure problematic.

Some researchers of interactionist persuasion may have been sympathetic towards forgoing the prescribed activities of the traditional, impersonal, universalistic ethical model. They have not been 'open' about role and purpose, or have told some research subjects and not others. Being in the world may be equated with developing moral awareness, confronting controversies and contingencies that force self-awareness and the need to wrestle with moral issues. Students have a moral choice; they need to be informed of a rational, impersonal ethical model and an alternative moral imperative. Denzin (1997) presents an alternative to the traditional ethical model; a 'feminist communitarian ethical model' for new 'postpragmatic' researchers, with critical, feminist persuasions, which students may be guided by.

The impersonal, tradional ethical model requires the researcher to engage in the prescribed spirit, consistent with the modern researcher who dwells in a particular world (academia). The researcher may be diverted by the traditional ethical model to a passage marked by many ethical and moral contingencies, and have difficulty finding their way back to a moral way of being a fieldworker. The researcher who adopts unprescribed ways (covert methods) may embark on a moral career of considerable personal difficulty, with many problems created that are without solutions.

Interpretive inquirers may begin fieldwork with simple ignorance; 'the less one know about something, the less one can reason about or even notice the problem' (Saks and Melton, 1996: 230). Ethical codes and guidelines incorporate moral standards into which the actor is socialized as a member of a community, and 'remind people about values they already share' (1996: 231). New ethnographers may know little about ethical and moral dilemmas of fieldwork because few university departments have courses on the topic and solutions, and few courses on research methods or textbooks include dilemmas as a topic. The interpretive inquirer cannot adequately foresee the ethical and moral consequences that may arise from the study of sensitive topics and back regions, use of dubious methods, multiple and overlapping roles and various types of relationships (power, intimate, social), and the necessary negotiations between self and others in professional and power relationships, the conditions of fieldwork (paradoxes, ambiguities, indeterminacies and dilemmas) that make researchers vulnerable and prone to personal stress, and the political, ethical and moral implications of disclosure and publication. The researcher has a responsibility to protect participants from harm and uphold their right to privacy. Importantly, recognition needs be given to the ethnographer's obligation to protect the self from being 'harmed' as a result of fieldwork.

CHAPTER 3

Scripts and staging the self

Scripts are essentially a metaphor for conceptualizing the production of behaviour in most social life. Scripts reflect the intellectual traditions of symbolic interactionists associated with Mead (1934) and Blumer (1969) and later sociologists like Strauss, Denzin and Plummer, and the theatrical or dramaturgical approach spawned by symbolic interactionism and Kenneth Burke's work (Simon and Gagnon, 1986). For behaviour to occur something resembling scripting must operate at the cultural, interpersonal and personal levels (Simon and Gagnon, 1986).

There are conventions governing how one behaves in organizations. Cultural scripts or scenarios inform of collective meanings of a group. Interpersonal scripts provide access to information to apply to role relationships in a specific social context. The enactment of virtually all roles reflects upon, either directly or indirectly, the appropriate cultural and interpersonal scripts for the context. The relevance of differing levels of scripting is far from identical in all social settings, and for all individuals in a given setting. Scripting is used in this chapter as a metaphor for staging appearances and performances. Reality is a staged performance and the metaphor of the theatre an interactional reality. Theatrical performances and the wearing of masks are no longer restricted to the stage but have 'creeped into everyday life' (Goffman, 1959: 254).

When staging appearances and performances, the social actor needs to give the impression of being a 'proper' researcher (she may be expected to take notes when interviewing), to gain the confidence of the audience members. Staging the self as a 'real' researcher does not simply involve 'real' achievements, however, since projecting a definition of the situation demands appropriate emotional and motivational attitude for the group. Appropriate expressivity equates with a 'belief in the part one is playing'. This creates confidence in others and contributes to building rapport with them in ongoing social interaction. Access to cultural and interpersonal scripts for performing the roles of observer and participant in a culture or subculture that is not one's own is a necessary part of successful 'impression management' in the new fieldwork setting.

The participant-observer, separated from her or his own familiar and relatively secure universe, may experience a disjunction between the customary interpretive schema and the cultural and interpersonal scripts that apply in the research setting, which could result in temporary disorientation, confusion and vulnerability. Vulnerability is one of the occupational hazards of fieldwork with which the social actor must deal in the fieldwork setting if they are to advance from novice to expert researcher. A consciousness of one's own vulnerability is not conducive to instilling in others feelings of confidence, could impede the establishment of trust and rapport and make access to people, places and documentation problematic.

The participant-observer who enters a setting to do fieldwork is required to engage in appropriate activities for the situation, while simultaneously observing people, activities and physical aspects of the situation (Spradley, 1980: 54). Access to the group's interpretive framework is needed for communicating with participants in ways they find immediately recognizable and acceptable. The actor who is able to suspend doubt in the security of their socially situated self and contribute to the group may find their properly staged performance rewarded by rich data.

New recruits to a moral community might pass through various roles during stages of socialization ('learner', 'collaborator', 'friend'), as they adapt to the moral order. The interactionist perspective would seem to depict how the researcher proceeds from 'outer' space to 'back-stage' regions of the participant's world with relative ease and control, manipulates people, manages impressions, engages in strategic action and generally performs in the other's social world without too much difficulty, and without fundamental transformations of self (Hunt, 1984). The new researcher or novitiate, with not much time spent internalizing the moral values and ideals of a group, may stumble in taking the role of the other. They must adjust appearances and talk in synchrony with the expectations of subjects if future ongoing performances are to be favourably received. One who needs to conform to the expectations of others must first know what those expectations are. Access comes from performing; the actor must have a willingness to make mistakes and an ability to learn from them.

Lee (1993: 133) acknowledges that 'physical access is a precondition for social access; that the latter may become problematic because the researcher is likely to be culturally incompetent and make mistakes. With rehearsals the novice actor is expected to make some mistakes. So it is with fieldwork. There may be protected time, or a preliminary period when mistakes with performing rules and roles (explicit and implicit) are not only understandable but also desirable. The preliminary period may have an overseer, who acts as director and gains the prestige that comes from performing the informal role. Ongoing access to the setting, the props and the people is contingent on learning roles and rules, in a manner not precocious, retarded or inhibited. Gaffes and indiscretions might be expected from the 'learner', but consistent and regular breaches of group ideals and principles could arouse the moral indignation of members, lead to negative evaluations and create lack of trust (Lee, 1993).

There are conventions governing behaviour in social settings that people internalize from having been socialized, tested, indoctrinated and taught. The researcher who is taken in by their own act and convinced by the reality they are busy staging, perhaps even gaining access to physical regions and back-stage repositories of information without invitation, may inadvertently lead to the creation of opposition. If minor infractions, deliberately or inadvertently performed, accumulate despite cues given by group members to modify behaviour, the actor could find himself or herself the central figure in a degradation ceremony (Garfinkel, 1956).

Within organizations and communities there are 'expert' performers who uphold the central principles and ideals of a community with regard to roles, rules and relationships. An expert may assume the role of spokesperson and moral entrepreneur whenever someone conveys lack of respect toward others and/or the moral order. Degradation ceremonies can provide insight to the moral norms and values of a group. These cultural scenarios make explicit previously unarticulated meanings that are appropriate for the collectivity. Some researchers no doubt have paid a high personal price for initial ignorance of others' implicit rules, having been caste in the role of 'perpetrator' in degradation ceremonies, but the literature in the social science is not generous in giving up such personal secrets about fieldwork experiences.

The participant-observer must interact with people with different assumptions about what behaviour is appropriate for the situation. The researcher's codes, 'recipes' or scripts may be at variance with cultural and interpersonal scripts by which members abide that have evolved in a setting with the duration of time. It is necessary to try to understand how the other person/s experienced you – what they expected *you* to do (Okun, Fried and Okun, 1999: 146) in order to make adjustments to one's behaviour. Those without a script, who throw themselves into a role, would not be expected to know the finer details of what is expected. Progress might need to be monitored by a co-worker. Interpersonal scripts have evolved from rules for context-specific situations; actors who perform before local audiences do so with improvised scripts. Awareness of these comes from having some ability to 'stand in their shoes' and begin to see yourself from their perspective (Okun, Fried and Okun, 1999). When the subject's cultural and interpersonal scripts differ from the researchers, the fieldworker could become disoriented, confused and stressed.

Different approaches to access

The main problem encountered when undertaking any research is often that of access (Alty and Rodham, 1998). Access has been linked with important elements of building rapport, like 'establishing trust and familiarity, showing genuine interest, assuring confidentiality and not being judgemental' (Glassner and Loughlin, 1987: 35). Access has been thought of as an initial phase of entry to the research setting around which a bargain is struck; a process in which the researcher's right to be present in a social setting may need to be continually renegotiated (Lee, 1993: 122). Some researchers consider access is best facilitated by reassuring 'gatekeepers' that confidentiality will be maintained, a report will be produced upon request, or at the completion of a study. Assurances of confidentiality may demonstrate the trustworthiness of a researcher, while a promised report may cause participants to feel they will also get something from the research (Alty and Rodham, 1998: 277). 'Gatekeepers' and sponsors may make access possible in the first place and 'conditional access' with ongoing fieldwork may involve trade-offs to satisfy 'gatekeepers'' interests and expectations (Lee, 1993).

With relationships that are fleeting (there are no formal institutional structures to bind parties in ongoing reciprocal relations), one may find a relaxation of moral expectations anticipated for people otherwise locked together in relationships of power, intimacy and sociability. This is not to say that strangers in one-off interviews make a conscious effort to deceive researchers. Rather, the relatively informal circumstances where trust has not been established may present conditions that favour the production of less than candid answers because people do not take seriously the questions which are asked.

The initial entry approach, where the researcher's official status and verbal assurances are influential to establishing confidence, reflects on the one-off prior to research contract of positivist-oriented quantitative inquiry. This approach to access has been made questionable by phenomenologists (Hunt, 1984). The alternative approach to access sees trust and rapport as an achieved outcome and not something established by explicit guarantees, verbal assurances of confidentiality and not being judgemental. Demonstrated ability to get on with people in the setting and a willingness to share experience in ongoing activities are important criteria of access. For this the researcher must feel comfortable and confident in the social setting. A successful and convincing performance that conveys belief in the part one is playing is likely to win the trust of others and facilitate the establishment of rapport. The researcher must first be at ease with the self in a strange setting in order to put others at ease. They must know the standards by which performances are judged appropriate and perform as an emotionally and motivationally well-equipped member of the group.

Discussion in the social science literature on access has reflected the guidance of both positivist and interpretive perspectives. For the positivist-oriented researcher, trust is assumed to be automatic because of the role played and the aura and respectability derived from the position of researcher (Hunt, 1984: 284). With traditional ethnographers (those who have been guided by symbolic interactionism and other theoretical perspectives), there has generally been recognition that rapport is an emergent phenomenon from ongoing fieldwork. The researcher must develop relationships with participants in order to create rapport (Hunt, 1984: 284). The traditional approach to access has obscured an understanding of the researcher's lived experience.

In textbooks on qualitative methods, a focus has usually been directed to the procedural aspects of participant-observation, emphasizing entrée, rapport and trust; the psychosocial aspects of 'participation' in participant-observation have generally been neglected (Ashworth, 1995). Yet being attuned to a group's concerns, having an ability to take for granted one's social placement in a socially constructed reality and knowing one can contribute without concern that their identity is under risk of threat are very real issues in the early phase of fieldwork. The researcher without access to the 'recipe' or knowledge framework for conceptualizing reality may be limited in staging appearances and performances. The actor could find himself or herself emotionally and motivationally ill equipped to take a place as member of a group (Ashworth, 1995).

Interactionist and phenomenological perspectives on staging appearances and performances

The first point of contact for sociological and anthropological analysis, from both the interactionist and phenomenological approaches, is access to the interpretive scheme or scripts which subjects use to guide behaviour and make sense of their social world. The methods used by fieldworkers to unearth codes, 'recipes' or scripts reflect upon various theoretical and philosophical persuasions. A phenomenological approach informs researchers to see 'participation' in participant-observation in ways that move beyond research concepts like 'detachment' (as the expression of involvement for positivist-oriented observations and analysis).

In the symbolic interactionist approach, social structure is a remote concern, always 'off stage', perhaps a backdrop against which action is played out or a parameter within which the social dramas of everyday life unfold. The symbolic interactionist approach is concentrated on micro social processes. The relatively free actor does not respond to internal stimuli (instincts) or external constraints (rules, regulations and culture), but to the interpretations they impose upon social phenomena (Jacob, 1987). Roles are to be activated into reality, infused with creativity and personal style. Actors can distance themselves from roles and embrace roles that are to their liking, within the boundaries of social acceptability for the situation. Roles are realized performances of actors motivationally and emotionally attuned to the attitude of the group. So too with rules, they can be played with and improvised to suit the ends

of those who work in organizations and institutions. Realized performances can give rise to informal and implicit rules operating alongside
formal and explicit ones in the same social or institutional setting.
Implicit and explicit roles and rules may command allegiance from
various segments of a group at different times.

Cultural and interpersonal scripts are significant for organizing
responses in a variety of community types (bureaucratic and moral),
and with various types of relationships (impersonal and hierarchical,
intimate and social). A good performance in the situation depends on
access to cultural and interpersonal scripts that have evolved for staging
appearances and performances. Settings are provided with scripts – the
codes or recipes for playing one's roles in different relationships (Okun,
Fried and Okun, 1999: 179), but these may need to be discovered by the
new researcher.

Within occupational settings, where people spend their working lives
and where the researcher may observe and participate over an extended
period of time, there is a kind of modus vivendi (Burns, 1992: 121).
Assumptions develop in differing groups in regard to determining
entitlements, communication processes, to expectations of power, rules,
roles and scripts. With large-scale departmental stores in the western
world one finds a hierarchy of authority, specialization of tasks and
task-oriented performances remunerated with money. Charity stores, by
way of contrast, vary in degree of bureaucratization (some are quite
undeveloped); implicit roles and rules apply and unpaid 'workers' may
value co-operative, co-ordinated group activities that reflect values of
freedom and equality. 'The explicit rules and roles are usually not a
problem; the implicit ones may present more of a challenge for . . .
outsiders' (Okun, Fried and Okun, 1999: 177).

Implicit expectations exist about communication and these vary across
cultures and within subcultures of a mainstream culture. Different
groups have ways of determining rules and roles. In the charity store
where I worked as a volunteer/researcher, the women were not paid a
wage and did not conform to roles and rules that apply to more
conventional trade outlets. Over time improvised scripts evolved for the
promotion of egalitarian relationships and a negotiated order. Fully
acculturated members of an institutional group may understand what
constitutes freedom and personal autonomy, what courtesies must be
extended, how to acknowledge deference and status differences, and
how to convey respect or disrespect through scripts. Procedures for
maintaining face across cultures vary widely (Okun, Fried and Okun,
1999: 60). Understanding our own culture is no guarantee that we will
understand how to act and communicate in another, because we belong
to various other groups at the same time. To identify both how the
setting of the moment may affect our behaviour and how we should
perform, we need to gain access to context-specific cultural and interpersonal scripts. The problems with adapting to interpersonal scripts

that are specific to local subcultures would seem an important issue for the fieldworker who is new to a setting and wanting ongoing access.

The moral community

A case study

Social scientists, inspired by the phenomenological movement, recognize the centrality of the natural attitude and an associated mode of knowing as the starting point of sociological analysis (Atkinson, 1997: 332). Attempting to understand what others expect of the researcher and how they experience her or him requires self-awareness and 'taking the role' of the other. In postmodern fieldwork, the interpretive inquirer who is interested in gaining access to the audience's interpretations of the performers' presentations seeks a position of being *with* other human beings – the *with* standing for a symmetrical relationship.

The natural attitude assumes a 'reciprocity of perspectives'. Inter-actants may understand each other in moral terms and act towards each other on these grounds. Morality is not embedded within individuals, but is a product of co-operative action. Morality may find expression in collective and co-ordinated group activities and decision making that is by negotiation rather than from formal rules and regulations and the directives of a staff member cast in the role of manager. A moral order evolves from, and is sustained by, moral actors engaging in ongoing social interaction with each other over time.

The researcher may access the moral meaning that pervades a particu-lar cultural arena by performing the 'full membership role' (Adler and Adler, 1987). A full membership role may mean offering everything that friendship could entail to cultivate trust. Members of the group may be involved in deviance; they could be drug dealers or otherwise engaged in illicit activities. The researcher who is inducted and acclimatized to a community may later realize the full implications of membership. What to do with 'guilty knowledge' emerges *ex post factum*.

Anthropologists use the phrase 'moral community' to 'refer to those who are prepared to make moral judgements about one another' (Bailey, 1971: 1–7). The members of such a community not only have an idea of shared rights and duties but also a shared pattern of norms and expectations against which behaviour may be judged and contained. By way of contrast the world outside is one where moral judgements are less important, where people are not to be treated 'in the round', where they are to be used 'instrumentally' (Bailey, 1971: 7). The moral com-munity is recognizable by the existence of people with shared ideas about how things ought to be and how they should be. Relationships between people are characterized by 'equality, a moral code and a personal ethic, those between the community and the outside being unequal and free from moral constraint' (Codd, 1971: 188).

A moral community may evolve within an institution established, ironically, for the promotion of trade. Access to a moral code, 'recipe' or script may be through being socialized, tested, taught and gradually granted positions of increasing intragroup responsibility (Mitchell, 1991). Extrapolation of implicit meanings is time consuming and demanding. The enthusiasm of early days in the field, when the researcher wants to observe everything, can blind one to some of the more discomforting aspects of observation, like manipulation of the researcher to foster a political agenda that may not be motivated from an entirely just cause. Acquiescing to the interests, expectations and even demands of subjects may form part of 'conditional access'. Some people may be threatened by the existence of a stranger in their midst. They might fear certain information they want kept secret could be disclosed to members of the upper echelon should they cultivate friendly relations with the new-comer, and they could present as an oppositional force to the ongoing involvement of the researcher.

Women with whom I worked and into whose community I was absorbed envisaged having a community where everyone was equal and no one 'bossed' another. Everyone was to have an opportunity to do both 'interesting' and 'boring' jobs and no one was open to blame. Rules, regulations, directives and guidelines for action, all perceived as constraints upon individual autonomy, as being in conflict with their expectations, were rejected by the women. The moral ideal was to have a community in which all women were equal and free; a place in which co-operation, co-ordination and group effort would foster harmonious sociability and where group life would be organized by consensus and negotiation.

Two complementary and at times quite opposed ways of ordering reality were combined in a welfare enterprise with strong commercial overtones. On the one hand there was the need to maximize efficiency and profit through the implementation of rules, regulations and personal supervision. On the other hand, volunteer women linked 'causes' and 'needs' to concern for adult interaction. Their social ends were fostered simultaneously with those of management. The impersonal order of the workplace, when introduced into the charity shop, contrasted with the familiarity found in friendship cliques. So, too, the specialization of tasks, which in more conventional commercial outlets linked women into specific duties, introduced a semblance of hierarchy to a moral com-munity made up of persons with equal status. Furthermore, rational, goal-oriented action, essential for the promotion of profit, belonged to business rather than social relationships. In the context of the second-hand clothing store, two possible ways of ordering reality were brought together in codes, explicit and implicit roles and rules and interpersonal scripts.

The anomalous and ambiguous quality of the setting meant multiple definitions of the situation were possible. The cultural and interpersonal scripts for more conventional business houses could not function to inform and guide roles and relationships in the unconventional trade outlet. Improvised scripts evolved in the local setting in which the women found themselves located together for a few days each week. The charity store may be at best qualified anomalous: women were simultaneously furnished with two ways of ordering reality and this had ramifications of moral significance.

Goffman takes for granted in his earlier work that 'institutional structures', 'occupational roles' and 'normative rules' set parameters within which action may take patterned form. But from my experience at the second-hand clothing store I know this is not always the case. The questions for the analyst became: 'How do the actors recognize and generate acceptable behavioural display for the situation when multiple definitions of the situation were emergent? How do they do this in a situation where the concept of role, relative to the more conventional business houses located a few streets away, could not be uniformly applied by a collectivity?' The problem faced by the ethnographer was to uncover the shared meanings which form part of the actors' inter-subjectivity. It was necessary for the researcher to perform activities!

Access to what co-workers said and did in response to customers could not be gained in the first fieldwork site. Access to the counter region site was limited by my status as a volunteer worker; only paid employees were allowed to handle customers and money. If access to 'transaction practices' and 'sales encounters', outlined as possible lines of enquiry in the research proposal, was to be granted, I needed to find another fieldwork site that placed no such barriers on the unpaid worker. I was able to observe the same phenomena under differing structural conditions, since the second organization to which I subsequently recruited was a recent addition to the 'salvage' enterprise and much less developed in the bureaucratic sense.

Access to sales work offered the researcher some means of under-standing how workers might use the self to create a reputation of honesty and trustworthiness, or 'face'. 'Face-work', the presentation of a line of action that conveys appropriate attributes and qualities and which includes communication and morality, is fairly circumscribed in society by cultural scripts and interpersonal scripts. Access to cultural and interpersonal scripts is needed to conform to, or correct for, a perform-ance when one was caught 'out of face' and needed to draw on a repertoire of face-saving strategies.

I found the 'one price rule' (the rule that workers pay the same price for goods as customers) was used in conjunction with concessions in the charity store to cover 'need'. While those who fixed prices stood to gain the prestige that comes from social control, those who were timid lost the control that otherwise might have been in their hands had they been able to assert the 'one price rule'. Bargain hunters talked them down and sometimes treated them with little respect. The confusion over roles and rules, which manifested at the level of interpersonal relations in conflict between salesladies and customers, between volunteers and those in positions of informal management, was structured at the level of twin goals of welfare and profit. No clear-cut means to provide unambiguous performances had evolved to order the reality; this was a negotiated order.

A critique of Goffman's earlier work

Goffman writes: 'To engage in a particular activity in the prescribed spirit is to accept being a particular kind of person who dwells in a particular kind of world' (1961a: 170). Furthermore, 'to forego prescribed activities, or to engage in them in unprescribed ways or for unprescribed purposes, is to withdraw from the official self' (1961a). Staging appearances and performances that convey the kind of person one anticipates for a role requires access to cultural and interpersonal scripts, since one who is caught 'out of face' and required to 'save face' must first engage in a process of perceptiveness (Goffman, 1967: 13). They must first interpret what it means to be in proper 'face' before they can correct for or save 'face'.

Goffman takes for granted in his earlier works that 'institutional structures', 'occupational roles' and 'normative rules' set parameters against which action may take patterned form; that projecting a definition of the situation will be unproblematic for 'normals'. Goffman says actors usually find a particular 'front' has already been established, 'a pattern of appropriate conduct, coherent and embellished, and well articulated' (1959: 81), ready to be infused with life and vitality. Thus 'a judge is supposed to be deliberate and sober . . . a bookkeeper to be accurate and neat in doing his work' (Goffman, 1961b: 87). Standard for action intentionally and unwittingly employed by the performer 'tends to become institutionalised in terms of distinct stereotyped expectations to which it gives rise' (1959: 37). Where the researcher enters a setting where roles and rules are implicit rather than explicit and not in conformity with conventional business practice, access to conceptual frames for defining and interpreting social processes become especially problematic.

Goffman says if a person is to employ his repertoire of face-saving practices, obviously she or he must first become aware of the interpretation that others have placed on his acts, and the interpretation that he ought to place on theirs. The relevance of this for a discussion of access is that with the ethnographer as 'stranger' to a subculture, they may be able to apprehend the *generality* of the new situation by drawing on the *specificity* of past experience in the more conventional departmental stores. They could face 'seemingly endless' contingencies in an unconventional setting because a shared definition of the situation is not applicable across segments of the audience. One learns from experience with one group what is appropriate, but a second set of propositions emerges higher in the echelon, beyond or outside the 'moral community', to confuse and make harmony problematic.

Access to members' cultural and interpersonal scripts for staging appearances and performances is necessary when correcting for roles and relationships that go astray. Researchers have sometimes been advised to write down their preconceived ideas about the people to be studied before any interviews are actually conducted (Okun, Fried and Okun, 1999: 144). A record in field notes of the researcher's interpretation and how this varied from the subject's interpretation is sometimes recommended, to capture both emic and etic perspectives in writing. The anthropological goal is to understand the 'native's point of view' (Malinowski, 1922: 25). The 'actor-oriented perspective' or emic approach has priority for promoting an understanding of latent or implicit meanings (Barrett, 1991: 151). Strangely, this does not seem to have been applied to researcher conduct in the field.

Theory and consent

The way researchers define reality and their relationship to that reality, has been linked with their choice of theories and methods (Sieber, 1996: 25). If reality is believed to be a construction established from interaction between the researcher and participants, as opposed to something that is 'out there' (as positivist-oriented quantitative inquiry would suggest), a consideration will be given 'trust and expectancy'. Any breaches to informed consent may then be considered a breach of trust established in social interaction and deception considered as a contingency in the management of trust. The relationship between researcher and researched, as defined by theory, influences how data are collected and organized, results are framed, disseminated and used (1996: 27).

Consent has been considered in terms of a 'continuum of consent' (from highly informed consent to deception and concealment (Patton, 1990; Sieber, 1996: 26). There exists in social science research the notion of a 'hierarchy of consent', with senior personnel acting as 'gatekeepers' and subordinates possibly being forced to participate (Woods, 1992: 379). The 'hierarchy of consent' and the 'continuum of consent' and the complexity of social and cultural choices and situational constraints of fieldwork make informed consent by no means straightforward, and possibly an ethical ideal that is unattainable in fieldwork. With the dramaturgical approach, there is a no sharp distinction between impression management and manipulation; the continuum suggests research is 'more or less overt and more or less manipulative' (Hunt and Benford, 1997: 117). At what point in research 'impression management' techniques (transferred into everyday understanding as 'tact' and public relations skills) are inappropriate, because they may endanger the physical and psycho-logical well being of others, is a serious ethical question that tends to be blurred by the dramaturgical approach (Hunt and Benford, 1997).

The gap between the ethical principle of informed consent and the actual practices of researchers has been variously argued about (Woods, 1992). Few researchers are willing to admit to unethical behaviour. One cannot be held in violation of an ethical principle when no one is harmed by research; the continuum of consent allows for variations in ethical compliance; or the benefits of covert critical research outweigh any negative connotations. Covert research can ease access to sensitive knowledge – 'sensitive' by virtue of being about private, deviant matters and social control (Lee, 1993) – but the use of sensitive methods some-times moves fieldworkers into situations they feel obliged to leave prematurely, or continue in under considerable personal anguish and ongoing personal regret.

Where subjects do not trust 'outsiders' they may create their own 'fronts' to impede the researcher's progress. Occasionally we read of concealment and deception being promoted by the researcher adopting a 'front', not revealing that participation was under cover and negotiated for the prime purpose of observing the practices of others. 'Fronts' conceal by ensuring the researcher has only a limited opportunity to observe what is going on (Lee, 1993: 133). 'Fronts' enable the researcher to 'pass', or in other words to conceal certain discrediting information, usually about identity. More control may be placed in the hands of the covert researcher when negotiating access, by engaging without consent, but continued presence in the field could undermine the 'front' of both the researcher and subjects.

The 'reactivity' issue may be negated by length of time spent in the field, since people tend to forget the researcher's presence, or find the effort to maintain a 'front' too onerous (Lee, 1993: 135). One cannot live amidst repeated social activity for any length of time without it having some influence on one (Liberman, 1999: 51). 'Carrying out a project of research you do not value for the sake of its own inquiry is corrupting' (1999: 51), and so too is carrying out a project of research using dubious research methods.

Questionable practices

Being socialized into a group's social world through a step-by-step learn-ing process, under the guidance of an 'expert' or 'director', can regulate the pace with which access to secret and private knowledge that is taken for granted by fully acculturated members is traversed. Assuming the 'naïve sympathizer' role, as one to be socialized, tested, indoctrinated and taught, and gradually granted increasing group responsibility, is a dangerous mission for a researcher who is performing under 'deep cover' (Mitchell, 1991). The actor who assumes the naïve learner role, but unknown to members of the group is simultaneously performing the role of observer under 'deep cover', would seem to have a problem with establishing moral equality with the subjects, since they are *looking at* and not really participating *with*.

Several ethical questions may be raised by research that is not necessarily covert yet involves concealment and deception. Informed consent may be procured, yet complicity and 'friend-like' relations between the researcher and researched may be developed to procure more information than people would want to divulge. Using our bodies, voices, demeanours and emotions to elicit responses from people may be a manipulative strategy that is employed in the context of informed consent. The closer the relationship the ethnographer has with participants, the more difficult it may be to avoid deception, since protecting what is shared from disclosure is at odds with the research goal.

Aggressive interviewing techniques with informed respondents can be defined as symbolic violence, yet ironically the covert participant-observer may resist any form of direct and indirect questioning (probing) because of a stubborn idea that doing so is immoral. A decision not to ask questions might be rationalized against notions of exploitation. Such responses promote the actor's research goals while offering very little return to the respondent. Alternatively, the researcher might be meticulous in procuring informed consent from all participants in a study, yet engage in the morally dubious act of cultivating relations of complicity with a subject to solicit private information from a third party. Informed consent is no guarantee of ethical fieldwork.

Is it ethical to talk to people when they do not know you will be recording their words? Is it ethical to encourage an informant to divulge what a friend has conveyed in private places? Is it ethical to develop a calculated stance toward other humans and be strategic in your relations? Is it ethical to 'use' people as allies or informants in order to gain entrée to other people, or elusive understandings? (Lofland and Lofland, 1995: 63). The researcher may fill a number of roles – 'learner', 'volunteer', 'friend', 'collaborator', 'therapist' – but none may be the researcher's principal interest. Is one exploiting the subjects if they do not have a genuine interest in performing the various roles?

Covert researchers who perform under the belief they can 'pass' unnoticed among attentive strangers run the risk of being taken in by their own act, whereas others may not be so gullible. The researcher who conceals the researcher role from members of a group may run the risk of concealing very little, least of all their ignorance of the audience (Mitchell, 1991). The ethical problems created by covert research can set up conflicts in the researcher's self. The fieldworker who performs roles of observation and participation is caught up in an interpretive and moral frame that rests on a certain code of conduct involving certain moral expectations (Woods, 1992: 379). Interaction is rule-bound but the meaning is implicit just as is the interaction being observed. If most of the relationships established with subjects are built on a sham, one is not only deceiving the subject, but also oneself. Woods says if deceiving subjects 'offends one's own values and runs counter to principles ingrained through years of socialization, not to mention allegiance to a professional code of ethics . . . one risks a damaged self and a "spoiled" project and possibly spoiled research career' (Woods, 1992: 380).

There is also the myth that misleading others about one's mission can release the researcher from the feeling world of subjects and the need to sympathize with them. Whatever the external appearances with covert practices, the researcher is open to the subject's feeling world (Mitchell, 1991). The covert researcher does not equate with a morally neutral and dispassionate positivistic-oriented 'scientist' detached from people who participate in the research. The represented self of the covert researcher might be experienced alternatively as a self not 'dispassionate', but sympathetic toward the feelings of the subjects and yet also a seemingly unfeeling and morally neutral observer for whom relationships and people are not personally meaningful. Secrecy in fieldwork might deceive others, but the veil of secrecy is an external barrier to assessing the identity of the researcher, not an internal one. Researchers who study sensitive topics or use sensitive methods may risk an 'ethical hangover' when fieldwork ends, because they are aware that the research goal requires they divulge information, which would go against what the performers would want.

The challenge of the researcher is to get to know about social phenomena by entering into ceremonies, rituals and other dramatic events and participating in social interaction and relationships. Researchers, including 'unknown researchers' (Lofland and Lofland, 1995), learn the ropes in order to take place in activities in a contributing way. To stand dispassionately aside at crucial moments is to risk exclusion from the privileged activity and to experience the self as 'outsider' (Mitchell, 1991: 106). In the dramatic episodes of fieldwork the boundary between appearing and being may be assessed, when the researcher is made consciously aware they are not 'acting' and the reality they confront is 'real' in its consequences for identity of self, in relation to others in the social world, and what is 'right' and 'proper' to do (McGettigan, 1997). There are no dispassionate observers, only researchers who are represented and experienced (Mitchell, 1991).

Sensitive topics have been defined as those relating to private and personal matters, deviance or social control (Lee, 1993). Researchers who study sensitive topics may access back regions and may use sensitive methods (covert participant-observation). The nature of the topic may set in motion forces of opposition; 'gatekeepers' may refuse access. Sometimes covert methods are rationalized against notions of a 'greater good'. The deception of a few is to be weighed up against exposure of ideologies, philosophies and institutions that exploit and marginalize certain categories of people.

Gaining access to back regions could mean uncovering data that reflect negatively on organizations, people and activities. Actors who gain access by ethical or other means to observe the 'inside' secrets of the troupe may be obliged as a member to perform dubious activities they would rather not know about. Researchers may be forced to reset or abandon their research priorities on ethical grounds. It may not be possible to disclose secrets without discrediting the image which the researcher is consciously attempting to present, as someone who is trusted. Deception and fear of being discredited may be risks that are characteristic of covert fieldwork and may cause the researcher to experience considerable research-related stress. One's sense of security may be placed under threat where deception has been used and disclosure is feared. With the risk of discrediting information being brought forth there are the attendant possibilities of humiliation, embarrassment and abuse, and a halt to the research. The 'real' ethnographer behind the mask may be one who is basically insecure.

Access to sensitive regions

The worker who is granted access to back regions may find through performing as a member they are gradually granted increasing intragroup responsibilities (Mitchell, 1991). This could involve performing activities that cause embarrassment, something you would not want people you respect to know about. The researcher may have some soul searching to do from having assumed an interpersonal script that is context specific. The status of group member is contingent on knowing the 'native's point of view' or perspective, and demonstrating the standard practices of the group. A crucial turning point in the researcher's moral career may come with the realization that all exit points are closed. The induction process may set in motion a course of action from which there is no escape for the researcher.

Moral qualms about 'guilty knowledge' could arise from access to a back-region vantage point. The inadequately anticipated ethical consequences of one's performances may begin to make their presence felt with disclosure and publication (Lee, 1993). Until then no harm may have been envisaged from research. The researcher might discover many reprehensible activities in the back region, but lack the warrant for disclosing them. The activities may be deemed by the subjects as something 'you don't want others to know about'. Is it ethical to tell others? The researcher may fear subjects will be embarrassed or angered by disclosure and that their identity will be exposed to censure of some sort. 'One's personal, even ethical, obligations to one's informants may stand *in conflict with* one's ethical obligations to one's discipline' (Liberman, 1999: 62).

During socialization the researcher may engage in activities that clearly pose questions about the organization, the group, the activities or the actors (Alty and Rodham, 1998: 278–279). How people solidify and stabilize their social environment and how, on occasion, play with it may constitute 'back-stage' information made accessible to the researcher through participant-observation. Access to a large amount of data that are private and secret creates problems with sifting out what should be kept 'off the record'.

The paradox of intimacy

Mitchell (1991) sees 'the paradox of intimacy' arising when affective relationships with participants are developed more rapidly than the researcher's knowledge of their practices. The researcher is advised to enter into intimacies with participants and be open to the others' feeling worlds and their taken-for-granted understanding of everyday life. The irony is that the ethnographer cannot know in advance what line of inquiry is appropriate to pursue (technical and procedural or emotional), what is personal and private and what things are not for public con- sumption. Forming friendships before establishing some knowledge of the implicit understandings of a group could result in overstepping the boundaries of acceptable behaviour and becoming offside with the members.

Once in the field and in contact with the people the researcher may find that what is expected is not so much enactment of a method, but engagement in a relationship, or the role of friend (Lipson, 1989: 50). The formation of intimate relations carries much the same sort of challenges as interpersonal relations in everyday life. Researchers who develop affective relations more rapidly than their knowledge of members' practices could overestimate the support given them by participants and pursue activities in places considered out of bounds for the *novice*. Being overzealous and too enthusiastic to become an 'insider', while not fully cognisant of the others' life-world could lead to one's rejection. One has to be equally mindful of the ethical implications of traversing terrains that are sanctified and out of bounds to the rank and file.

Mitchell (1991) found mountaineers expected trusted intimates to understand and avoid certain activities and lines of inquiry that related to emotions and feelings; expressivity in relation to mountaineering was a personal and private matter. Such implicit understandings were some- thing newcomers could not be expected to know about; they formed part of the insider's implicit meaning structure. A breach of members' expectations may occur where the degree of intimacy is achieved early in fieldwork that is not commensurate with the fieldworker's understand- ing of group values and shared sentiments. Probing to get people to say more about an issue may be offensive in some situations where that issue is taboo. An occasional mistake in pursuing certain taboo lines of inquiry may be admissible for the *novice*, but repeated mistakes that violate the members' code of conduct would not be tolerated.

Researcher as prey

Mitchell (1991) acknowledges the participant-observer, new to fieldwork, may be socialized, tested, indoctrinated and trained, and gradually granted positions of increasing intragroup responsibility. Researchers may variously become objects of fun and ridicule and the butt of jokes. They may be manipulated to serve the political interests of group members or duped into thinking that some of the self-presentations are honest, when in effect members have intentionally dramatized experiences and exaggerated positions, practices and prowess (Mitchell, 1991). In the early days of fieldwork, the researcher might take at face value the expressions of others and miss the theatrical aspect of their performances. Time is needed to get to know the expectations that subjects have of the researcher and to be appropriately and adequately informed of social and cultural phenomena, in a grounded, theoretical and ethical sense.

The juggling act

As rapport develops and friendships are established, the danger of betrayal is created. Lofland and Lofland (1995) see the 'dilemma of distance' arising from the researcher's attempt to become immersed more deeply in the social reality of group members, and the need to maintain the distance considered appropriate by the researcher for critical analysis and interpretation. The modern ethnographer had to juggle between becoming immersed in the local phenomena with putting distance between the self and the subjects. The paradox of the research relationship that requires rapport and intimacy be established, yet sees the need for critical distance, creates potential for ethical and moral dilemmas.

In any field setting there are plenty of unanticipated social activities to distract researchers *entirely* from their agenda without just cause and entice them into 'going native'. One needs to balance the stance of the 'disinterested scientist' who lacks a human face and stands aloof, *looking at* the other, with the temptation to become a 'real' participant who internalizes the reference group as their own, and to disengage from the academic audience. Marginality and the temptation to 'go native' may be placed at the two opposite ends of a continuum: either condition may cause fieldwork related stress. The closeness/distance dilemma is a contingency of modern fieldwork which continues to plague fieldworkers in contemporary times (Reinharz, 1992). Friendships may be deliberately promoted with the research agenda and when fieldwork ends the subjects could be left wondering whether the friendship was 'real' or only 'friend-like' and whether they had been exploited.

With modern fieldwork, the delicate balance between involvement and detachment was thought to maintain conditions of rapport adequate to fieldwork. Spradley (1980) assumed that being made to feel 'strange' would better facilitate a capacity to unearth tacit rules and implicit meanings. The idea behind such an assumption is the more you know about a situation, the more difficult it is to study. The cultural logic of this argument is that the ethnographer who does fieldwork at home is limited by 'lived experience' and immersion in their own community. Full participant-observation by an ethnographer who is socialized to a group that is not their own is perceived to be an ideal position from which to learn the ropes and gain an understanding of a people's life-world that approximates closely with how the subjects would conceive of this (Mitchell, 1991: 102).

There are likely to be frequent and unavoidable conflicts arising from the need for researchers to open themselves to the social world of others and the desire to pursue their own research agenda. Participants may cause the researcher to experience feelings of guilt and embarrassment from pressure applied to 'get involved' in activities that take her away from research, for reasons that are not just and moral (political intrigues make demands on researchers to take sides and help workers engage in underhand activities, sometimes in opposition to management). Political manoeuvrings are a fact of fieldwork life of which the researcher must be aware, but something that cannot be specifically known in advance or planned for.

Mitchell (1991) suggests the researcher engage in 'passionate observation' rather than 'dispassionate observation'. There is an implied sense here of the postmodern thrust towards engaging in ways suggested by the 'feminist ethic of care'; of *being with* and *for* the other, rather than *looking at* (Schwandt, 1995). An ethical and moral imperative of the new social research enterprise is that researchers 'respect' and take seriously the other's world and engage in genuine caring and sharing.

Fieldworker control?

Far from being in a position of control, the fieldworker may be dependent on the host population for 'conditional access'; and ongoing access may require an exchange of gifts and services. Some interviewers and observers 'trade off' with more concrete provisions: like offering rides or loans, delivering messages, serving coffee, giving advice and opinions (Lofland and Lofland, 1995: 59). Financial support, clerical assistance and political advice may be exchanged for information with people, some of whom may be engaged in deviance and have something to hide from the authorities (Adler and Adler, 1994). You can expect to pay some 'dues' and, moreover, unless you wish to be seen as odd and cold, perhaps risking being completely shut out from the research setting, 'you cannot forego the helper role altogether, it may be your trade-off for access' (Lofland and Lofland, 1995: 60). The customary exchange practices raise the question: 'Is it ethical to "pay" people with trade-offs for access to their lives and minds?' (Lofland and Lofland, 1995: 63).

One may feel obliged to provide some substantive benefit to the research subjects for tolerating intrusion into their lives. What the 'service' should be is something the people must decide or require of the researcher. It may be that the subjects want assistance in the composition of letters to some bureaucratic organization, translation of texts, computer advice or small monetary contributions (Liberman, 1999: 59). Contributions that benefit the people may go a long way towards requiting one's indebtedness, but the subjects must be able to make requests and determine what they want. There can be formal guidelines for ethics, but ethics in fieldwork are relational and subject to local contingencies.

Commitment to the research agenda

Postgraduates who embark on a PhD study by research need to do so for the right reasons and be able to withstand the criticism of others (Liberman, 1999). The decision as to whether to proceed with a study of some aspect of social life is a personal and ethical matter that the researcher must address. The question of whether it is ethically appropriate to study a particular group, setting, situation or question, or whether such phenomena are appropriate for you to study (given your set of values and the values of other people you admire), requires you to make a conscious decision and articulate the basis for making it early in the research process (Lofland and Lofland, 1995).

The researcher may have their confident self rendered totally irrelevant, bourgeois or superfluous by the expressions of a member of the subject group (Liberman, 1999: 51). Liberman speaks of a graduate student doing fieldwork in India who, in her first interview, was thrown into self-doubt and in need of counsel because the subject conveyed his belief that her scholarly interests were useless (1999). One who is not able to withstand the criticism of a subject with regard to their research project may need to reconsider whether the intentions to study a particular topic or area are grounded solidly on the right reasons; that they are committed to the integrity of their own research. Superficiality can lead to moral dilemmas and reflect on the integrity of the researcher to engage honestly and seriously with subjects with whom they share activities.

The ethics of relationships in the field

Anthropology has a tradition that would lend itself to the task of trying to understand what the other person expected you to do rather than trying to understand what went wrong. An understanding of the culture provides some ability to begin to see from the insider's perspective (Okun, Fried and Okun, 1999: 146). Yet paradoxically most social science writing on field research in general, and with problems of access in particular, is based, as it inevitably must be, on the researcher's own account (Lee, 1993: 120). What are usually lost thereby are the understandings of those being researched on being studied (1993). The understanding of how subjects experienced the researcher and what they expected of her or him is usually overlooked.

With long-term fieldwork, trust is usually facilitated because those in relationships with the researcher have much information about her or him that is conveyed through self-disclosure, and from observation of past actions (Lee, 1993: 123). When initial access to a new setting is made, when interviewing people in one-off sessions, the subjects or respondents have little information about how the 'stranger' is likely to act. On-going access crucially depends on 'establishing *interpersonal trust*' (Lee, 1993). Over the course of fieldwork, impersonal relationships are transformed into interpersonal and often intimate relations. Some risks of threat derived from dealing with the stranger might be averted once the researcher is actually inside a setting and immersed in the regular practices.

Ongoing access to certain physical locations, such as back-stage vantage points and private gatherings, may need to be tempered by a genuine respect for the privacy of the social world of the people the fieldworker engages with if social research is to be ethical and moral. Fieldworkers should not be driven by their research protocols and topics of inquiry to the extent that they cannot engage seriously with the subjects, and understand and appreciate what the people are doing from their own perspective (close to the way the world appears to the people themselves). They should not stand aloof from them and allow the self to be a 'disinterested observer' with feigned respect for the social practices they study (Liberman, 1999). We need to be more than willing not to take the shortest route to 'conveying the local social phenomena to our analytical reductions of them' (1999: 56) and engage wholeheartedly in the local social phenomena, irrespective of the fact that such practice is not included in the research agenda.

Where qualitative fieldworkers participate in local activities that go beyond the research agenda there is a potential for fieldwork to be transformative. This does not mean the researcher is actually transformed, 'only that they do not make themselves immune to the effects of the insights and local practices that they are investigating' (Liberman, 1999: 56). A vital component of being open to local contingencies is that we expose the self to the reductions which people have made of us; we become, in other words, an object for another. Each social situation in the field poses its own unique contingencies and the researcher is advised to respond to them skilfully, with innovative methodological and ethical solutions (Liberman, 1999: 60). An ethical imperative is to have honest engagement with local contingencies of fieldwork. Contingencies of fieldwork are to be viewed not only as obstacles to observation, but opportunities for celebration and transformation.

Barriers to access: the subjects

The major problem with access in fieldwork has generally been recognized as the involvement of the researcher with other people, perhaps the 'gatekeepers' who fill both facilitative and constructive roles (Lee, 1993). These are the people who may or may not be accepting of the researcher and can block access. Some see research subjects as the major problem with access in fieldwork, since they too can make problematic the presentation of self.

The traditional attitude taken toward the subjects, and possibly the major view, is to find ways to connect with subjects in relations of mutual trust and reciprocity. The opposing attitude towards subjects is that of suspicion. One expects to suspect others and expects others to suspect them (Lofland and Lofland, 1995: 55). They acknowledge the existence of two main contrasting attitudes toward the subjects and these should be seen as representing two opposite ends of a continuum. Most fieldworkers adopt a stance that is somewhere in the middle of the continuum, 'trust combined with a heady dose of skepticism; suspicion mixed in with large portions of faith' (Lofland and Lofland, 1995: 55).

The researcher in fieldwork nonetheless may be a major problem of access and ongoing research. Fieldwork is about observation and participation on several levels simultaneously: verbal and non-verbal expressions; the management of emotions and of self in a variety of relationships (power, intimate and social); and in 'face-work' (communication and morality). The ethnographic quest has been to understand the beliefs, values, fears and aspirations; the implicit meanings of a people and how they make sense of their world. Grasp the 'native's point of view' is the message that successive generations of fieldworkers in Malinowski's (1922) footsteps have headed. The 'insider's point of view' of their social and cultural world has been emphasized as the focal concern, in the first instance. Little interest has been given to the researcher's beliefs, values, expectations and fears prior to and during fieldwork. Even less attention has been given to trying to understand how the subjects experience the fieldworker's presence.

How subjects experienced the researcher may have to be assessed by being open to the 'attitude of the other'. The subjects' interpretation of the researcher's presentation, through verbal and non-verbal symbolism given and given off, in role-related activities and a range of relationships, might be addressed. In fieldwork, the 'ethics of relationships' may require the researcher not so much to take special care to capture 'the subjective reality' of the people that one studies as to leave oneself open to the objectifications that the people make of us (Liberman, 1999: 57).

The researcher needs to become an object for another and capture the image that is reflected back through the 'looking-glass effect' of micro sociology. Embracing the 'looking-glass effect' may heighten one's awareness of 'what doing research' means in ethical and moral terms (Richard-son, 1992). Taking 'the role of the other' could facilitate self-awareness and help the researcher to get to know the self. Being open to other people's responses to you, however, means making the self vulnerable.

Witnessing the person he was for the aboriginal people studied in Australia made Liberman (1999) aware of his ethnocentrism, and the customary practice (interruptions) he employed to make himself at the centre of the social interaction. The researcher's stance stood in stark relief against the desire for 'congenial fellowship' aspired to by the aboriginal people from sharing the social solidarity of a group of con-sociates (Liberman, 1999: 57).

The researchers are advised not to pursue only their self-interests. A reading of the researcher, from the subject's responses, as yet another of those 'scientists' who look at others and lack a human side, may impel one to adopt a more self-aware and self-critical stance. If one is mimicked and ridiculed by others in the field, it might be better to seek to understand what the subjects expected and experienced you to be, rather than trying to understand what went wrong with your plans to collect data for the research agenda. But this requires a certain amount of maturity and security of self in the situation.

Barriers to access: the self

Negotiation of self is central to the symbolic interactionist approach. The self emerges in social interaction and is modified as the other and the situation undergo change. Verbal and non-verbal expressions are in a dialectical process. Some would say appearance has a priority over language as the dominant symbol, since appearance sets the scene for verbal interaction to occur. Appearance means many things, including body size and shape, 'reputation' and 'image', clothing, stances and facial expressions (Stone, 1962). Through appearances the actor may announce the self as an identity for social placement in structural terms (title, status, class, race and gender) and provide a glimpse of values, moods and attitudes for an audience's appraisal.

Appearance 'represents the person *as there, stratified* or assigned a particular distance, and *rapt* or engrossed' (Stone, 1962: 100). The path one has travelled and intends to travel in the research process may be part of the staged appearance of the researcher. Appearances are staged to arouse in others the assignment of words embodying responses to one's presence (1962: 101). The audience serves as a mirror reflecting one's appearance back to the actor. Responses may be in the form of challenges that suggest a new programme should be aroused.

The researcher's understanding of how they communicate non-verbally is an important step in communicating effectively with members of one's own and other cultures (Okun, Fried and Okun, 1999: 75). The actor, however, may be unaware of the specificity of standards for non-verbal behaviours in local settings. Anger, fear, disgust and surprise are basic emotions one sees across cultures through facial expressions by people experiencing them (1999: 78). Some cultures believe feelings should be expressed while others do not. Potential differences can hamper communications and cause misunderstandings in research relationships. Differences in the meaning of facial gestures cross-culturally may insert an element of confusion in the communication process. Thus, it is important for staging appearances that researchers become aware of how non-verbal expressions are experienced by audience members.

The researcher who is new to a research setting and appears before audiences as a stranger may be without a code, 'recipe' or scripts to inform an appropriate appearance. Without some knowledge of how appropriately to project one's 'programme' can be a pretty unsettling affair. Those with an inability to tolerate uncertainty and a willingness to make mistakes may experience a fair degree of anxiety (Lipson, 1989: 68). An inability to take for granted the security of one's identity can mean the actor is emotionally ill-equipped to present the self and perform appropriately. In the immediate situation there may be little the researcher can do to ameliorate the anxiety that could impede progress towards establishing rapport and trust.

Researchers are obligated to ensure that their appearance does not intimidate others they are interviewing. The way the researcher presents the self through appearance (dress and non-verbal as well as verbal expressions – moments of silence strategically interspersed to extract information) are all aspects of 'impression management' that the field-worker may need to modify in response to subjects' non-verbal expressions. Rather than researchers trying to understand what they were doing wrong when things do not go as planned, it might be better to try to understand what the subjects expected they would do, and how what they did differed from this.

Access to certain information might be appropriate for men but not for women, and vice versa. According to Barrett, 'a priest may be the best informant in religious questions, women are generally superior to men in discussing childbearing; and a few elderly men and women may be the last repositories of a waning tradition' (1991: 35). Access to certain areas of information may be limited by gender, age, status and occupation. Self-awareness of the culture may help determine why responses to certain questions were unfavourable. It helps researchers to be self-aware of emotional expressivity and what roles and regions they may enter and exit from in the field.

Access to specific physical locations, pieces of information and privileges may be regulated in local settings by role relationships. One may engage as a participant-observer in a hierarchical organization where tasks are fixed and performances determined by role, whereas in relatively egalitarian community groups access may not be so explicitly proscribed, but only implicitly understood by the members. The 'stranger', with little time spent in an organization for the internalization of its moral values, may stumble in taking the role of others. She or he may be so taken in with their own act that they fail to see the cues others give off to warn one to proceed with caution. Failure to heed the warning could convey lack of respect for cultural mores and stimulate negative and hostile responses from audience members.

Implicit rules that deal with values, principles, ideals, aspirations and fears are more difficult to unearth. They are usually taken for granted, not spoken about and culture or context specific. Some understanding of cultural and interpersonal scripts is needed to assist in understanding audience expectations with regard to the way strangers should perform. The actors must not be so taken in by their act that they fail to be sensitive to audience receptivity, and should modify behaviour when modifications are due.

Fieldwork has the potential significantly to change people both in their own eyes and in the eyes of others (Lipson, 1989: 70). The researcher may become self-aware: 'Self-awareness is not only necessary for good field-work but fieldwork itself is a potent source of self-awareness'. Fieldwork brings researchers face to face with their values, beliefs, aspirations, fears and concerns. Self-awareness comes from trying to understand what others expect of you and how you match up to these expectations through demonstrated practices; how subjects experienced the researcher's presence and what they expected the researcher to do.

One may become vulnerable when crossing boundaries between public and private spaces, conventional and sensitive topics, overt and covert methods, professional and personal roles and relationships, ethical codes and moral scripts, modern and postmodern approaches, and so on. More specifically speaking, vulnerabilities in fieldwork arise from: admitting ignorance of subject's knowledge; relinquishing control in interviewing when control is assumed; recognizing personal experiences when this is not assumed for analysis and interpretation; not knowing whether to act in the role of 'marginal native' or 'real' native when the observer role is assumed; not knowing whether you want to be friend or therapist when not overlapping roles is assumed. The researcher is advised to see vital contingencies as opportunities to celebrate opportunities for self-awareness, despite the vulnerability (Liberman, 1999). It is rare to find accounts of consequences of fieldwork for subjectively felt experiences (Richardson, 1992).

Symbolic interactionism and the inner 'I'

The interactionist perspective of self embodies the notion of development over the entire lifetime; the self is subject to the many contingencies of everyday life. In symbolic interactionism the social self has an inner 'I' that distinguishes any misconceptions the social actor may feel they are sowing among others by virtue of subjects' responses to appearance ('fronts'). The 'I' manages the role-playing self into and through social situations, establishments and settings (Burns, 1992: 107). The inner portion of self may retreat from the self-image being projected to the subject/s and might ask what kind of 'I' do I want to be? With scripting theory one gets the impression that the self is an autonomous being and located in the obscurity of the individual's behaviour. Yet personal scripts in most vital contingencies are a derivative of the social process. Contingencies of fieldwork have a capacity to call into question the very organization of the self and demand a reshuffling and reformulation of self. A contingency of fieldwork may precipitate a 'crisis of identity'; the ecology of the self could be so radically disturbed as to require major reformulation of self and validation of self in interaction with others.

The inner 'I' that distinguishes between self-image and discrepancies may retreat from the self-image of 'betrayer'. The inner 'I' may feel the need to modify behaviour and adapt to a script written by others, or alternatively become a partial scriptwriter or adaptor as she or he improvises with interpersonal and personal scripts to suit the local context. In social settings where most actors find it difficult to conceive of them as being anything other than what they are, personal scripts may be the best way of accounting for minor variations in performance (Simon and Gagnon, 1986).

Conclusion

Discussion of rapport and participant-observation has highlighted the influence of the positivist and interpretivist approaches, according to two major criteria. The first involves the position of the researcher in relation to the subjects and the setting (whether the researcher is perceived primarily as an observer of a reality outside the self, or a participant in a reality they have participated in creating). The second criterion involves the type of act or interaction by which rapport is accomplished: trust automatically granted as a result of the researcher's official status; or must the researcher develop relationships with participants in the course of the social construction of intersubjective meanings (Hunt, 1984: 284)?

From the positivist perspective, the observer role dominates the partici-pant role; the researcher is an outsider who exists apart from the research setting. Traditional ethnographers do not generally assume the researcher participates in the construction of the world, but they do recognize rapport needs to be negotiated in fieldwork. Traditional accounts of fieldwork assume the researcher is not changed by the journey through the fieldwork setting. The researcher proceeds from the 'outer' to the 'back-stage' regions of the participant's world (Goffman, 1959). The assumption is that the researcher manipulates people, manages impression management, engages in strategic acting, and manages to perform without fundamental transformation to his or her identity.

In a sense then, traditionalist ethnographers share a positivist view that the cultural setting is an objective reality external to the researcher, and not altered or transformed by the researcher's presence. The traditional perspective on fieldwork obscures an understanding of the researcher's lived experience of the other's world. 'Phenomenological' literature on participant-observation pays close attention to the active role of the researcher. Fieldwork is not defined as a journey through which a sociologist penetrates back-stage regions with relative ease. Instead it is a 'process of intersubjective construction' by which the researcher and researched develop a shared system of symbols (Hunt, 1984: 286). Rapport from this perspective is not the result of the formal role, or technical skills involved in strategic interaction and impression management. Rapport comes from the intersubjective construction of reality. In particular, it is the process whereby the researcher accomplishes membership of a group by displaying the very features by which subjects distinguish themselves from others that underpins rapport and ongoing access. Feminist research, although not a unified theoretical position, offers another approach to the analysis of rapport and participant-observation. The gender of the researcher is considered in the context of access to social areas and the participant's perceptions in turn effect permission to observe.

The researcher wants both to look in at the setting as a 'stranger' but also be immersed within the social reality of group members. To make problematic or 'bracket' social life requires distance, to become immersed sets up a tension in the other direction; the participant-observer role is ambiguous. Implicit in social science discussions of rapport is an assumption that separation between the researcher and researched is an essential aspect of field relations. With survey and experimental research, the 'scientific' stance is rationalized with avoiding bias and contaminated data. With qualitative inquiry the researcher is advised to 'achieve intimate familiarity with the setting' and 'engage in face-to-face interaction so as to participate in the minds of the settings' participants' (Lofland and Lofland, 1995: 17). The researcher's relationship to a setting captures the 'dilemma of distance'.

To maximize the research opportunity, the researcher needs to express the appropriate intellectual and emotional attitude towards the participants; trust has to be established between the researcher and the researched. The researcher needs to determine how to act or present the self so as to keep the flow of information coming. The researcher who has emotional difficulties may deflect energy and time away from the task of data collection. More seriously, however, does inadequate impression management create the potential barrier between the self and others? The researcher who can be non-threatening to participants (to their beliefs, self-confidence and existing social arrangements through argument, ridicule, sarcasm, disinterest) can be anticipated to receive more information than someone who is not sensitive and responsible in such matters. Being sensitive and attentive to others relates to appearances (gestures and dress) and to being appropriately situated relative to the audience. One who fills the role of 'learner' may be better placed than someone who is not so cautious in the situation, but treats the audience to a performance to which they may not be receptive.

A great portion of the ethics of sociological and anthropological practice derives from genuine respect for the social world and social practices of a group, and from taking seriously the opinions and values of the people we observe (Kellehear, 1993). The conditions of fieldwork, the paradoxes, impasses and dilemmas that arise from close social interaction with others, make ethical practice problematic in qualitative fieldwork (Fabian, 1991). The irony is that social science research requires the researcher to know in advance how to perform activities that convey respect for the social world and social practices of a group, and the opinions and values of people in the local situation. The scene is set for mistakes to happen and for ethical and moral dilemmas to emerge. The drama of fieldwork, as played out on the stage between ethnographer and subjects, implies both intrusion into another's social world and a certain pressure exerted to elicit information necessary for drawing some general conclusions; and a degree of researcher vulnerability derived from assumptions that the fieldworker knows in advance how to carry out activities appropriately.

The notion of the self-directed actor in the fieldworker role should not be overstressed. Researchers are well aware that the roles they play in the field are not strictly and exclusively their own choosing. The risk of threat that is emergent from the fieldwork setting and with problems of access cannot always be adequately anticipated. Research roles in practice are tentative offerings and possible forms of self that are subject to negotiation and to the vicissitudes of the action setting (Mitchell, 1991: 101). Subjects have their own pre-conceptualizations of researchers and what is expected of them and can take advantage of those who are taken in by their own acts, and show overconcern with self-interests. On the other hand, positions of increasing intragroup responsibility may be gradually granted to those who are willing to be taught, trained, tested and indoctrinated (Mitchell, 1991).

Without access to context-specific cultural and interpersonal scripts, however, the researcher initially is not well equipped for staging appearances; performances in the early phase of fieldwork may be akin to rehearsals. The researcher, under the guidance of an 'expert' or 'director', may be taken through a step-by-step procedure. Their progress may be monitored and they may be provided with a sounding board against which to bounce off ideas and gradually learn how to perform to group expectations. Relationships may be formed and roles played in ways approved by others, and a willingness to make mistakes and learn from them considered necessary to perfecting the role.

Access to cultural scenarios or degradation ceremonies can be a valuable learning process, enabling you to grasp implicit rules and roles that apply in a local situation. Such dramatic events have a capacity to bring together implied meanings that may otherwise gradually come together from numerous observations. The assembling capacity of such ceremonies may contribute to an understanding of the socially con- structed moral order of a social organization in which the researcher is located for purposes of research. Degradation ceremonies can show how the social actor who is an 'insider' is expected to act by projecting a definition of an 'outsider' who is guilty of moral infraction (Garfinkel, 1956). An actor who may not have known the rules, or was unwilling to respond to cues from others because they got in the way of their own agenda, who was subsequently joked about, ridiculed, mimicked and subjected to horseplay, can provide a role model in the learning process. The new researcher is well advised to internalize ways they and others are experienced by subjects, as 'outsiders', 'strangers', perhaps even figures of fun and ridicule, since subjects' responses provide opportunities for self-awareness, cues that signal the need for corrective 'face-work' and representations of moral significance.

Local contingencies of fieldwork are seen as both obstacles to research inquiry and opportunities to learn about other people's social world and about the self (Liberman, 1999). One must not overlook entirely the fact that researchers intrude into other people's lives and *systematically* violate others with their probing and questioning to gain access to information that the subjects may not want to disclose. The point is that '*systematics* are defined and redefined by the ethnographer's involvement in a particular social drama, for which she could only in part prepare herself' (Hastrup, 1992: 118). Reality is a joint production and the subjects are by no means dupes and suckers who are open to exploitation.

Contingencies convey insights into local practices. Researchers are advised not to make themselves immune to their effects and insights if personal transformation is to be achieved through fieldwork (Liberman, 1999). Vital contingencies are where the real discoveries are made; they offer both challenges and opportunities for celebration. Those who are genuinely sympathetic towards the interests and concerns of subjects, so much so that they are prepared *temporarily* to forgo the sole pursuit of research and become involved with other activities in the field, and demonstrate a more caring and sharing attitude towards others, may be defined as moral fieldworkers.

'Informed-sympathetic others' who become allies with subjects may confirm the worthiness of their *craft* or methodology. Such actors may become back-stage visitors who are free to examine the make-up and props used by a people to stage their appearances and performances in the field (Liberman, 1999). The ethnographic goal should be more than simply finding the shortest route to conveying local social phenomena to our analytic reductions of them (Berg, 1988; Liberman, 1999). The basis of moral inquiry and social interaction in general is to facilitate a genuine interchange, where each party to the encounter engages in transforming the other (Liberman, 1999).

CHAPTER 4

Back regions and sensitive methods

When we think of back regions we think of private space, where personal activities take place and only 'insiders' participate. Areas which are private introduce the need to be sensitive to the confidences and intimacies of others, if you are a researcher. One who intrudes into private space may pose a threat of risk to actors who fear exposure and sanctions. Access to such places by researchers may be rejected on such grounds and less 'open' methods may be used to infiltrate such places (covert observations, probing and 'strategic complicity' (Wong, 1998)).

The 'darker side' of fieldwork relates to deception, betrayal and clandestine observation. Researchers have aligned themselves with the 'darker arts' to study deviance in back regions (Wolcott, 1995). A particular study may encompass all aspects of sensitivity (private space, deviance, social control and use of devious methods), or any number of these aspects of sensitivity. One who has been granted consent may betray subjects' trust through use of ethically suspicious strategies (probing and complicity) to infiltrate back regions. Where research is defined 'sensitive', by virtue of being about personal and private matters, deviance or social control (Lee, 1993), the researcher may be at some risk of threat. Stigma may attach itself to those who align with deviance in any form and this can impact on the research's identity, the status of research itself and career opportunities.

An unanticipated consequence of engaging in sensitive research, and one that is not commonly spoken of in social science literature, relates to the personal and professional risk to self from having engaged with deviance and having to live with 'guilty knowledge'. The interior identity (or back-stage person that lies behind the public image of self, or within the inner and basic layers of the researcher) may need protection where the boundaries have been crossed between conventional and sensitive topics, regions and research methods. Excuses and justifications and other accounting devices in natural settings and the segregation of audiences may provide some means of neutralizing actors and actions; but these are part of the props and practices of self-preservation. Whatever the external appearance and practices suggest, ethnographers are not hidden from themselves. They are open to the feelings of others, often share the subject's outlooks and are broadened in understanding by their acceptance (Mitchell, 1991). They must confront the duality of the represented and experienced selves simultaneously (1991: 106). When this involves questionable practices the represented and the experienced selves are conflicted and may cause a 'conflict of consciousness'.

Early interactionist work

Many of the topics studied by the Chicago sociologists would be regarded as sensitive. There was intrusion in private spheres and the study of deviance (Lee, 1993: 11). The researchers recognized difficulties with gaining access to research sites, but were relatively unselfconscious about their methods. A number of symbolic interactionists used covert methods to study deviance. In some cases subjects were not told about the researcher's role and the purpose of research. From the interactionist perspective life may be seen as a masquerade, with people wearing many masks to conceal identity. Research may intrude into everyday activities; covert methods may be rationalized as yet another instance of masked activity to get behind the 'fronts' people use. The researcher like everyone else is engaged in the treacherous task of 'impression management'. The motivating force or spur to action may be that of reputation, the creation and consolidation of it through fieldwork and publications.

A lack of ethical awareness among first generation interactionists may have allowed many scholars to sidestep the ethical issues raised by sensitive topics and intrusion into private spheres. Those who carried out undercover research would have not have been able to use tape recorders or openly record field notes before an audience in the field. Thus they would have been limited when it came to establishing credibility by recourse to methods. Feelings of anguish over deception and regret from use of 'sneaky' strategies have been recorded in the literature. Whyte (1955) experienced considerable personal anguish over the deception he felt compelled to use in his study of Cornerville (Woods, 1992: 379) and Humphreys, (1975) later regretted the various deceptions engaged in with his study of homosexual encounters. The evidence suggests there are ethical and moral implications with sensitive methods and topics as well as methodological implications.

Later, generations of interactionists have shown a preoccupation with ethical dilemmas of fieldwork and a number have published accounts of their own fieldwork dilemmas for teaching purposes. Hansen (1976) locates the source of ethical dilemma in a symbolic interactionist inspired ethnographic study of family life in Denmark. The dual roles of researcher and friend enabled Hansen to enter the private sphere of the home to observe family relations and engage in personal interchanges and intimacies. The personal interchanges and intimacies that were openly spoken of between the researcher and the researched and the confidences and private information shared were not necessarily intended for an uncensored public airing; this raised problems with disclosure. Decisions had to be made on what material was considered personal and private and what to set aside for disclosure and publication.

The roles of objective analyst, friend and voyeur to promote an understanding of the subtle dynamics of Danish family life led the researcher to a back-stage vantage point in the private home, to promote an understanding of the subtle dynamics of Danish family life; and to ethical implications of *anonymity* and *confidentiality* that personal relationships create. The ethical implications can be at least as compelling on moral standards of behaviour as the rules of a discipline to document 'scientific' analysis by references to the concrete data to which friendships facilitated access in back regions.

Back regions and front regions

Goffman (1959), in talking about back and front regions in the context of shops, acknowledges how a mode of conduct to frame social behaviour has evolved over time. The back region is characterized by relaxed composure, appearance, interactional style, etc. Normative back-stage language consists of 'reciprocal first-naming, cooperative decision-making . . . playful aggressivity and kidding' (1959: 129). By contrast front-region behaviour conveys formal composure, involvement patterns and an interactional style to capture and maintain respect for the activity in progress. When we examine Goffman's handling of social space and standards of behaviour we find that the order maintained in a given physical region is governed by two kinds of demands – 'moral and instrumental'. In the front region there are moral rules regarding respect for people and places and instrumental duties that an employer might demand of an employee, care of property, maintenance of work levels, etc. (Goffman, 1959). In the world of shops, front-region actors express appropriate conduct for the sphere of activity in progress (work). Such actors may accord others and themselves a moral as well as an official identity. For it is as Goffman writes: 'To engage in a particular activity in the prescribed spirit is to accept being a particular kind of person who dwells in a particular kind of world' (1961a: 170). Conversely, to express inappropriate conduct for the sphere of activity in progress (work), 'to forgo prescribed activities, or to engage in them in unprescribed ways or for unprescribed purposes, is to withdraw from the official self' (1961a). The covert interpretive inquirer who has used participant-observation to infiltrate back regions to collect data most likely performs the role of worker as well. Immersed in the work role, they may engage in the prescribed spirit, respecting the propriety boundaries between front and back regions and the code of conduct for the back region, but there could be a problem with the prescribed spirit with regard to research where the role is covert and concealed. The particular kind of person who engages in participant-observation in unprescribed ways (secret), or for an unprescribed purpose, may be thought of as having withdrawn from the official role and professional identity accorded a person who dwells in a particular situation (the field), as judged by the standards of the biomedical ethical model. Such a person may be defined *deviant*.

With fieldwork done prior to and including part of the 1980s, the researcher's reference group was probably the academic audience, who were most likely accepting of underdeveloped ethics in anthropology and perhaps not so conscious about intrusion without consent as today, when anthropologists place greater emphasis on informed consent, permission and rights to privacy (Barrett, 1996). The *novice* interpretivist researcher of a past era gave first loyalty to colleagues and the profession rather than subjects in the field. Although allegiances may have been divided at times and relations between researcher and staff members occasionally strained, the ultimate test of loyalty was that the student remained committed to the goal of interpretivism and did not 'go native'. Debate on ethics in the published literature has more recently questioned the traditional impersonal ethical model that guided ethnographers of various persuasions in the field (Denzin, 1997), as objective, rational and bureaucratic, not situational and context specific or amenable to individual variations that require personal values, intuitiveness and emotions be taken into account when dealing with dilemmas.

In traditional ethnography, the reasons why and for whom research was done gradually unfolded as relationships were formed between the researcher and group members and people generally got to know each other. Consent was usually secured prior to entry to a fieldwork site. While there are few exchanges in the literature where consent was not granted, there is now enough information to realize that all parties to a research enterprise do not have equal rights of control over what happens to their ideas and actions. There is in the literature an acknowledgement of a 'hierarchy of consent', whereby senior personnel may act as 'gatekeepers' over subordinates, whom they force to participate in research (Woods, 1992).

Inmates in Goffman's famous study *Asylums* (1961a) were not informed that research was being carried out, whereas members of the upper echelon were. The control wielded by powerful members of an establishment in this case might suggest those lower in the hierarchy were considered not capable of making informed decisions on matters of consent. With covert research that is consciously entered into as a strategy, the point to emphasize is that the ethnographer is walking on thin ice (Punch, 1986). Where no one is told about the research and when most relationships created with participants over time in the field are built on a sham, the researcher is not only deceiving the participants, but are also deceiving the self (Woods, 1992). At some future point in time the researcher will probably need to face an 'ethical hangover' through having engaged in sensitive research and much soul-searching may be needed.

A case in question

A brief overview of personal experience is an attempt to illuminate how the study of back-region activities can impact on phases of actual fieldwork, 'writing up' and teaching practice. The aim is to put into perspective the threat of risk that sensitive research poses for the researcher and to contribute knowledge of practical ways to deal with ethical and moral dilemmas.

Fieldwork in back regions

In my first fieldwork placement, entry to the back region was made possible through a formal recruitment procedure. An official interviewed me as was customary practice and allocated a shop in which to work. Characteristically of qualitative fieldwork, analysis took the researcher to numerous field sites to study the same phenomena under different structural conditions. The later arrangement did not involve formal recruitment procedures. The second organization to which I recruited was new to the 'salvage' scene and relatively undeveloped in terms of bureaucratic rules and procedures. Members of the public could walk in off the street and arrange to work in one of the shops, and even start immediately as I had done. There was no formal recruitment procedure in place, although there was a committee that met to discuss the 'world of shops' and business practice.

The new recruit was inducted into formal and informal activities (in that order) and gradually acclimatized to a range of activities not anticipated by an 'outsider'. Such activities took place in the back region of stores run by the two unconnected organizations or welfare groups. Informal practices operated alongside the formal procedures; group norms and values sometimes deviated from company policy. As in other work situations, a system had evolved whereby workers negotiated concession rates for purchases made by and for the self. Informal practices performed in the back region provided the workers with a measure of control over the conditions in which they found themselves lodged for a few days each week. Control in occupational life is a feature of the sociology of the workplace and has been studied in relation to the dockyard (Mars, 1974) and the bakery (Ditton, 1977a). 'Working the load of the boat' among longshore boatmen has been seen as a feature of work life and a context for establishing trust among workers (Mars, 1974).

The dual roles of researcher and member of the group enabled the immersed participant-observer to gather data while performing activities which co-workers considered appropriate for the situation. The learner was socialized into the standards of appropriate conduct for the situation and, not unlike other researchers, became immersed in the 'complete membership' role (Adler and Adler, 1987). One of the unanticipated consequences of dealing with sensitive topics, regions and methods was the internalization of a fair amount of moral transformation. Ethical sensitivity was undeveloped in the postgraduate. There was an unquestioning attitude towards anything of an ethical nature that possibly stemmed from ignorance, since ethics was not a topic taught at undergraduate or postgraduate level and not an issue in the literature that the researcher's attention may have been drawn to. The anthropological debates seem to have emerged in the literature during my fieldwork in the early 1980s.

'Writing up' sensitive materials

Researchers may not adequately anticipate or even foresee the potential harms of fieldwork. Fabian (1991) did not anticipate ethical and moral dilemmas would arise from his attempt to understand how African workers of a religious movement coped with their world. Ethical and moral dilemmas present themselves *ex post factum* and they involve what to do with materials. Fabian later realized that the ideas and actions of the African workers he observed could be used to repress people if they became lodged in the wrong hands. The problem with dealing with secret and private matters moves beyond 'how to get it' to include 'what to do with it' (Fabian, 1991). Data in themselves are not necessarily sensitive or particularly harmful, but the possibilities of their becoming so are 'real' with disclosure. Information may be used for purposes other than originally intended. Harms from fieldwork occur with disclosure and publishing (Lee, 1993).

After fieldwork was completed, the researcher embraced fully the task of 'writing up'; decisions had to be made on what to include in the text. How to avoid taking a moralizing stance toward others was a concern, combined with importance of maintaining anonymity of people, places and organizations. Tracing the moral career of the researcher by drawing on Goffman's (1961a) 'moral career' concept, and the twofold accompanying concepts of self-image and felt identity, was a strategy consciously deployed to handle in a sociological fashion the issue of women's control of the informal reward system. The role of the 'stranger', a notion elucidated in the anthropological literature (Frankenburg, 1957), was appropriated to deflect attention away from others and enable the responsibility for activities to be absorbed by the ethnographer. The strategy provided a means to avoid being cast in a moralizing stance by the reader audience. There was apprehension of possible conflict between opposing groups being avoided by use of the strategy. Ironically, the autobiographical account was underpinned by a moral sensitivity. The researcher was made aware of the ethical and moral interpretations that an audience might place on the author's representations.

Teaching sensitive topics

A considerable number of years after research was completed the researcher revisited her field notes and considered using fieldwork experience for teaching purposes. Many of the women with whom I had worked in the shops were by then quite elderly as near on fifteen years had passed since fieldwork ended, and many were in their sixties and early seventies at that time. Given the considerable time lapse between fieldwork and disclosure it was assumed that any adverse ramifications from revelatory information would be minimal. Such rationalization was balanced with the notion that actual fieldwork experience was a good source from which to draw examples to illuminate abstract theoretical concepts in courses on qualitative research for postgraduate students. A provocative stance towards research methods was taken in the sense that no attempt was made to conceal my lived experience. I had hoped something positive would come from past fieldwork. A moral lesson in what *not* to do in the field was being promoted at the same time as providing information that might make abstract theoretical concepts more understandable by having been made personal.

Personal accounts were presented to audiences from a variety of disciplines and with differing theoretical persuasions (positivist, interpretivist, critical and feminist), and with varying degrees of actual research experience. Audience receptivity varied. Some members openly expressed their gratitude for an honest approach to ethics. Others thought the message had not gone far enough, that experiences should be recorded for the publication of a book on ethics and fieldwork. There were those (thankfully very few) who were morally outraged and indignant over my revelations, which they found objectionable on ideological, methodological, political and ethical grounds. An attempt on my part to salvage something from fieldwork that had gone wrong from the start was thwarted by opponents who were ideologically opposed to interpretivism and the self-indulgence of someone who drew on personal experiences.

On one occasion my fieldwork experience was used to illuminate assumptions about the social world and human behaviour held by symbolic interactionists; in particular to contrast the interactionist's emphasis of process to that of structure by positivist inspired researchers. An attempt was made to illuminate how, from the interactionist perspective on human behaviour, the individual is not assumed merely to respond to an internal stimulus (impulse or instinct), or to an external influence (rules, regulation, culture). The social actor responds to the definition she or he projects on to phenomena (Jacob, 1987). Processes of *definition* and *interpretation* are inserted between the giving and receiving of a message (Blumer, 1969). I thought that by drawing on my own fieldwork experience I would be able to make more understandable Blumer's basic premises (1969: 2).

I set out to demonstrate the social 'constructedness' of reality with a focus on 'situational honesty'. By showing that what was 'legitimate' for women with whom I worked had less to do with rules and regulations and more to do with group values, ideals, norms and shared sentiments, as they related these to notions of work rendered, I hoped that the first two basic interactionist premises outlined by Blumer would be illuminated. These are 'that human beings act toward things on the basis of the meanings that the things have for them . . . that meaning is derived from, and arises out of, the social interaction that one has with one's fellows' (1969: 2). Morality was to be shown as situational and relative and policed by workers. I was aware that Ditton (1977a) and Mars (1974) had shown how workers construed workplace activities as a morally justifiable addition to wages and an entitlement due from exploiting employers. Although there was never any suggestion that these women spoke of privilege in terms of redress for exploitative contractual arrangements, there were parallels to be made since they had a notion that they were entitled to 'perks'.

In attempting to salvage something positive from fieldwork in back regions I was to learn how the presenter risks stigma by association with sensitive issues and methods. The attempt to illuminate the point that actors respond to meaning which is projected onto the situation and not to some internal or external stimuli, rules and regulations went without a hitch, but following this there were dramatic unanticipated consequences for the presenter. During question time an agitated audience member expressed her moral indignation over what had just transpired in the session, which took the presenter completely by surprise. It was unclear whether negotiating prices in the back region, dubious methods of observation or both were being attacked by her interpretation of deviance, which either way seemed to reinforce the argument I was attempting to get across: people project meaning onto social phenomena and they act in terms of the meaning this has for them. But in this case there was an ironical twist.

I assume the audience member spoke from the position of another theoretical perspective and philosophical persuasion with which she was more in sympathy, and she was at some remove from symbolic interactionism as a modern or traditional sociological approach. She defined either the topic or research method or both as *deviance*, and by association the actor was stigmatized too. The members said, in a half-hearted questioning and revelatory sort of way, 'So you were engaged in deviance were you?' I retorted automatically from a taken-for-granted point of view, 'No, I was engaged in participant-observation.' In retrospect there came the realization how changed circumstances coloured and shaped an audience's ethical and moral interpretations of the actor's representations, as indeed it had blinkered the student to moral choice. A different historical moment in the unfolding of qualitative research when ethics and morality were being debated, and a different audience constituted of more ethically conscious members, rendered my interpretation of lived experience, for whatever purpose promoted, questionable on moral and ethical grounds. What I had accepted without question as a postgraduate student as normative fieldwork practice was now defined as an ethical and moral choice, and a dubious one at that. The lecturer and the student before her seemed unaware their definition was coloured and shaped by different historical and sociological circumstances.

The threat of stigma from the study of a sensitive topic, back regions and immersion in the participant-observation role, which attached itself to the fieldworker, contaminated the identity of the lecturer when teaching sensitive topics. Much has been said on what the researcher must do to avoid harming participants in the social science literature, but less is written of the potential risk of harms for the researcher who studies sensitive topics and uses sensitive methods. Within anthropological research the notion of 'the sly manoeuvres of crafty professors' has been debunked, and so too has the notion of 'innocent subjects' who need to be 'protected' (Wax, 1977: 324). The *novice* is not always in control and can be seen as performing to a script largely written by other people (supervisors and hosts). Even very experienced ethnographers must rely on the goodwill of hosts to protect them in the field (Mitchell, 1991; Wax, 1977).

A number of options have been presented to address the problem of dealing with 'ouch' factors in the research process, or obstacles of fieldwork which require the researcher to step back and reconsider options (Alty and Rodham, 1998). With regard to sensitive issues, Alty and Rodham (1998) provide three options:

1. Plan another project entirely.
2. Proceed with caution.
3. Publish and be damned.

None of these options seem particularly satisfactory where sensitive topics are concerned and anticipatory measures are needed. Planning another project might be easier in the long run, but this does not adequately deal with the public's right to know about social phenomena. Proceeding with caution could mean the public's right to know is at least being addressed, but this could be at the expense of plunging the self into 'a conflict of interests'. To publish and be damned is a calculated risk that is littered with problems which could draw the researcher into debates and legal wrangles. Deciding what should be disclosed is a central anticipatory issue of fieldwork, especially where sensitive topics are concerned, and should be taken seriously (Lee, 1993). Ethnographers possess few precise ideas of what they will confront in the field. While there may be no satisfactory answer to obstacles that arise in fieldwork, the option of proceeding with caution would seem the best one to adopt.

Confronting local contingencies of fieldwork may be the first real experience that the interpretive inquirer has with ethics. Fieldwork can trap the *novice* into performing activities appropriate for the situation without their necessarily knowing what appropriate activities will involve. With ethnography it is impossible to provide in the proposal an explicit and precise description of the 'problem' to be explored and the activities that fieldwork will involve. The field site may be described in geographical and organizational terms but the socio-political and cultural nature of the region can only be speculated upon and discovered. The same applies whether fieldwork is carried out in remote and unknown locations or at home in the urban area. It may be enough in the proposal to say fieldwork will take place in an urban or metropolitan area of a known city, but circumstances are largely unknown and can change during the research process. The grounded theory approach (where the researcher relocates to another site to study the same phenomena under differing structural conditions) captures the indeterminacy that is characteristic of ethnography (particularly in disciplines like anthropology); and the need for the *novice* who is without clear-cut guidelines to tread cautiously.

Deception and betrayal

Betrayal may be most explicitly addressed when ethnographers are asked the question 'Did the participants know you were a researcher?' Even where informed consent has been granted and observations are unambiguously overt, there are many interactional sequences in the field that can give rise to deception and betrayal. Researchers may use the art of seduction to discover confidences and personal matters in the course of pursuing ethnography's goal of revelation. Respondents may be betrayed by virtue of the contrived nature of using the self as an instrument to get people to 'open up'.

A propensity for being gossipy and prying may be a personal style that the researcher brings to the setting, in contrast to the impersonal, objective stance of the fully detached quantitative researcher. The personal style may be particularly amenable to establishing intimacy and confidences in the field, but engaging in the art of seduction raises the question 'How ethically appropriate is it to seduce people?' Wong (1998) admits recording information gathered from corridors by seductive means was an ethical violation he could have avoided. Extending from extraction of information is the problem of what to do with the information: 'Does the fieldworkers have a licence to tell all?' 'What does one disclose and at what cost, and for what audience?' Wolcott (1995) advises, 'No fieldworker ever has a licence to tell all.' Wong (1998) did not have to record confidences in field notes and he could have fore-warned people their confidences would be recorded. The researcher has a responsibility periodically to remind people why they are there. What should be disclosed is to a large extent a problem of reportage and is discussed in Chapter 8.

The qualitative researcher may inadvertently find out too much of the 'wrong' information when learning to become a member of the institution under study, and when establishing how the participant-observer is going to proceed. Revealing aspects of one's socialization in the role of 'learner' may provide a means to divert attention away from the subjects, but doing so could constitute betrayal, because autobiographical accounts can identify mentors and co-workers in association with the author.

Face-to-face contact puts people in touch in sensitive ways

Some strategies in fieldwork are more problematic than others. Participant-observation is an interactive technique that brings the researcher into close relationship with participants, and with the same sorts of inter-actional difficulties experienced with social relations in everyday life. Feminists argue for a more egalitarian and less exploitive relationship between researcher and researched in qualitative interviewing (Oakley, 1981). Face-to-face contact, however, puts people in touch in sensitive ways, characterized by intimate relationships of trust, mutual caring and regard, and demands extra attention be given to handling relations in sensitive ways. The very closeness recommended by the 'feminist communitarian ethical model' Denzin (1997) would seem to require greater sensitivity, authenticity and discretion than previously required of modern researchers in social science.

Participant-observation is a technique of fieldwork that is by definition a sensitive issue by virtue of the intimate human interaction that is thus facilitated. When empathy, trust and support are used to forge strong supportive links between the researcher–researched, the potential for complicity and betrayal is created. The researcher needs to be mindful of ways of knowing and ways of relating to those who assist her investigation of social phenomena. The way the researcher uses the self as an instrument to draw out the narratives from respondents and styles of interviewing are ethical and moral choices. The ethnographer who establishes rapport and intimate relationships in the field may be granted access to information about illicit affairs, illicit activities and 'deviance', and could become entangled in a 'conflict of interests' when partners in the field fight over allegiance with the researcher (Stacey, 1988).

Deception and betrayal may be linked with interviewing strategies and with physical space. Corridors and women's bathrooms are places where they trade stories, share gossip and generally exchange confidences. Such back regions would normally be out of bounds to a male researcher, but it is possible for a male to access women's stories, gossip and confidences vicariously, by exercising seductive skills and engaging in complicity. Wong gained access to private space for his dissertation and research by engaging in a strategy he calls 'strategic complicity' (Wong, 1998). He encouraged women to reveal the confidences and gossip they shared in private space, and thus aided and abetted betrayal among women. One of the interviewees showed signs of having been beaten and was badly bruised. She gossiped about a relationship between her batterer ex-boyfriend and an administrator in the programme under study, and the researcher wanted more information about the personal abuse that everyone was talking about. Wong asked women questions that drew on the collective exchanges that had transpired in the bathroom, corridor and self-esteem class. Women divulged confidences in response to questions asked about the private concerns of others (but not of them). Asking women to betray one another breached ethical boundaries and double standards applied (the researcher did not reveal intimate details of his private, sexual life). Wong admits to having accessed the bathroom, the corridor and the self-esteem class by asking questions about information shared in private spaces, which subsequently meant the trust among women, their relationships and confidences were betrayed.

The ethical and moral dilemmas recounted in Wong's (1998) article are made understandable against a professed overzealous and enthusiastic approach to data collecting, without being sensitive to the terrain traversed. Deception is a fact of life and of fieldwork, but the researcher has a moral obligation to act responsibly in the field. Normally the bathroom would be a safe space for women to conceal confidences, but in Wong's study the back region was infiltrated through complicity rather than covert observations (there was informed consent). Wong admits he should have forewarned women that the confidences so enthusiastically proffered constituted data which would be recorded in field notes. He was under no obligation to write up confidences and could have expressed an appreciation of participants' input on the matter. People who participate in research need not only to know about the role of the researcher and the purpose of research, but also be periodically reminded why the researcher is in the field (Wolcott, 1995). Contemporary fieldwork puts people in touch with others in more intimate and personal ways than previous moments in social science. It demands more integrity, authenticity and maturity, and has the potential to create problems with the management of *anonymity* and *confidentiality* (Lincoln, 1995).

Strategies used in fieldwork are moral and ethical choices that reflect responsibility and a sense of justice. Harm to participants can arise from feelings of having been betrayed. Mistakes of fieldwork and the quandaries experienced by the researcher often emerge in the post-fieldwork phase. Having observed too closely and found out too much of the 'wrong' sort of information, the problem becomes how to proceed with what has been revealed and understood. I would suggest that how and how much to report are complicated even further where back-region space has been explored through use of sensitive strategies. Every fieldwork situation brings its own set of ethical problems, many of which are without a solution, but we can learn from the mistakes made by others and their attempts at being accountable.

Probing

Techniques of interviewing in natural settings to break silences, oppose resistances and unravel thoughts on matters people prefer to keep hidden are hardly new in ethnography. Probing which stimulates an informant to produce more information and allows the researcher to be relatively uninvolved in a questioning stance is linked with successful interviewing in anthropology (de Laine, 1997: 174–175). Probing to extract information that is in some way intimate or personally discrediting is ethically questionable, particularly if the material is to be subjected to uncensored public airing.

Bernard (1994) has specifically addressed the ethical implications of probing and outlined the researcher's responsibilities to subjects. As rapport develops and respondents are treated as friends, they are likely to 'open up' with partial biographies and accounts of difficult moments, hopes, dreams, sufferings and aspirations. It becomes an ethical issue as to whether such information should be recorded as data in field notes and whether the researcher should prompt. People who tell too much of what they consider secret can later have real regrets and even experience loss of self-esteem. Establishing a mutually trusting relationship provides a base from which to negotiate what should and should not be probed (Mitchell, 1991), but the rapport and intimacy established with fieldwork relations would seem to provide opportunities to get more intimate and confidential material.

The silent probe is characterized by the researcher remaining silent and waiting for the informant to continue. The strategy may increase the uncertainty of participants about how much the researcher knows. They may be prompted to fill in more detail than previously envisaged or desired. Members may be at some disadvantage with researchers who have become friends. Researchers are often able to read very subtle cues and anticipate what respondents have not made explicit, by virtue of sociological training, whereas subjects have not been trained to pry professionally. The researcher who has been granted access to personal and private space in back regions may observe much by virtue of the participant-observation role. They are in a position to manipulate informants to reveal more than they intended through probing, which could constitute an invasion of privacy, or collect information that is inadvertently conveyed through non-verbal expressions. A difference in biographies can be differentiated in terms of sociological imagination and manipulation. Bernard says 'the first ethical decision you make in research is whether to collect certain kinds of information at all. Once that decision is made *you* are responsible for what is done with that information, and *you* must protect informants from becoming emotionally burdened for having talked to you' (Bernard, 1994: 220).

Foddy (1993) acknowledges that questions which are idiosyncratic and relative to specific individuals' (cancer and some forms of sexual behaviour) may generate personal fear and feelings of guilt among those afflicted. Questions that concern normative issues (social morality and responsibility, hygiene, and so on) and political and economic interests may create the threat of social rejection and economic and political sanctions respectively. Questions that pose a threat to respondents have been matched with strategies to reduce the threat, so as to ensure that interviews and questionnaires will work the way that fieldworkers and survey researchers intend them to work (Foddy, 1993: 125).

The study of sensitive topics which provoke the disclosure of highly personal and confidential information requires strategies be imported into the interview encounter to protect the respondent and interviewer alike (Brannen, 1988). Research on sensitive topics like HIV and AIDS, marital relations or specific sexual behaviour can identify respondents in written reports both by themselves and with others (including the researcher), because of the personal and unique nature of the data. Identification carries with it the associated risk of sanctions and stigma (Brannen, 1988). In addition, the respondent who is encouraged to confront and tell her or his story may be led into a stressful experience, which could be a problem for the researcher as well as the respondent. The researcher has some responsibility to protect the respondent, both with respect to the confidences disclosed and the emotions which may be aroused and expressed (Brannen, 1988).

Problems in conducting sensitive research, which may challenge both the researcher's and the respondent's values and assumptions, are not always easily anticipated (Alty and Rodham, 1998). Focusing on sensitive topics, for example, HIV and AIDS in an organizational context, can highlight the researcher versus therapist dilemma. The researcher may be torn between the decision to follow the interview protocol and an equally strong desire to take on a therapeutic role toward the respondent. The interviewer who strays from the research role may place the self in a position of hearing too much and contribute to the respondent becoming stirred up emotionally, which could be seen as irresponsible, given the researcher is not usually trained to administer counselling.

Listening to people's stories and distress may be exhausting and emotionally disturbing for both parties, but the respondent can turn to the professional support of a therapist whereas the researcher lacks this supportive back-up. The counsellor or psychotherapist is supported by professional practice guidelines that safeguard client and therapist alike, but the researcher is treading on ethically sensitive grounds when she strays from the prescribed role and engages as a confidante (more on this in the following chapter). Hearing too much about off-the-record comments and activities (by encouraging respondents to discuss feelings stirred up by emotional issues) may cause difficulties for the researcher, yet it could be considered unethical not to provide an opportunity to talk (Schmied, 1995).

Respondents who reveal highly personal details about their lives are vulnerable to their own emotions. They could experience feelings of guilt and regret afterwards and may be at risk from other people, especially partners who are implicated in the respondent's confidences (Brannen, 1988: 559). Partners may be angered that they have not been told of the research, or that a view has been presented which they do not agree with. The researcher could be drawn into a relationship of complicity by one member, and thus placed in opposition to the member's partner. Researchers doing sensitive research have a special responsibility to anticipate the ways in which research may be risky for respondents and researchers alike.

Social control as a sensitive issue

A number of researchers may have decided to study health-related problems ethnographically. The decision has been made to use qualitative methods of inquiry (perhaps participant-observation instead of survey or experimental design). Although relatively experienced with quantitative research, the choice of qualitative inquiry may be thought better suited to the 'problem'. Being without the structure provided by a hypothesis in quantitative research (which requires relations between variables be tested) may create feelings of insecurity. This is understandable since quantitative research on human behaviour has a more clearly defined research agenda, whereas ethnography and other kinds of qualitative inquiry are characterized by the concept 'discovery' (Hammersley, 1990).

The notion of discovery does not mean the researcher enters the field without any idea of what to look for and where to look for it. Sensitizing concepts 'provide a general sense of reference' and point out 'directions along which to look' (Blumer, 1969: 148). Group process and *control* are sensitizing concepts that have origins in sociological theory and are pertinent to symbolic interactionism. The researcher who chooses symbolic interactionism as a theoretical perspective may adopt these concepts to guide first observations. Preliminary observations in the field may have established the value in following certain lines of inquiry for first observation that feature interactionist concepts like *process* and *control*. From preliminary observation of one store, and conversations with friends who purchased second-hand garments from such shops, I was sensitized to a problem worthy of further study.

In response to admiring a pair of trousers worn by one friend I learned she had purchased them from a second-hand store. She informed of the price she had paid and said, 'If you want a bargain you'll have to dress down.' The reasoning behind the statement was that appearances mattered where prices were fixed at the counter. If my appearance indicated a capacity to pay a higher price then that was what I might be charged. Soon after this conversation another friend reiterated the negotiable price arrangement at the shop counter, and elaborated further on the notion of control in them of access to goods. My observation of one store verified what my friends had previously told me. The seller produced items from under the counter for a dealer's perusal and purchase.

The worker who controlled the flow of goods and adjusted prices stood to gain the prestige that comes from social control. Social control and deviance have been defined as sensitive topics (Lee, 1993). Had I been alerted to the sensitive nature of the topics I may have been more cautious with the choice of problem, but at the time such an emphasis on sensitive topics was unheard of. In point of fact, the undergraduate and early postgraduate years were inspired by allegiance with interactionists (Becker, 1963; Goffman, 1961a; Whyte, 1955), each of whom had studied topics that were sensitive (drug use, mental illness and street gangs), with deviant connotations.

From the outset I was interested in a topic that was deemed sensitive. Where access to goods and prices was being granted to some people and not others, there was an element of secrecy, deviance and control. *Buyer–seller transactions* and *pricing dictates* suggested by my preliminary observation, featured in my research proposal as lines of inquiry to pursue in first observations. Other lines of inquiry addressed the questions: 'Why was there a bell for customers to ring for service when workers could see them at all times?' 'Why did some workers consider serving customers the least important part of their work?'

The notion of *control* was of significance not only because of preliminary observations and conversations, but because *control* is a sociological concept of some considerable import to symbolic interaction, the theoretical perspective that I intended to use. From the perspective of symbolic interactionism, *control* is concentrated in the hands of the self-determining actor, who is not merely responding to some biological stimulus or instinct, or an external stimulus such as rules, regulations or culture, but to the interpretation projected on to the situation. When I proposed the study of *buyer–seller relations* and *pricing dictates* I was not aware that participant-observation would take me into back regions to participate in activities which co-workers (but not necessarily upper management) considered appropriate for the situation, the details of which they may have wanted to keep secret. I unwittingly embarked on a study that was ridden with ethical problems by virtue of being a sensitive topic in back regions which created problems with disclosure. 'Insiders' are allies who frequent back regions, and allies are not supposed to divulge secrets to 'outsiders' (Mitchell, 1991).

Performances are usually constructed with an audience in mind. The members of the organization I studied performed for an audience mainly constituted of peers with whom they formed friendships on a base of shared activities. Women volunteer workers who processed second-hand garments in the back region of various stores were out of sight of customers. They hoped they would appreciate the presentation of the display area and reward their work effort with purchases. The paying clientele was prevented from gaining uninvited glimpses of backstage activities by a curtain that partitioned the front from the back region. Audience segregation assisted information control in another sense. Friends of the participants generally belonged to a different social circle outside the store. As these social circles and those formed inside the store were unlikely to overlap, information was unable to filter from one social circle to another and mar the impressions women were busy creating. Secrecy surrounded the 'day out' since women were heard to say on a number of occasions, 'You don't tell your friends where you get your clothes?' and 'You don't tell your friends where you go on your day out.'

Where ethnographers do fieldwork in the urban setting the post-graduate body and dissertation supervisors may be in regular contact and form an audience before which to discuss fieldwork. Audiences have different interests and expectations and exert different degrees of moral pressure to perform in certain ways and demonstrate loyalty and com-mitment. An academic audience may exert considerable influence over the *novice* at every phase of the research process. The formulation of a problem, choice of methods and field site, duration of fieldwork and so forth may be negotiated within such a body. Dissertation supervisors may prescribe in particular ways how the *novice* will perform and may disattend personal preferences and moral dilemmas.

When information about performances in the back regions was con-veyed to the academic audience before which I regularly performed during fieldwork, it was not the trials and tribulations in the day in the life-world of the researcher or moral career of the interpretive inquirer that was of any relevance. An investigator who happened also to be a participant had collected the data discussed; the audience expected to hear about observations and analyses. The personal and private were mildly interesting, perhaps as asides with some light relief or amusement value. Participating before an academic audience during fieldwork pro-vided some relief from being the 'complete group member' (boring and frustrating when fieldwork was near completion), and a friend (demand-ing when combined with the research role), but did not necessarily provide any escape from sensitive issues. The shared understanding of a variety of issues gathered from the field, when placed before an academic audience, assumed analytical significance, but anything idio-syncratic or impressionistic was irrelevant.

Being a participant-observer in the urban setting meant performing before two audiences; each had evolved cultural and interpersonal scripts to which the actor was required to perform, but which she had no part in writing. Had a member of the organizational group under study enquired about the research in progress, challenge to the identity as the group member could have resulted in some form of redress; the performance could have been drawn to a premature halt. Protection from discrediting information was facilitated by the physical separation of the audiences, but the differing expectations of staff members on what was appropriate behaviour for the fieldworker made more complex the moral career of the interpretive inquirer, since she could not take for granted that the academic setting was a safe haven either, because the seminar sessions were rigorous and personally intimidating to a new researcher.

Reparation work on the identity may be a consequence of the researcher having been involved with sensitive topics and/or sensitive methods involving secrecy. I found the mildly illicit activities, considered appropriate for the situation, in the future (when fieldwork is completed) could be entirely divorced from the customary routines and values of everyday life – the academic milieu, which was the paramount reality. But self-apprehension of self-as-violator was a contingency of the moral career of the interpretive inquirer. Where dubious methods are used in the study of deviance, as was the case with Laud Humphreys' (1970, 1975) study, reparation work would be considered more extensive than for fieldworkers generally (see below). The self-apprehension of self-as-a violator may be an occupational hazard of fieldwork that the covert researcher has to confront long after fieldwork is completed.

Rationalizing sensitive topics and methods

Research that deals with areas which are private or relates to the study of deviance and social control is threatening both to the participants and researcher alike (Lee, 1993). Where deviance has been studied the researcher may be stigmatized by colleagues and students. Research or teaching fieldwork methods produces personal and professional risk where the topic is sensitive. Charges of self-indulgence and being overly narcissistic have been brought against those who engage in confessionals and produce cookbook style publications that feature the ethnographer's experiences in the field. Such accounts have been trivialized by those who regard unbiased and generalizable information as 'scientific' and noteworthy, and anything personal and idiosyncratic not acceptable for an academic audience. The researcher and the research can be displaced out of the mainstream of a discipline by virtue of lower status or marginal character.

As indicated previously, many of the topics studied by the Chicago sociologists would today be regarded as 'sensitive'. Much attention was focused on family networks, friendships or neighbourhood groups, any one of which might implicitly involve intrusion in the private sphere (Lee, 1993: 11). There was also an interest in the study of deviance, and involvement with asking questions, which might yield incriminating information. Some early interactionists were relatively unselfconscious about their methods, which in part may have allowed them to get around some of the difficult ethical issues raised by the study of sensitive topics today. Later interactionist writing within the sociology of deviance was confronted by dilemmas which arise from possession of 'guilty knowledge' or knowledge of deviant activities (Lee, 1993: 15).

The trend for future ethnographic inquiry seems set for more rather than less research done on sensitive topics, given the problems and issues that require researching. This would suggest a need to be aware of the pitfalls with sensitive research in terms of personal and professional identity. Ethnography is now being recognized as one of the most important approaches in qualitative research. It is popular in the health sciences where problems like AIDS, drug use, child abuse, marital breakdown and diverse sexual practices require investigation. An understanding of such problems implies entry to private and/or deviant worlds and of finding ways of dealing with the threat of risk for participants and researchers alike, especially the unknown ramifications for self, research and career.

Laud Humphreys' well-known, if not notorious, study *Tearoom trade* (1970, 1975), features a covert study of homosexuals in a public toilet (a private realm in the public arena). In this study Humphreys assumed a covert observer-as-a-participant role. In the role of 'watchqueen' or lookout, he was able to observe all impersonal homosexual activities that took place between men in the bathroom, which were highly deviant. Following from this, Humphreys recorded car licence plate numbers and traced men to private residences, where he interviewed them under the pretence of another study and was physically disguised to avoid identification. It was the fact that he traced the men to their residences and changed his appearance which raised objections in the academic audience (Fontana and Frey, 1994: 373).

The stigma associated with his topic and the unorthodox methods used were rationalized by Humphreys against the need for sociological investigation and by recognition that the methods used were the least obtrusive possible (Adler and Adler, 1994: 388). In his published work Humphreys (1970) successfully hid evidence of his participation in the tearooms and this reticence might be interpreted generally as stemming from embarrassment, or because the researcher feared disapproval and sanctions. Feelings of outrage and betrayal on the part of those studied typically follow the disclosure that a covert study has taken place (Lee, 1993: 146).

Adler and Adler's (1994) research on upper level drug dealers and smugglers involved them in a peripheral membership role. They refrained from participating in actual trafficking, but in order to gain the trust of the drug dealers and smugglers they cultivated friendships and provided support, advice, loans, use of their car and so on (Lee, 1993). The researchers later experienced feelings of guilt for services they had provided and felt insincere for having feigned friendships to gain information. They sometimes felt resentment because those they studied took advantage of them in various ways and exploited them (Adler and Adler, 1994). Expending resources on individuals and paying dues to those harnessed to deviant activities could lead those observing the research to ask, 'Whose side are you on?'

Accounts recorded in the sociological literature of moral dilemmas encountered in the field are valuable for promoting an understanding of the pitfalls of ethnography and other kinds of qualitative research, and for the promotion of more professional and ethical research. Woods (1992: 380) informs the reader that where fieldwork offends one's own values and runs counter to years of socialization, to say nothing of allegiance to a professional code of ethics, the researcher risks a damaged self, a 'spoiled' project, and possibly a spoiled research career. The question becomes not *why* do they do it, but *how* do they do it. How does the researcher maintain a favourable self-image and manage a positive felt-identity when carrying 'guilty knowledge'? A contingency in the moral career of the covert interpretive inquirer may be to ensure that the partial researcher self as 'rule breaker' remains an auxiliary role, and does not become a master and controlling status that could damage the production of a total social 'Me' (to use the terminology of symbolic interactionism). In other words, embarrassment, shame or guilt, which stem from breaching one's own moral values, must not spread into the inner and basic layers of the self and affect the perception of self as a person worthy of self-esteem.

Interpretation of past dubious experience seems generally to occur in an ad hoc fashion, sometimes well after fieldwork is completed. Whyte's (1955) famous study of Italian men of Cornerville, which depicted illicit operations and informed many sociologists and other educated people about the nature of 'ethnic slums', is alleged to have portrayed 'corner boys' in demeaning ways. A symposium in the early 1990s, some forty to fifty years after the study was completed, provided scholars with an opportunity to reflect on the production of the text and differing interpretations of Whyte's ethnography. Participant response to the alleged 'trashing' nomenclature – *slums, gangs, rackets* – suggested Whyte imposed normative judgements on Cornerville life, misinterpreted street-corner activity for *gang* activity and the community as a *slum*, overlooked the place of the family in the community, while at the same time placing too much emphasis on *racketeers*. He breached confidences when he published his book without informing the men that he was doing so (Denzin, 1992b: 123). Whyte is thought to have experienced considerable personal anguish over the deception he was compelled to use in his study of Cornerville (Woods, 1992: 379).

Social actors may excuse, justify or clarify motives by producing accounts that address blame publicly and embarrassment or shame privately. Verbal accounts are part of 'face-saving' work that might be used to bring the act and/or actor in alignment with the norm, or at least make them acceptable given the circumstances. Where questions are asked in natural settings the researcher might in defence provide verbal responses to neutralize blame and feelings of shame, or they might mount a defence with a published text to distance the self from stigma. Other people's responses to the role performance become part of the actor's perception of self and are crucial to relations to self as a person. The interior identity (the 'back-stage' person) needs protection where devious practices are concerned. The researcher, who has performed activity in unprescribed ways but wants to avoid the *deviant* label, must find ways to insulate the total 'me' from the rule-breaker part of self.

Types of accounts

Social actors may attempt to excuse, justify or legitimate behaviour or clarify motivations by producing different types of accounts with different audiences in mind. Accounts take the form of justification and excuses; other accounting devices like 'the indeterminacy repertoire' appeal to the apprenticeship status of the ethnographer.

Research-based rationales

For the past couple of decades anthropologists have conducted a great deal of soul-searching about research done at home or abroad (Barrett, 1996). Terms such as deception and informed consent reflect a new concern for the rights of the individual. Within anthropology little attention seems to have been given the ethics of fieldwork prior to the 1960s, but sensitivity seems to have gradually increased with the input of feminism and scholarship, the emergence of participatory and critical types of research with applied outcomes, and a general interest in individual rights that is reflected in the rise in importance given to ethical codes, guidelines and committees in universities and other bodies entrusted with research (Punch, 1986). No longer is it considered appropriate to intrude into the lives of other people to collect information without making research goals explicit. Permission must be sought and granted and the privacy of individuals respected. Knowledge for its own sake is no longer sufficient reason to study human social life. In some instances research has to have practical or applied outcome to be ethical, and the findings of esoteric topics that exercise the minds of academics, but have no other pragmatic outcome, could be deemed unethical.

Postgraduate training in the past did not include ethical issues. Methods and theory classes were considered sufficient to prepare the *novice* for the field. During fieldwork the researcher might recognize the ethical aspect of some situations (Rynkiewich, 1976). The underdevelopment of anthropological ethics became an excuse for dubious ethical practices, like not making research goals explicit or not seeking permission to observe practices and not attempting to change the status quo. Confessionals which depict the trials and tribulations of ethnographers as they go about conducting research, which can prepare *novices* for the pitfalls of fieldwork, are more prevalent in the social science literature today, much to the concern of modernists who reject such practices as narcissistic and self-indulgent. The traditional goal of ethnography, to produce unbiased and generalized findings, is not advanced by 'textual radicals' who engage in new ways of textual representation (Hammersley, 1995).

'The indeterminacy repertoire'

It has been the tradition in anthropology for neophytes to learn on the job. How to do fieldwork was not so much something considered a teachable activity as an art that draws on public relations skills that have been developed over a lifetime. Those for whom such qualities as empathy, sympathy or at least everyday courtesy come naturally may be well placed to handle the human relations aspect of fieldwork. Participant-observation is something you learn by doing, and you do this alone. Each encounter might be anticipated as an element of the unknown, since the actor can never be sure the other will treat him or her with the respect a person of specific standing may consider deserving. There is an element of mystique perpetuated by an inability or reluctance to explicate fieldwork processes.

The novice enters the field a neophyte and comes out an ethnographer. An accounting device like 'the indeterminacy repertoire' (Coffey and Atkinson, 1996) might emphasize the field setting as a context for ritual transformation, where the *novice* experiences 'becoming', of betwixt and between, where structure is not. The indeterminacy of the liminal phase of fieldwork can influence the meaning that is imposed on the act and the actor. The 'liminal' or marginal act or actor may not be defined unethical, but the possibility could be revealed.

Relativist-oriented rationales

Symbolic interactionists have generally embraced a strongly relativistic streak in the past. Some have debunked absolutist claims because the standards of ethical absolutism (universal and impersonal) in relation to consent, privacy, harm and confidentiality fail to respect the researcher's conscience. Ethical relativists have questioned the relevance of the biomedical model of ethics for disciplines outside medicine and the health sciences (such as sociology and anthropology). Those who subscribe to absolute freedom to pursue activities as they see fit, and consider no method of sociological research is intrinsically more ethical than any other, may bring a distinctively liberal and individualistic approach to consent, confidentiality and disclosure. The relativist may support the notion that the researcher who has intimate knowledge of others knows the consequences of her or his actions, and must exercise individual conscience on such matters. A symbolic interactionist who is guided by a relativistic approach to ethics may reject fixed ethical standards and rely on the individual's conscience. This approach perhaps fits more closely with the constructionist perspective on motivation that is based on the individual's perception and interpretation rather than adherence to rules and regulations or cultural norms, which characterize in part an absolutist perspective on the social world and human behaviour.

Questions have been raised over the ethical standing of covert studies because such 'undercover' work negates the principle of informed consent, involves deception and frequently cannot be carried out without invading the privacy of those being studied (Lee, 1993). The sceptical perspective accepts the need to protect the rights of participants and an obligation not to harm them, but covert research may be engaged in and even regarded reluctantly as an acceptable method where the study is not typical and there is no other way to obtain the data (1993: 144). The sceptical position may justify covert research, or reject the notion of refraining from covert research where doing so would favour the powerful at the expense of the powerless. Some conflict methodologists consider covert research justifiable on grounds that it opens up a window on elite and powerful groups. The abstract ethical principle of informed consent tends to inhibit such exposure and can lead to wider ethical concerns. Thorne says 'elite groups are less in need of the protection granted by the principle of informed consent: they may also *warrant* less protection' (1980: 294).

Justifications and excuses

Justifications neutralize or attach positive value to questionable evidence. The activity may be situated in a justificatory context or the consequences or the victim may be trivialized. Accounts that seek to justify rather than deny responsibility should be coherent and plausible (Coffey and Atkinson, 1996: 101). 'Denial of the victim' (Matza and Sykes, 1957), a neutralization technique that serves to negate the moral indignation which an actor may have about the self or another, does so with the insistence that any inquiry perpetrated is not wrong in the light of the circumstances. Acts of infraction may thus be changed to permissible conduct by this technique of neutralization. For example, where no harm to subjects can be shown to come from research, there would be no victim and therefore no case to answer; a category of person or category of act may be influenced by 'denial of the victim'.

On a number of occasions a member at a lecture on qualitative research methods has asked me whether I thought my presence in the field had influenced the participants. Underpinning the question was the 'reactivity problem' (individuals changing their behaviour in direct response to the researcher), and the notion of harm which is inscribed in the professional code of ethics. Where subjects were unaware that research was being conducted it could *not* be said that subjects provided the researcher with information they thought she or he wanted to hear; and thus findings might be less biased and distorted. On the other hand, as long as information that was provided remained undisclosed it could be said that subjects were not 'harmed' by the research. Harm in qualitative inquiry refers to people being embarrassed or angered rather than physically hurt. On hearing rationalizations of covert methods along these lines some audience members have taken the attitude 'why worry?'

The researcher may offer a rhetoric of self-reconciliation (I cannot do anything about what has been done, but I might be able to prevent someone else from falling into the trap), or engage in corrective 'face work' with a ready-made line of excuse to deflect blame away from the self: 'There were no ethics committees in anthropology when I did my fieldwork.' 'Anthropologists have a long history of free access to infor-mation.' 'I worked under supervision.' Excuses that are persuasive may be thought of as socially approved accounts to mitigate or relieve questionable action or conduct (Coffey and Atkinson, 1996: 101). Excuses are attempts to gain social approval for questionable action or conduct and may appeal to accidents, biological drives, fatalistic forces, lack of information and scapegoating.

Conclusion

In back regions violation of traditional or ideal rules may take place, and animosities, jealousies, conflicts of interests and other human weaknesses could surface. Back regions are places where people relax composure and the norms of formal practice and presentations. The role of participant-observer may facilitate access to back regions where strangers ordinarily are not permitted to go, to observe and participate in secret and private activities. The topic studied, which takes the researcher into back regions, is usually sensitive by virtue of being about secrecy, deviance and social control (Lee, 1993). Back regions are sometimes accessed by 'undercover' means; sensitive methods are used that conceal the identity of the researcher and the purpose of her or his research. Sensitive topics, regions and methods are dilemmas of fieldwork that carry risk of threat to researchers and subjects.

Risks are not to be understood in physical terms, although actual bodily harm may be a potential hazard of fieldwork where the researcher participates in the world of trafficking, petty crime or police work. The risks relate more to personal stress that comes from use of undercover methods and knowing what to do with the material. There are few accounts in the literature where researchers discuss emotional stress from fear of being discredited from having 'passed' in the field, yet the fear of being unmasked (and of the attendant possibilities of humiliation, embarrassment and abuse) may be a constant companion of the covert interpretivist researcher. One's sense of insecurity and self may be under threat where deception is concerned and disclosure is feared. The potential of being discredited can create additional emotional stress in the fieldwork situation.

Risks of back-region study more commonly relate to the stigma that attaches to one's identity from having participated in marginalized or mildly illicit activities. The field is a possibility of numerous roles, as we shall presently see, some of which draw the researcher into full group membership. They may be taught, trained, tested and indoctrinated into a subculture and to the workplace confidences and experiences of co-workers and gradually granted increasing intragroup responsibilities for activities that deviate from the norm in other similar situations; the extent of which could never have been anticipated by the researcher. Fieldworkers who choose to study sensitive topics (those relating to deviance, secret matters and social control), or be situated within sensitive areas where such matters are enacted, or who use sensitive methods (covert participant-observation) might experience an 'ethical hangover' when fieldwork ends, because they have to carry around 'guilty knowl-edge' that plays on the conscience. Access to secret and private infor-mation creates problems with disclosure. The closer the relationship the researcher forms with participants, the more the importance that might be attached to transforming that information into public knowledge without incurring feelings of betrayal.

The goal of interpretivist research advances an understanding of human behaviour, and descriptions in print are to be supported by information about individuals and activities in back regions. The sub-ject's expectation that the participant will maintain confidentiality and anonymity might be at divergence with the research goal and the expectations of colleagues, gatekeepers and sponsors. Complying with the research goal could mean betraying the trust established between the self and members, and membership previously granted, that made access to information possible in the first place. Apart from the anger that may be caused through disclosure or publication, some forms of research (covert) may generate criticism and accusations from colleagues and other professionals. Disclosure of sensitive activities in which the researcher participated draws attention to all parties involved and this could evoke accusations of betrayal.

Part of the unanticipated consequences of participating in back regions as a group member engaged with mildly illicit activities, and using dubious research methods to observe practices engaged in by others, is the potential that such activities have to contaminate the self and make problematic the production of an untarnished total social 'me'. Researchers who have engaged in sensitive sites have exhibited a sense of remorse and anxiety that requires identity reformulation work and explanation. Sociology includes understanding the ways in which social actors, including researchers, manage secrecy and disclosure of their motives, identities and practices (Mitchell, 1991: 101). Social actors may attempt to excuse, justify or legitimate behaviour or clarify motives by producing a variety of accounts or rationales. The conciliatory reactions of the covert researcher in terms of ethical deficiencies, or those who are guilty of ethical oversights and divergences, are part of the repertoire of face-saving strategies and part of presentation of self. The social actor has a ready-made or predefined line or two to draw upon for purposes of neutralization, but the props and practices are part of cosmetics for an outward show that conceals what they do not want revealed; the strategies do not detract from how one sees the self. Whatever the external appearances suggest, fieldworkers are not hidden from themselves.

In the field the researcher has to confront the represented and experienced self simultaneously; appearance is not separable from being (Mitchell, 1991). Those who engage with sensitive topics, regions and methods could find the experience problematic because self-image and felt-identity (the public and private dimensions of self) are in conflict. The modern image of the objective researcher, who hides behind the participant role, is questionable, and so too is the notion that appearance can be wholly separate from *being*. The notion of the wholly detached observer in long-term fieldwork is a myth. The self you are at the beginning of the research may be a different self to the one that will emerge at the end because fieldwork can be a transformative experience.

The new researcher, when evaluating the appropriateness of the setting, might ask the self whether this particular setting or situation should be studied by anyone. Or more specifically, should I study this situation or topic? The potential negative consequences of studying sensitive topics or situations for the various parties, including importantly the self, should form part of assessing the appropriateness of the study. Traditionally such questions were not considered necessary in anthropology, but nowadays the appropriateness of a topic or situation for study has been challenged on a number of levels. Some studies have been considered ethically inappropriate because they are 'trivial' or too esoteric. Other arguments are political (the protection of less powerful groups may necessitate that knowledge about them be made available by whatever means thought necessary). Some individuals criticize fieldwork because of the implied tendency to link covert research and deception with it. The emphasis in some ethical committees in relation to qualitative research is overwhelmingly directed toward stamping out covert research (Daly and McDonald, 1996). Many feminists argue that research which supports power differentials and treats subjects as objects violates feminist ethics and is to be avoided. With critical and partici-patory approaches the emphasis is on social change and applied out-comes as an ethical imperative.

The risk that is attached to a setting or topic needs to be seen as a problem over and beyond that of access, although admittedly barriers may be put up where activities are secret or need to be kept secret to protect the interests of powerful groups in society. There are personal consequences of sensitive fieldwork that need to be addressed, but one cannot be expected adequately to anticipate all the ethical implications of fieldwork, nor be truly prepared for the ethical problems and dilemmas that are emergent because of the futuristic nature of the phenomena. An understanding of a number of potential difficulties and a capacity to be flexible may smooth the way to dealing with some pitfalls that revolve around sensitive topics, regions and methods. As Lofland and Lofland (1995: 30) advise, 'to be *forewarned* is at least to some degree, to be *forearmed*'.

You should, at the minimum, make yourself familiar with the code of ethics of the discipline to which you are attached. You should know how covert research is viewed by categories of researchers (anthro-pologists, sociologists, feminists), perhaps in relation to modern and contemporary approaches and/or theoretical perspectives (critical and participatory approaches may take a different approach to ethics from interpretivist approaches). It is well worth treading cautiously in a 'grey area' of fieldwork that is defined as sensitive, and in the planning stage incorporate an ethical agenda into your proposal to address ethical problems which may occur. Rather than proceed with the attitude that if and should ethical issues arise they will be dealt with later, the advice is, where possible, to anticipate certain problems may occur and take precautions against them; and bear in mind that to avoid the study of certain issues is not a completely satisfactory option either.

CHAPTER 5

Roles and role performance

Defining the fieldwork role one wants to play and how to participate appropriately in the field are challenges confronting the fieldworker. Performing to scripts written by others and directing the social role-playing self into and through social situations and relationships in the field is by no means clear-cut, and involves negotiation with various parties at the beginning of research and during the ongoing research process. Negotiations within fieldwork are about the roles to be performed that link the researcher into a variety of relationships (power, intimate and social), and with activities within the boundaries of the professional and personal spheres, and ethical and moral practice. 'How far will the self be allowed to intrude into the group to be studied?' 'How far should it?' These are ethical and moral questions to ask oneself. Various parties with their own agendas and power differences may determine how far one will be allowed to intrude into the lives of other people, and what activities the researcher will be expected to participate in. The actualities of fieldwork demand the fieldworker be flexible and inventive with roles and relationships and prepared to modify behaviour to suit context-specific requirements.

One might turn to the textbooks on qualitative methods to see what fieldworkers do when they perform the role of researcher, but this would not advance very far our understanding of role and role performance. There is more to a role than what is formally designated in abstract and idealized form found in textbooks on qualitative methods. Observing what those who are not fieldworkers do not do which fieldworkers actually do might advance an understanding of role-related activities performed by ethnographers when in research mode. Ordinary members do not observe activities, people and situations in order to understand them sociologically. Nor do they perform a role that consciously requires balancing participation with observation, and closeness with distance. Ordinary citizens do not probe into the lives of their friends with a view to gathering information about them which later they may disseminate uncensored for a wider public viewing. They do not have to avoid breaching privacy rights, which could arise from prompts and questions about personal and intimate affairs that are secret and confidential.

The difficulties with directing the social role-playing self into and through social situations in the field tends to be downplayed in textbooks on qualitative methods that treat methods and roles in abstract and idealized form (not in context), and provide few examples of actual fieldwork. In textbooks there is a failure to provide the reader with ways to wrestle with, adapt and sometimes even abandon roles in the context of complex political, ethical and moral circumstances. What activities are likely to be involved with a particular role or roles are neglected in literature that prescribes, idealizes and presents role in abstract form. The point to emphasize is that the research role is neither uniform nor unvarying (there are many roles the fieldworker might assume). Fieldwork commonly requires the researcher to perform dual roles of researcher and friend, but additional roles may be performed and overlapping of roles and relationships may occur when the researcher role is combined with that of therapist, counsellor or nurse. Crossing boundaries of disciplines and professions can create ethical and practical dilemmas.

In fieldwork, role is not some fixed entity, negotiated in a one-off contract prior to fieldwork, like the role one fills when recruiting for paid employment. Roles may be differentiated in terms of researcher involvement as a member of the subject group, with 'peripheral', 'active' or 'complete membership' roles options available (Adler and Adler, 1987). Roles may vary in relation to the degree of closeness that is created with subjects by way of contrast to distance, as with the detached, objective and impersonal researcher. The role/s the fieldworker is allowed to take on in the field could depend on the state of harmony or tension in the group or community (Barrett, 1996: 122). Roles in fieldwork vary with the advent of political unrest and conflict or the demands of different parties with an agenda to promote which differs from the researcher's. The participation aspect of participant-observation and the observation dimension of role could change over time in relation to factors totally beyond the control of the researcher, as we shall presently see.

Each setting might require the researcher to assume a different role, or a number of roles (Ram, 1996). Some settings might require anonymous relationships (see Laud Humphreys, 1970), and others intensely personal relationships (Adler and Adler, 1987; Reinharz, 1992). The setting rather than methodological ideology may be used to rationalize choice of role and define appropriate role/s to perform. Role, not unlike informed consent, might be more appropriately defined as processual and ever-changing, and subject to negotiation over and over again.

The textbook approach to roles

In textbooks roles have been defined as 'consciously articulated and abstracted categories of social "types of persons" ' (Lofland and Lofland, 1995: 105). A role is a label people use to organize their own activity and make sense of what others do in organizations. Formal and informal or de facto roles are commonly found in organizations. The person identified in relation to a position within a hierarchy of authority performs activities that are consistent with those prescribed for the role. In the organization where most of my fieldwork was done there had over time developed an informal managerial role which women identified by the term 'the lady in charge for the day'. The person who performed the role each day was responsible for opening and closing the shop, handling customers and money, including banking the day's 'takings'. One who handled money engaged in serious responsible 'work' by way of contrast to those who did not handle money, who were more appropriately defined as engaged in light-hearted fun and not 'work'.

Formal roles are linked to the notion of 'position', 'office' and 'occupation' in organizations and some societies feature an abundance of formal organizations (Lofland and Lofland, 1995: 105). Goffman says, 'A self, then, virtually awaits the individual entering a position; he need only conform to the pressures on him' (Goffman, 1961b: 88). Personal qualities are effectively imputed to the individual: 'a judge is supposed to be deliberate and sober; a pilot to be cool' (Goffman, 1961b: 87). A type of performance is anticipated: 'a bookkeeper to be accurate and neat in doing his work' (Goffman, 1961b: 87). A ready-made *me* virtually awaits the person fitted to the role, who in turn is expected to infuse the role with life and vitality, enabling the role to become a realized entity. The role is subject to individual improvization, even invention, a measure of contrivance and inventiveness (Burns, 1992: 22).

Both the formal and informal aspects of the participant-observation role yield data. In traditional fieldwork, the formal aspects of role might apply to the collection of census and survey data, genealogical data and data about rituals and ceremonies. The informal aspects of the field role are not so easily designated and are sometimes even referred to as 'hanging about'. Literally, this means performing everyday activities of ongoing social life, like going to the market, taking an evening stroll, stopping and chatting to people in their homes and generally becoming friendly with a range of people at church, picnics and other leisure time activities. The family, the neighbourhood, circles of friends and acquaintances, these cover most of the obvious situations and settings where a variety of roles is waiting for each researcher to activate into a lived reality.

Added to this list we might include the 'field', somewhere abroad, a place the ethnographer travels to and returns from, but not necessarily, since nowadays fieldwork is frequently done in the urban setting, and within establishments that provide health care, education, employment, entertainment, and so on. The fieldworker could perform a number of roles, which are differentiated in terms of participation and observation, distance–closeness and insider–outsider status. With role performance, involvement in social relationships and group formations in the 'field' might coincide with the boundaries of various administrative units or work teams, and could include working relationships with people outside the workplace.

Where the researcher is unable to access a setting by virtue of gatekeepers or other limitations and wants to acquire information, they might decide to act out a 'discrepant' role. The covert role of the interpretive inquirer might be defined as a 'discrepant role' because it is inconsistent with the ethnographic norm of 'openness'. The role of impostor (a covert role opposite to the overt role) has been used to mediate back and front regions. With the 'discrepant role' a potential is there to damage the impression that team members seek to promote through disclosure or publication of secret and private or 'in-group' information). Few researchers would rationalize the use of anonymous relationships (see Humphreys, 1970) in any situation other than public settings, since there are ethical implications of deceit and betrayal to contend with. The extent to which those observed know they are being studied is not only a methodological choice but also an ethical issue.

A multiplicity of roles goes to make up the social self; the researcher may be a mother, student, nurse or therapist. The individual performs multiple roles in the field, to be held in abeyance in some situations, or combined with others in differing circumstances. Defining which is the salient role and holding in abeyance involvement in other roles is a process that might be defined as 'scheduling'. The roles of researcher and friend intertwine in the practice of qualitative research, sometimes resulting in a 'conflicts of interest' and ethical and moral dilemma (Stacey, 1988). The role demands of loyalty and commitment owed to various parties cannot always be met and cross-cutting demands could incur 'role-conflict' and 'role-detachment' (Adler and Adler, 1987). Attempting to meet various conflicting demands of role in the field could result in the researcher experiencing a 'conflict of consciousness'.

Personal qualities for the role

As indicated in previous chapters, in fieldwork the researchers must establish and maintain rapport, tolerate ambiguity and have a capacity to keep self-doubt in check as they go about their work in the field in circumstances of considerable indeterminacy. Individuals need to have a capacity to withstand ambiguity, indeterminacy and insecurity, to be flexible, inventive and accommodating in their role performance, and willing to make adjustments to role. An ability to tolerate uncertainty is critical 'because uncertainty creates anxiety and a willingness to make mistakes' (Lipson, 1989: 68). 'Good' ethnographers are said often to be able to maintain a kind of detached involvement and can cope with culture shock (1989). In order to enhance the human relations aspect of fieldwork empathy, sympathy and patience are needed, qualities thought not to be directly teachable but acquired over a lifetime participating with 'one's fellow human beings'.

How to participate effectively while maintaining control of one's own presence is a challenge of psychosocial import attached to the 'partici-pant' dimension of participant-observation (Ashworth, 1995). Our 'being there' in the field, whether in terms of a sojourn in some distant land or doing fieldwork in the local community, is a social experience different from participating in the taken-for-granted life world of everyday reality in one's own community. The self-conscious role of participant-observer requires the fieldworker to question everything, which in my opinion can be every bit as challenging as it sounds.

Nowadays there are many more texts available on ethnography to demystify what goes on in the field and no shortage of critics ready to dismiss as self-indulgent and narcissistic the development of rich bio-graphical and confessional accounts which depict fieldworkers as they go about their work. Scholars are increasingly more willing to take risks and write about personal experiences which many conventional ethno-graphers object to because the personal emphasis detracts from the prime goal of ethnography – to foster analytical and theoretical infor-mation (interpreted as social facts). The worst sin is to be 'too personal' (Behar, 1996: 13). While a good supply of textbooks that address access and role is available, publications tend to disappoint some educators who want more than prescriptive, abstract and idealized versions of role to inform their students. Qualitative texts which treat access, role and methods in a vacuum, with few examples of actual fieldwork experience, fail to provide the reader with ways to wrestle with, adapt and some-times even abandon roles in the context of complex political, ethical and moral circumstances (Barrett, 1996; Crick, 1993). Knowing what to participate in and how to participate appropriately can be more difficult than envisaged prior to fieldwork, or from a reading of literature on qualitative research where roles are sketched out in abstract and idealized form.

Accounts of ethnographers' actual experiences in the field seem to have been sidestepped by the emphases in ethnography on textual representation (see Clifford and Marcus, 1986). There is a need for original fieldwork projects to be published which make sense of the practice of fieldwork in ethically and morally responsible ways. A focus on ethics and fieldwork is missing from the pre-1960s literature, but with the forces of feminism and feminist scholarship, action research and participatory approaches, a consciousness about ethical and moral aspects of fieldwork has been aroused, especially in terms of how ethics intertwine in feminist scholarship with epistemology (ways of knowing), to make greater moral demands on fieldworkers.

Crick captures something of the complexities of role when he asserts fieldworkers are not 'genderless, ageless, classless, raceless observation machines'; that age gender, ethnicity, marital status and so on affect what roles we are allowed to take on in another culture and often whom one has access to (Crick, 1993: 6). Doing fieldwork in an organization within one's own culture may not be qualitatively different to fieldwork in a traditional village in some far-off land; the same major difficulties apply. One must gradually gain an understanding of the setting and the interpersonal dynamics of group life in context before being able to participate in appropriate role activities. The fieldworker at home might not have to learn a new language, but the social rules of an establishment have to be discovered and role relationships developed with other people in situations that are strange.

The fieldworker could find access to many activities limited by virtue of being male, an unpaid worker and not a friend of someone whose opinion counts. Other roles from the fieldworker's repertoire of roles, which constitute a social *me*, could assist or impede access to and observation of people in the field. A teacher might be granted permission to interact with children and observe written materials, whereas someone without the teacher role in their repertoire could be deprived the opportunity (Ganguly-Scrase, 1993). Being a female might limit one's perspective to a women's reality and restrict access to men's social circles and leisure activities (Ganguly-Scrase, 1993).

With interviewing, it cannot be assumed that the feminist researcher will establish rapport on a basis of empathy or sympathy. Class, race and ethnicity could present a challenge to feminist claims of equality, sharing and caring. The responses of the interviewer might illicit negative personal reactions, making a genuine caring experience virtually impossible to sustain (Phoenix, 1994: 56). The potential for gender, age, ethnicity, class and race to impact adversely on subject's responses makes questionable the establishment of caring and sharing relationships prescribed by 'the feminist communitarian ethical model' (Denzin, 1997).

Varying degrees of difficulty might be linked with formal and informal aspects of role. The researcher might aspire to being immersed in the lives of the people being studied, but group members could insist that the formal aspects of the role of researcher have priority or exclusive attention ('just interview and take notes!'). The formal aspects of the research role may assume priority in the minds of researchers, like 'talking to people, collecting data of various kinds, and writing up notes' (Fordham, 1993: 20). Funders, community members or group members of an organization can determine what the ethnographer will do in the field. With my first fieldwork placement I anticipated the role of saleslady would help me pursue two lines of inquiry outlined in my proposal (transaction practices and buyer–seller relations), but I was a volunteer, not a paid worker, and only paid workers were permitted to work at the counter region site. Volunteer workers handled clothing in the back region of the various stores. Rules that had evolved in the organization determined what roles volunteer workers would perform and the saleslady role was not included in the more bureaucratized welfare organizations.

In actual fieldwork the members' political and/or personal agendas might become an 'aside' to be dealt with by the researcher, above and beyond the research goal or agenda (Shakespeare, 1993). Members could perceive the researcher as a friendly person who is genuinely interested in them and their personal concerns, someone to be trusted with confidences, a sort of confidante. Members have role models with which the researcher may be aligned and against which their performances may be judged, and the expectations may be at variance with the social actor's research agenda (Atkinson, 1993; Shakespeare, 1993). My decision after four months' fieldwork to combine work for the first group with that done in another organization was linked with failure to gain access to the counter region site and observe buyer–seller relations and sales transactions. A previous decision to work alone in the back region of a store one day a week was a consequence of moral pressure exerted upon me by superiors in the organizational hierarchy for political reasons (see below).

A case in question

The fieldworker might anticipate dual roles of researcher and friend, but these may be combined with a mediator role. Members of a group might envisage a mediator role for the 'stranger' with the benefits derived from having someone deflect blame away from them and absorb responsibility for activities they do not want to accept. They may push the researcher forward as a spokesperson to advise management of discontents; political neutrality is not a possibility in long-term fieldwork (Fordham, 1993). Professing political neutrality could lay the foundations for mistrust, imputed motives, strained relations and even open conflict. The fieldworker might not want to participate in the political scene and become involved in factions and intrigue, but others could have different ideas about this and bring moral pressure to bear on the researcher to conform to their demands.

Early in fieldwork I realized how vulnerable ethnographers could be when drawn by groups in opposition to other groups, and expected to perform activities of a political and personal nature outside the research agenda. Failure to conform could put the researcher outside the group and establish him or her as a candidate for a future 'degradation ceremony' (Garfinkel, 1956). Middle management in one organization connived with workers in the shops in opposition to top management on a number of work-related issues. As a member of the rank and file, my assistance was solicited on one such matter. A fellow volunteer and co-worker had been appointed to a new position as a paid manageress of a shop that was without any regular staff. She would have to handle customers and garments. She was pregnant and this could be detrimental to holding down the position should it become common knowledge, as the work involved heaving and lifting. She was a single-supporting mother who desperately needed the position. Women were morally obligated to protect the secret and support the transfer to the new job.

The initial request by my superior that I change my roster and work alone in the back region of the store to do the heavy dirty work of unpacking boxes of garments and taking them to the display failed to elicit a positive response immediately. Detachment from social inter-action had to be balanced somehow with the research goal, which was a problem in an interactionist study that relied on personal relationships for the collection of data. The manageress called in the district supervisor who wanted to know exactly why I was so hesitant; support was expected of group members, especially in the circumstances. A resolution was found. I decided to work an extra day each week doing heavy, dirty work on my own without an opportunity to observe the social dynamics of group life. I was morally obligated to conform to the role my superiors had chosen for me and to participate in the plot. Had I not been accommodating, my chance of ongoing work in the group would have been difficult. As it was, the hesitancy over becoming involved with the intrigue caused workers to be suspicious and possibly laid the foundation for strained relations that emerged later between the pro-tective manageress and myself, which was to erupt in an epiphany (Denzin, 1992a).

Classic anthropological goals

The goal of classical anthropology established by Malinowski is 'to grasp the native's point of view, his relation to his life, to realise "his" vision of "his" world' (1922: 25). The approach prescribed for successive genera-tions of interpretivist ethnographers was an 'actor-oriented perspective' or emic position, thought best to facilitate an understanding of partici-pants' circumstances, pleasures and satisfactions (Barrett, 1991: 150). The two major tasks of the modern fieldworker are:

- to engage in activities appropriate to the situation;
- to observe the activities, people, and physical aspects of the situation (Spradley, 1980: 54).

Participant-observation would facilitate these tasks in the field, but the fieldwork technique would involve a delicate balancing act between participation and observation.

The beginning of modern fieldwork was marked by intensive participant-observation studies, carried out by the lone researcher over a period of at least a year (Behar, 1996). Fieldwork was a rite of passage and the hallmark of ethnography. Reliance was placed on informants and use of unstructured interviews, life histories and census work. It was assumed that only those who were extremely flexible and perceptive, with a strong constitution and ability to be good listeners, possessed the personal qualities required for the fieldwork role (Behar, 1996). The early social anthropologists belonged to the 'sink or swim school'; they had to have a willingness and determination to survive in a strange setting for considerable periods of time. Modern participant-observation was deeply paradoxical: 'get the "native point of view", act as a participant, but don't forget to keep your eyes open' (Behar, 1996: 5).

The modern social anthropologist was to become involved in the community, take part in some activities and become familiar with the routine daily life of village members. Specific activities became a focal concern, knowledge of decision making by members of the group, perhaps in relation to ritual practice, or the promotion of understanding of social organization or culture. Being a participant-observer was realized through coming to terms with a range of issues, problems and uncertainties. Nowadays fieldwork is done at home as well as abroad and the long-term duration in the field has undergone considerable change due to the pressures of time, funding, and so on. Fieldwork, irrespective of whether it is done at home or abroad, remains surrounded by indeterminacy (nothing can be taken for granted and everything must be questioned). The inability to take for granted the reality of the life-world makes impression management problematic (Ashworth, 1995).

Defining fieldwork roles

Observation and participant-observation

Fieldwork connotes very different practices for different disciplines. Fieldwork is often thought to be synonymous with participant-observation, ethnography and anthropology. There are distinctions to be made, however, between fieldwork as positivist-oriented researchers and qualitative researchers within anthropology and other disciplines practise it. Major changes have occurred within anthropology since the 1980s, with new approaches like action research, critical ethnography and feminist ethnography introducing a preference for critical rather than interpretivist approaches. Anthropologists of feminist persuasion have been in the fore-front in experimenting with more ethical and less exploitative methods (Wolf, 1996: 8). The preoccupations of poststructuralism and post-modernism have stimulated interest in issues surrounding the role of participant-observer. They have introduced a critical view to 'the tensions between disinterested observation and political advocacy, between the "scientific" and the "humane", between the "objective" and the "aesthetic" ' (Atkinson and Hammersley, 1994: 249).

Large-scale surveys or quantitative research using formal question-naires have sometimes been called fieldwork, as too have qualitative in-depth interviews and focus interviews which rely on (usually group) discussion, and participant-observation. There has been a tendency in the past to define research that goes beyond merely interviewing people as fieldwork. While the interview has pride of place in qualitative and quantitative sociological research, ethnographers or anthropologists focus less on talk and more upon 'conversation and chatter' (Eipper, 1998: 6). Ethnographers orient themselves to codes of conduct as they are lived rather than reported upon. Modes of engagement are enhanced by *empathy*. Interpretivist specialties such as symbolic interactionism and grounded theory have adopted and adapted an ethnographic perspective which encapsulates the 'insider's perspective, with the inter-actionist concept 'taking the role' of the other (Blumer, 1969).

Fieldworker roles have been defined in terms of observation and participant-observation (Jackson, 1987). Observation and participant-observation are sometimes taken to mean the same. There is, however a distinction to be made: all participant-observation is fieldwork, but not all fieldwork is participant-observation:

> If you take a random sample of a community, go door to door, and do a series of face-to-face interviews, that *is* field research – but it's not participant-observation. If you . . . monitor the behavior of patrons and clients as they go through their transactions, that, too, is field research, but it isn't participant-observation. It's just plain observation. (Bernard, 1994: 137)

Interpretivists use quantitative methods and positivists use qualitative fieldwork techniques without contradicting their epistemological per-suasions. The survey researcher who observes in the field is not attempt-ing to immerse himself in a culture being studied. She or he is more appropriately fitted to the observer role, a role that is not informed and guided by the ideas of humanistic and subjectivist approaches to field-work, and an elaboration of empathy, where the key concept is participa-tion. A quantitative researcher who uses observation and fieldwork techniques is not taking on board the methodology of ethnography and the ideas embedded in a constructivist paradigm. The complete detach-ment of the observer role, characteristic of survey research, is incompat-ible with the anthropological goal, which is to live intimately as a member of the community chosen for study. On the other hand, the immersed ethnographer who uses survey approach is not contradict-ing the humanistic approach to inquiry, but combines survey with participant-observation because the kind of numeracy provided seems to offer a route along which empirical and theoretical advances are likely to be possible.

A number of scholars have provided typologies of fieldwork strategies and observation techniques, which depict variations in terms of specified dimensions of role. For example, Patton (1990) developed a series of continua for thinking about one's role during the conduct of qualitative, evaluative research. The evaluator-observer's role could vary in terms of the degree of actual participation or observation in daily life. At one extreme was complete participation and at the other complete observation, with all possible complementary mixes along the continua available. The researcher's role could vary in terms of the extent to which the study being conducted is known to participants. Full disclosure lies at one end and complete secrecy at the other, with variations of the extremes in portrayal of role available. The researcher's role could vary in terms of time spent in the field. The researcher could be minimally intrusive in the short term, but a longer stay could facilitate the development of relationships in the field with others. The researcher's role could vary in terms of focus of observations (the degree of specificity or diffuseness). A narrow focus might cover a single element or component in a programme under inquiry; a broad focus could provide a holistic view of an entire programme and all its elements (Patton, 1990: 217).

Gold's fourfold typology

Gold (1958) defined four modes through which observers might gather data:

- the 'participant-as-observer';
- the 'complete participant';
- the 'observer-as-participant';
- the 'complete-observer'.

The 'participant-as-observer/observer-as-participant' roles balance involvement with detachment, familiarity with strangeness and closeness with distance (Adler and Adler, 1987).

The 'complete observer/complete participant' roles, as distinct roles, mark the extent to which those who are observed know they are being studied, and how much the researcher participates in the ongoing activities (Reinharz, 1992: 69). Immersion in the social world and eliminating distance from those studied, or assuming the position of 'onlooker', 'spectator' or detached observer, these are aspects of role and ethical components of fieldwork. Portrayal of role to others is a dimension of fieldwork that has raised considerable concern within ethics committees, who are on guard against the use of covert research. Most ethnographers today would agree that deliberately concealing the researcher's role from others in the setting is probably unethical, but that being completely 'open' about role as the ideal is probably unachievable given the actualities of fieldwork (everything is changing, the setting, the people, social relationships, and so on; Wax, 1982). Ram (1996) interprets the totally detached observer role or 'participant-as-observer role' (Gold, 1958) as involving the researcher in developing a relationship only with key informants. Such a role was considered to limit a capacity fully to comprehend the dynamics of the processes at play within the clothing factory he studied, and therefore to understand behaviour as aberrant, or without logic (Ram, 1996).

Various scholars for various reasons, some of which are sketched out below, have rejected both the 'complete observer' and 'complete participant' roles as distinct research roles. The 'complete observer' role, where individuals in the setting have not been informed they are being observed, is considered appropriate only in public settings, where people and relations are anonymous and impersonal (Kellehear, 1993). Understandably, the 'complete observer' role would not be popular among social anthropologists because it nullifies empathy, which is interwoven with interactionist theory and the concept 'taking the role' of the other (Blumer, 1969).

'Going native'

Over-involvement has often been conceptualized as the problem of 'going native', of 'developing an over-rapport with the research subjects that could harm the data-gathering process' (Adler and Adler, 1987: 17). Those who participate fully in the world they are studying might become so attached to goals of the member group that they cease to consider their own cultural or professional subgroup as the reference group, and the research agenda as the prime one. They could lose sight of the 'scientific' perspective, or sense of 'detached wonder', and refuse to publish the results of field studies (Lincoln and Guba, 1985: 304). Overrapport might bias the researcher's perspective, leading them to accept uncritically the views of the members, or one group of members over another (Adler and Adler, 1987: 17).

'Complete participation' or the 'insider' approach has been seen as running the risk of 'telling it how it is without sufficiently questioning the vagaries of workplace behaviour and the existing order' (Ram, 1996: 127). Ram avoided 'going native' by 'going academic'. He combined fieldwork with lecturing in the university department. In the clothing factory where he did fieldwork, Ram assumed an 'active membership role' with men and a 'peripheral membership role' with women. He maintained regular contact during fieldwork with the collegiate as a postgraduate student by lecturing. An 'insider' by virtue of familial ties and membership of an ethnic minority group, he embraced core activities of male members of the clothing factory but did not commit himself totally to the goals and values of the group (Ram, 1996).

Gold's fourfold typology has been criticized on the grounds that it runs together several dimensions of variation: the portrayal and purpose of the role; activities performed in the field; insider/outsider orientations, and so on (Atkinson and Hammersley, 1994: 249). The space created by respectful distance is thought to be essential among some modern ethnographers for the progress of unbiased, analytical work. Avoidance of autobiographies, confessionals or accounts of personal conversion is implied (Hammersley and Atkinson, 1995: 115).

Adler and Adler's typology

Adler and Adler (1987) work with the notion of membership roles, which predominate in the field:

- the 'peripheral membership' role;
- the 'active membership' role;
- the 'complete membership' role.

Researchers who feel an outsider perspective is vital to formal and accurate appraisal of human group life might prefer the 'peripheral membership' role. Alignment with a 'peripheral' role might be context and gender specific. Active membership role among women was found unacceptable in the family clothing factory which Ram (1996) studied. He was obliged to assume a 'peripheral' role in relation to women who worked in the family factory. Despite Ram's vantage point as an insider, cultural prescriptions on gender relations made problematic the task of engaging individual women machinists in conversation. The particular nature of gender relations in the factory was influential to ways of gaining access and the role to be performed. An understanding of ways to go about talking to women machinists in the setting was negotiated in the process of winning people's trust. Ram acted on the advice of insiders who judged the appropriate role for the researcher for that situation. Ram was obliged to interview individual women machinists always in the company of a senior machinist who acted as chaperone and support.

The 'active membership' role reflects the activities of researchers who become more involved in the central activities of an organization and assume responsibility in helping advance the group's goals, but without fully committing themselves to group members' values and goals. The 'active' role is ideal for the researcher who wants to learn the ropes. It is the role with which I am most familiar, having been inducted and acclimatized to the moral order of the secondhand clothing store and practised the full range of activities attached to the volunteer worker role. For Ram, the 'complete membership' role (Adler and Adler, 1987) did not transpire from enactment of the 'active' membership role, although an 'insider' role was made possible through ethnic and familial affiliations and work background in the ethnic minority clothing firm in the West Midlands. Ram participated in the core activities of the factory worker but was not committed to the goals and values expected of a 'complete member'. The diversity of roles elaborated upon in Ram's study (1996), that of 'insider', with 'active' membership among men, 'peripheral' membership among women, but never 'complete' member-ship, proved beneficial to avoiding a partial presentation of data for analytical scrutiny.

Outsider–insider roles

In more recent times, the emphasis given to interventionist and partici-patory action research has been on the partnership formed between the researcher and those who are researched and research roles, identified as the outside–insider approach and the inside facilitator approach (Prideaux, 1994). Participatory action research focuses on the research process and the degree of participation that subjects have with a range of research tasks (data collection, analysis, interpretation, editing, and so on). Fieldwork techniques are favoured that erode distance between the researcher and subjects and methods encouraged which facilitate social interaction with subjects and self-reflection.

An 'outsider' might perform the role of 'broker', evaluating the ideas of subjects in an organization (perhaps a university department), and in the process become increasingly absorbed in the activities of the group. They might make the transition from 'outsider' to 'insider', although this would not be easy since building alliances to promote change requires the researcher learn about practices as an 'insider' and then critique such practices as an 'outsider'. A group member occupying a senior manage-ment position in an organization might be appointed as an 'internal' facilitator of action research, assume the 'inside facilitator role' and be supported by external facilitators from an institute of education (Prideaux, 1994).

In participatory action research citizens often become full participants in the research process and are sometimes referred to as co-researchers. Control of the research process might be transferred to subjects who select the problem, methods and process. The perspective on who determines major decision-making processes, whether the researcher or subjects, in relation to the 'problem', methods, role and interpretation, is crucial to a discussion of role and the promotion of injustice (Altheide and Johnson, 1997: 179). Relinquishing control in participatory action research is seen as an ethical dimension of the feminist approach (Archibald and Crnkovich, 1995: 116–117).

In participatory action research, participants are invariably granted the right to define the problem, the methods for study (including questions to be asked in the interview and in what order), analyses, interpretation and textual representation. When member definitions predominate, a transfer of expertise from the privileged to the 'underdog' may be acknowledged, with participants placed on a more equal footing with the researcher, as traditional 'authorized knower'. The control that changes hands and role performance of subjects challenges traditional ethnographic practice. A feminist ethical concern to put on equal footing those less privileged and from minority or dispossessed groups renders questionable the expertise of the authorized 'knowers'. The transfer of decision making renders the researcher less powerful and more vulnerable. Subjects' active involvement in the research process often leads to ownership of the findings. The joint sharing, learning, analyses and interpretation can generate bonds of solidarity and a common cause, and provide the groundwork for the development of friendships in the field. More participation and consciousness-raising has become the groundwork of friendship in feminist ethnography.

Caution is needed to ensure the researcher does not undermine the progress that is advanced by collaboration with subjects. Use of heavy abstract theoretical models to assist with analysis and leaving the field when a strong researcher presence is needed can disrupt participant motivation and the momentum of ongoing research of subjects. The action researcher assists members to learn skills and techniques that will allow them to continue investigating their own life-world and community problems and issues. Steps may need to be taken to ensure research continues when the fieldworker is gone. To this end some researchers have emphasized the need to focus research on 'really useful knowledge' that is relevant to the community and which members relate to and understand, rather than pay allegiance to critical theories and theoretically heavy perspectives which perpetuate limited assumptions of members' self-understandings, as ideological and distorted misrepresentations of reality (Jordan and Yeomans, 1995). Action research should be a strategy to address a particular problem of relevance to the research participants.

The closeness–distance dilemma

Both interpretivists and criticalists (feminists, structuralists and postmodernists) participate more fully in the lives of members than do positivists and postpositivists, who tend to assume a 'scientific' attitude towards participation to avoid bias and contamination of results. With quantitative research, distance is required from subjects and social relationships in the field, the researcher does not see the self as a participant in social interaction; positivist-inspired data collection is advanced by an impersonal role. The distance established between the researcher and the researched reflects the impersonal, objective and analytical 'scientific' attitude. The qualitative participant-observer, by way of contrast, accepts a degree of contamination as an inevitable outcome of intrusion in the daily lives of people, and in full knowledge of this asserts the value of social interaction to the production of data.

'Sympathetic detachment' was the preferred mode of practice in modern ethnography (Barrett, 1991). Tradition set a pattern of involvement for modern ethnographers; they were to balance 'complete involvement' with 'complete detachment'. 'Going native' and becoming detached from the research agenda and colleagues was a matter of over-involvement that had to be avoided. The balance between 'complete involvement' and 'complete detachment' is a challenge derived from 'being there' (Wolcott, 1995: 95). Today every fieldworker has to achieve some workable balance between participation and observation. New conceptions of role in fieldwork suggest contemporary fieldworkers' attitudes have turned towards more participation and less observation (Wolcott, 1995).

The 'reactivity' issue

The past three decades have witnessed the social scientist's concern with the role of the researcher in influencing results (Altheide and Johnson, 1997). The 'reactivity' issue (how the research act might influence an optimal understanding of the phenomena under inquiry) has been an issue of contention in the social sciences over the years, and thought to be corrected for by lengthy participant-observation in the field. People take less and less notice of the fieldworker's comings and goings over time. With long-term participant-observation, however, there is a risk of losing sight of the fact that the friend with whom many confidences are shared is also a researcher collecting data. To reiterate a point already made, the participant-observer inevitably performs two roles, that of researcher and friend. The role of friend has been rationalized as inherently problematic in terms of eliciting information that makes disclosure problematic and for creating a 'conflict of interests' (Stacey, 1988).

Feminist approaches

There is a tendency for each of the methodological traditions to emphasize particular aspects of fieldwork. Notable feminist scholars have claimed qualitative methods, particularly the face-to-face interview, as the feminist approach (Kelly, Regan and Burton, 1992: 149). A commitment to exploring members' understanding or definition of the situation, characteristic of phenomenological inquiry and symbolic interaction, is encapsulated within feminist scholarship, with an emphasis on the interview rather than participant-observation.

Participatory action research is also popular in the feminist methodological literature. Much feminist research defined critical is underscored by notions of oppression owing to sexism, 'conscious-raising', increased politicization and activism (Punch, 1994: 85). Politicization and activism are central aspects of feminist research and not found in survey research or modern interpretivist inquiry. Strands of feminist research that promote liberation as an ethical goal have profound implications for methods and roles. Participatory action research models emphasize participation and collaboration and the erosion of distance between the researcher and subjects. Methods and social interaction blur the lines between 'outsider' and 'insider' status.

Many feminists subscribe to qualitative in-depth, face-to-face interviewing, more involvement and sharing of fate (Kelly, Regan and Burton, 1992: 151). Many seek to transform traditional impersonal relationships into relations of equality and reciprocity; and some aspire to the development of close friendships. The feminist challenge to modern fieldwork methods (quantitative and qualitative) is underscored by a belief that the key to ethically and morally responsible fieldwork resides with participating more fully in social relations and playing the role of detached observer less. What is consciously eliminated from participant-observation relations and the interviewer–interviewee relationship is social distance between the researcher and the subject. Many feminist ethnographers, cultural and social anthropologists and sociologists subscribe to the notion of taking seriously the challenge of fieldwork or participant-observation that requires participating more and playing the role of observer less.

Feminist methodological literature on participant-observation reflects a division among feminists who advocate 'closeness' and those who advocate respectful distance between the researcher and the person studied (Reinharz, 1992: 67). Whether to develop social relations in personal and intimate ways and play the role of observer less is an ethical and moral matter as well as a methodological choice. The ethical and moral import of the close relationship is fostered through promotion of the 'feminist ethic of care' or 'the feminist communitarian ethical model' (Denzin, 1997). The closeness–distance dilemma, which relates to both quantitative and qualitative research approaches, directs a focus on fieldwork ethics and moral fieldworkers.

Feminists have criticized positivist-oriented, quantitative research for objectifying and exploiting subjects. The kinds of relational forms and interpersonal dynamics reflected with survey research are 'distant', 'rational', 'uninvolved', 'hierarchical' and 'unrelated' (Wolf, 1996: 4). In rejecting the possibility of social science being objective and value free, Mies (1983) proposed a 'conscious partiality' that was to be achieved through partial identification with those being studied (Archibald and Crnkovich, 1995: 114). Mies's (1983) guidelines have provided a framework that allows feminist researchers to reflect on role and refine their research practice (Archibald and Crnkovich, 1995). Mies's postulates have the status of ethical imperatives; theory must be intertwined with research process. Mies directs feminist scholars to support the development of reciprocal relationships between the researcher and those being researched. This is a significant departure from traditional fieldwork where objectivity was valued in regard to relations in the field. Mies

(1983) urged female scholars to incorporate their own subjective experiences of oppression into their research projects.

The new 'feminist ethic of care'

Avoiding undue intrusion, obtaining informed consent (and renegotiating consent), protecting the interest of subjects, maintaining confidentiality and preventing disclosure of identities (where this might adversely impact on individuals and groups), are universal principles encapsulated in ethical codes and guidelines (Peace, 1993). The traditional ethical model offers some protection to vulnerable people against being exploited through use of intrusive methods. Codes which address universal principles of consent, privacy and protection from harm are referred to when teaching students about ethical issues in social research, both qualitative and quantitative. Anthropologists have long considered the ethical codes are not fine-grained enough to deal with the actualities of fieldwork; they prefer guidelines instead. A processual and negotiated approach to informed consent is thought best for fieldwork rather than the one-off contract, prior to research, the 'scientific' model (Wax, 1982).

The traditional impersonal–universalistic ethic (which covers both absolutist and relativistic approaches) is under challenge from the relational or care-based ethic, 'the feminist communitarian model' or 'ethic of care' (Denzin, 1997). The 'ethic of care' provides moral imperatives, to form relations of solidarity, foster empowerment and more involvement with participants, and 'close' connectedness between researcher and the researched. Social inquiry is to be communal and shared, with friendship, trust and support the foundation stones of the new relational form of research (see Chapter 2). Reconfiguration of what we consider ethics in qualitative research is warranted, since the whole issue of face-to-face contact, which puts the researcher in touch with people in sensitive ways and requires more integrity, authenticity and intuition than in other moments in the history of social science, demands moral imperatives that apply to problems of human interaction (Lincoln, 1995). The new ethic and moral imperative of feminist research is warranted, but the new ethic and moral imperatives are not well codified yet (1995: 47). In the meantime researchers must abide by ethical codes and guidelines that have traditionally informed fieldworkers, which imply a belief that risk of threat to subjects is negated by informed consent.

Marja-Liisa Swantz (1996) raises issues that can be seen as theoretical implications of her work, but also speak directly of personal and ethical concerns for those who engage in participatory research. Some of the key issues that Swantz addresses include whether there is self-deception in the scheme whereby the researcher participates in a double role, as fellow human being sharing the interests of the people she works with, but as a researcher or a developmental worker employed for a research purpose; whether genuine involvement of the studied people is possible, or whether the situation purposely created for intercommunication is only a way of camouflaging the existing power differential; and whether the research situation is always one of domination by what is conceived to be superior knowledge (Swantz, 1996: 134).

Swantz (1996) points out that there are always conflicts between the ethnographer's personal quest for knowledge, which is directly connected with working in the interests of ordinary people in their life situations, and with what the ethnographer wants to gain from research itself. How to conduct research *together* with other people has become the core problem of participatory and feminist research, rather than how not to treat people as 'objects'. Researchers can be guilty of conducting research that is not morally acceptable, but nevertheless meets the ethical guidelines on protection of rights and subjects from harm. The assertion of feminist research, that the 'personal' is 'political', has influenced the way scholars in a wide range of disciplines think about the subject of ethnography and their work (Behar, 1996: 28). From the modernist's or traditionalist's point of view, fieldwork is person specific, yet somehow has not to be 'personal'. What do we do when ethnography grows 'too personal'?

Close participation may be an intrusion, imposition and irritation more than a responsibility and a benefit. The 'openness' that is linked with more effective and ethically responsible treatment of women and intimacy can create a measure of abuse not previously seen with quantitative research that does not go under the guise of friendship. Friendships in the field may foster more effective and ethically responsible treatment of people (individuals are treated as total human beings, with feelings and emotions), but social relationships formed in the field on a base of sharing personal experiences and shared fate can lead to more intimate topics and issues being discussed, the potential for more abuse from probing, and breaches of confidentiality with disclosure and publication.

While many feminist scholars favour ethnographic techniques and fieldwork, some feminist researchers argue shifting from quantitative to qualitative methods of inquiry will not solve ethical questions because ethical and moral dilemmas are characteristic of fieldwork and participant-observation (Stacey, 1988). Not all feminist researchers want more participation or seek to perform the role of detached observer less. They fail to see more participation and less detachment the key to ethically and morally responsible fieldwork, since engaging in close relations with interviewees and members of a community is not without risk of threat to respondents.

The notion of women interviewing women, in terms of ease, comfort and involvement, is considered problematic for a variety of reasons (Phoenix, 1994; Young and Lee, 1996). Judith Stacey (1988) and Daphne Patai (1991) question the ethical possibilities of ethnographic techniques that argue for intensity of ethnographic relationships. While some feminist researchers tend to emphasize the importance of feelings and experientially based knowledge which draw on 'feminine' qualities of intuition and empathy in interviews, close friendships formed in the field are seen by others as potentially exploitative relations that can create a 'conflict of interests' and cause ethical dilemma (Stacey, 1988: 122). The fieldworker could find that the moral obligation to preserve the secrecy of intimate and personal accounts divulged between friends and retain the integrity of friendships formed in the field at some considerable variance with the professional rule to treat information as supportive evidence for analytical findings and interpretations.

Friendships formed in the field – are they different?

Participant-observation includes the development of various kinds of relationships with people in the field, some of which over time develop into friendships. These friendships have been defined as slightly different from those developed outside the research project because they are fundamentally unequal and duplicitous. Intimacy is created between the researchers and researched to uncover a great deal of sensitive information, which is then used as information to be disseminated for a wider public viewing. People who share confidences and secrets and assist the ethnographer to understand their culture can be betrayed by fieldworkers who are committed to the research agenda. Stacey (1988) came to the conclusion that the ethnographic method exposes subjects to far greater danger and exploitation than positivist research methods.

The 'closeness–distance dilemma' raises questions like: 'How real is the participation?' 'Is the role of participant-observer a pretence?' 'How real are the friendships?' 'Is the role of friend a pretence?' Some say that striving for empathy and intimacy should not be confused with friendships, that most friendships cultivated in the field are short-lived and the purported solidarity is often a fraud, perpetuated by feminists with good intentions (Reinharz, 1992). Perhaps at times friendships are 'real' and at other times they are not. Certainly, where most of the social relations formed in the field are built on a sham (as with covert research), pretence would seem to predominate. Many relations presumed 'close' are not long term and might only be 'friend-like' rather than genuine and ongoing. The researcher usually is only a temporary member of a group or community and is primarily in the field to collect data. The transitory nature of the researcher's role and purpose are considerations that enter into the question of pretence.

Despite having made the transition from observation to participant, my primary aim in the field was to observe (make notes on paper and in my mind). While it is true to say that my immersion in the field as a volunteer worker was authentic, a decision to leave was determined by analysis, as was my entry, and relationships were sacrificed. Much of what was observed was recorded in field notes and analysed with the aid of theoretical concepts, but questions to elicit responses that would advantage my agenda were never asked. From observations certain data were recorded in field notes, but much was not recorded. The personal challenges, disappointments, aspirations and concerns of both the researcher and subjects, which evoked emotional response and affected individuals deeply, were never mentioned in the notes. I was engaged in a filtering process but largely unconscious of it and in retrospect I have come to a realization that there was a pattern of disregard recorded by what was missing in terms of personal, idiosyncratic and impressionist attitudes deemed not 'scientific' by virtue of being 'personal'.

While I observed social processes that linked women together in an assembly-line fashion to do the formal work tasks and participated informally with the women in casual conversations, they in turn observed me. That my mind was not always on the social activities which were currently in progress did not escape their watchful eyes. My detached or not totally involved stance was noticed and my reputation of being a daydreamer was established, which elicited casual comments now and again from observers who were friends: 'There she goes again . . . life passes Marlene by.' Contacts with friends ceased when fieldwork was concluded; they could not be continued given the circumstances. When informed in lectures of my fieldwork experience, postgraduate students have asked, 'Can't you go back and tell them about the study?' My fieldwork experience, albeit extreme in terms of the silence allowed to surround the fieldwork role and purpose, addresses the notion that friendships in the field are only 'friend-like', established by the researcher talking about herself, sharing confidences and tasks (Wolf, 1996: 20).

There is an inequality about the research relationship that is established and maintained, despite the best of intentions to rid qualitative research of imbalances of power in the researcher and researched relationship. A trained ethnographer can arguably claim to be more adept at reading subtle cues than a layperson who is without sociological or anthropological training. An unsuspecting informant might be placed at some disadvantage and potential risk of harm because a great deal of information conveyed through non-verbal symbolism is data that can be used to promote research goals. My access to education and the influence of a collegiate culture and research agenda, in terms of being a friend, placed me in a different situation to subjects.

In some circumstances the fieldworker might be genuinely unable to ascertain whether informants actually tolerated silences and prompts in the knowledge that these were to promote research, or because subjects did not want to alienate friends with whom continued interaction was valued for personal reasons. The skilful deployment of pauses, affirmative noises, nods of approval and/or understanding, used to encourage individuals to continue talking without the researcher having to assume a directive role, is one of the 'tricks of the trade' ethnographers commonly use to avoid taking the lead in interviews. The question to be asked is whether probing is ethical among friends. Researchers need to take seriously the discrepancies between self and others that professional training creates, and consider the questionable nature of probing in the context of promoting genuine equality of experience in participant-observation relationships. Where information is revealed without informants realizing its usefulness as data, an infringement of another's privacy may occur. Being involved in the daily life-world of members of a group has to be balanced by a concern not to 'melt' into the group to such a degree that members forget the research role is the salient one, and this may occur in more subtle ways than with covert observations.

Quantitative survey methods and structured interviewing have been rejected by feminist scholars who find objectionable the power differential incorporated within the researcher–researched relationship, and because of the potential for exploitation endemic to quantitative research. My discussion would suggest qualitative fieldwork techniques are not without a capacity also to create and perpetuate unequal relations in the field. Does each party to the qualitative research act have equal opportunity to protect the self from intrusion? Ethical problems arise from the dual roles the fieldworker invariably performs (researcher and friend), and from a disparity between what is willingly shared and what is revealed without subjects realizing this (Hansen, 1976: 132). The fieldworker could be faced with major ethical problems by virtue of having 'been there'. Other roles may conflict with the research role (for example, friend, therapist, counsellor) and make demands that test professionalism and expertise. Ethical and practical dilemmas may be created by overlapping roles and relationships that have to do with disclosure of personal and secret information and breaches of privacy rights.

The first ethical problem underscores the importance of reminding individuals during fieldwork that you are actually performing fieldwork, this way securing dominance of the research role. The second ethical problem might be corrected for by editing field notes and text so that informants cannot recognize themselves from links made with activities. Hansen (1976) admits to selecting data judiciously so as not to violate responsibilities to protect privacy and subjects from harm. But some evidence which violated implicit expectations about privacy was included and the informants were able to recognize themselves, despite the use of pseudonyms and editing.

Ethnographic methods, which reduce distance and move the researcher in closer interaction and intimate relations with others, demand greater sensitivity, authenticity and discretion than required in previous moments in social science (Lincoln, 1995: 45). Where the moral imperative in research is for closer relations, expressions of feelings and sympathy, and patient listening, there seems to be a demand for researchers with personal qualities to handle the human relations side of research. Since this may not be possible in all cases, it would seem that fieldwork studies in the future that are underscored by a 'feminist, communitarian ethic of care' Denzin (1997) could be hampered by new role-related problems to do with personal characteristics for the job.

Skeggs (1994) reports positive outcome for participants from having been involved in close personal relationship with the interviewer. Students she interviewed were given the opportunity to discuss violence, child abuse and sexual harassment. The opportunity to discuss such matters was believed to outweigh any risks since positive self-worth was derived from having been usefully involved in a research project. On a less favourable note, Skeggs admits a great amount of time was spent counselling subjects rather than interviewing, and to some extent this 'jeopardised the research'. The outcome was rationalized as inevitable, ethical and consistent with feminist research practice. In light of Mies's (1983) moral appeal and ethical imperative for feminist researchers to identify with respondents and those less privileged, such a rationalization would seem reasonable, yet problematic.

The researcher–therapist dilemma

The researcher takes to the field a bundle of roles that constitute the total social 'me'. Which role will be allowed to assume a master and determining status in any social setting, and which roles are to be relegated subsidiary positions in the repertoire of roles, might be a matter to be negotiated with another/others. While some roles may be compatible and allow multiple identities to be managed simultaneously without putting the researcher or subjects at risk of threat, overlapping other roles and relationships could lead to ethical and practical dilemmas.

It has been suggested that phenomenological and interactionist concepts provide valuable resource for researchers engaged in social work; that social workers might 'take the role of the other' when engaged with those adjusting to bereavement. The 'significant other' or confidante may be a role that the social worker could adopt when visiting, listening and encouraging a widow to 'live out the grief by talking about it' (Smith, 1975). The activities thus prescribed are consistent with the caring, sharing and nurturing role of feminist scholarship (sharing women's interests and concerns and assisting them to achieve liberation from forces that adversely affect identity, social relations and well-being).

The researcher and therapist or counsellor roles seem compatible at face value, but on closer examination, straying into the preserve of counsellor or therapist could present the researcher with some ethical and practical dilemmas. That one should overlap roles in fieldwork is understandable since during an interview subjects may address topics that arouse emotional response, which in turn elicit a reaction of concern from researchers. Over-concern, however, with the emotional aspects caused when the respondent 'opened up' with confidential information, can lead the sociologist to cross the boundary into another discipline or profession considered the preserve of the therapist. Without the necessary training to handle feelings and emotions, the researcher could inadvertently create additional stress for self and other. In the past, the traditional researcher could feel they were not being professional should they express over-concern for the feelings and emotions of respondents or members because the 'personal' was not part of the researcher's responsibility. Nowadays, nurturing and caring in feminist research is a moral and methodological issue, but those who do what they consider 'right' could become targets for criticism because they lack the training necessary to ensure the subject is adequately protected from risk of harm.

Researchers need to be particularly sensitive to the emotional expressions of respondents during an in-depth interview; uneasiness might be an indicator of stress from probing, which could result in withdrawal from future encounters (Baker, Yoels and Clair, 1996). The researcher might seek to gather information about personal histories of those interviewed, unaware that demographic factors in some circumstances have a potential to create distress in respondents. In a debriefing interview with a therapist with whom she had professional relations, a respondent who had been interviewed by Young (Young and Lee, 1996) expressed her personal distress. The sociologist sought confirmation of family size, but information on family size was a sensitive issue for this woman, since it raised the matter of contact with a child she was no longer in touch with. The subsequent session between the client and her counsellor precipitated the woman's withdrawal from a further planned interview with the sociologist. Nurses of the hospice interpreted the withdrawal as 'typical of a counselling response', after exposure, the person withdraws (Young and Lee, 1996: 106). The nurses believed that concern with emotional response was appropriate for a counsellor or therapist, but not appropriate for a sociologist/researcher and not what 'good' interviewing was about.

Other scholars have found interviews offered few opportunities for respondents to discuss at length their concerns, needs and feelings about AIDS with someone perceived as objective and sympathetic (Alty and Rodham, 1998: 278). Where subjects felt safe to express their views and discuss their own experiences of sensitive issues and how these affected them, there was a potential for the researcher to stray from the interview protocol and to take on a therapeutic stance toward the subjects. While it may be advisable and quite appropriate to provide an opportunity for the respondent to discuss in more detail an issue that causes them much distress after the interview is completed, this practice can open up the possibility of hearing too much of the wrong sort of information ('off the

record'), and make problematic the selection of information for disclosure. The researcher is then faced with the ethical and moral dilemma
of what to do with sensitive information that is secret and private and
not for wider uncensored public viewing. The problem could then
become 'is one to use the information or forget it altogether?'

In a conference paper presented at the International Nursing Conference (Schmied, 1995) there was reported a case where a heterosexual
couple, who had been recruited to a study of couples' first experience of
parenthood, were in default because the death of their child ruled out
their ability further to meet the criteria of inclusion. On moral and ethical
grounds team members were reluctant to exclude themselves altogether
from ongoing interactions with the couple. Having already established
rapport with them in the first few interviews, it was thought 'callous' if
not unethical not to visit them and give them the opportunity to talk
about their experience. However, it was not considered appropriate for
interviewers to take on a clinical role and provide grief counselling.

Unlike health professionals who have back-up support provided with
debriefing sessions, researchers may have to find their own solutions to
personal experiences which are outside the formally prescribed research
role (Brannen, 1988). Without the necessary training to handle feelings
and emotions and without professional back-up support for debriefing,
there is a potential that the researcher could be considered irresponsible
and perhaps even unethical.

Conclusion

From this discussion it is apparent that the role/s one is allowed to
play in a different culture or subculture are a matter of negotiation and
renegotiation between the self and others in a context of shifting power
relations. Directing the self into and through roles is a staged performance that is affected as much by a setting as by ideological, methodological, cultural and personal factors.

The point to emphasize is that roles performed in the field are neither
fixed nor unvarying. One may start out as an 'insider' in a group and
gradually assume 'outsider' status (as with feminist standpoint research),
or vice versa, and one may perform a variety of roles simultaneously
within the same piece of research. The concrete field context may
influence the roles the researcher is allowed to play before a specific
audience because age, gender, ethnicity, and so on are involved. An
occupational setting may have personnel residing there to designate
what is the best role for the fieldworker to perform in the situation.
Those in positions of authority and power sometimes have their own
agendas which are at variance with the research goal, and they may
decide on interpersonal scripts and role relationships for the researcher
with this in mind.

With role performance, the researcher often must contend with the expectations and demands of colleagues in team research, supervisors who invest much time and interest in their students' projects, funders who dictate methods and roles, and members with whom they have formed friendships. Cross-cutting ties of loyalty and obligation to various audiences can impact on role performance, make ethical and moral action problematic and cause a 'conflict of interests', and perhaps a 'conflict of consciousness'.

The issue of overlapping roles and relationships needs to be addressed in relation to the potential for creating ethical and practical dilemmas. Once researchers cross the boundaries into other disciplines and professions, like psychology and therapy, there is the problem of risk of threat to self and others to consider. Those who are not trained to deal with other people's emotions could risk creating a situation that has the potential to run out of control. Researchers without psychological training and professional back-up support in the form of sessions could run the risk of being defined irresponsible and their actions judged unethical should they import into their interviewing a concern with emotional matters that ideally should be handled by health professionals. There is a need to be aware that becoming too familiar with members can create ethical problems with disclosure of information.

Textbooks on qualitative research methods tend to present an idealized and abstract version of a role that is not realistic and context related. We need accounts that extend upon the notion of role as a fixed entity, to be filled like a formal position in an organization. Fieldwork roles are varied. The field is a potential opportunity for selecting a variety of roles to be realized in performances that unfold over time. From the repertoire of roles which the researcher carries into the field, the selection of a few may be made and choice will link the researcher in relationships of various types (power, intimate and social). Role demands can weaken the establishment of social solidarity with some people in the field, or work against the formation of relationships (quantitative researchers do not form close relations with subjects).

The fieldworker is sometimes required to perform a delicate balancing act to meet the obligations and responsibilities owed to various parties, and still promote their own research agenda. The fieldworker might be required to balance involvement with detachment, familiarity with strangeness and closeness with distance. The fieldworker needs to be flexible, creative and willing to experiment with role and able to withstand the insecurity that can come from the indeterminacies of the field.

CHAPTER 6

Ethical dilemmas: the demands and expectations of various audiences

---

F ieldwork ethics in this chapter is considered not so much in terms of the self-directing and autonomous social actor, who anticipates problems and makes adequate plans to combat pitfalls and dangers at the outset of research; the notion of deliberate, calculated acts on the part of the researcher is replaced by a concern with inadequately anticipated consequences of fieldwork that may occur throughout the research process, are possibly unavoidable and can create ethical and practical dilemmas. The notion of the researcher deliberately refraining from what is obviously unethical activity, like fudging data and claiming credit for work done by others, misappropriating funds, stealing from one's research grant, and so on, is not a concern here (Sieber, 1996). Staging and performing fieldwork rests on a foundation of negotiations with various parties, each with their own interests and expectations (sponsors and funders, gatekeepers, colleagues and subjects), which may or may not clash and could rise to conflict.

Negotiations are an ongoing part of the fieldwork process and concern relationships: 'relationships that may be between parties with vested interests, hidden agendas and unequal power' (Peace, 1993: 35). During negotiations the position of researcher can vary 'depending on the circumstances, and the power and powerlessness of all those involved' (Peace, 1993). The interests of one or more parties may be compromised at times, and the researcher could be plunged into a dilemma. The privacy rights of subjects may be compromised by the professional rules of a discipline to provide confidential information as evidence to support analyses and interpretation. The researcher could find himself in the unenviable position of being caught in cross-cutting ties of allegiance and loyalties, and faced with a dilemma for which there is no satisfactory solution. Ethical problems and dilemmas can be an outcome of having to balance responsibilities and interests of the various parties in the research enterprise, rather than a consequence of deliberate acts that reflect deception, manipulation and exploitation of people and resources.

Gatekeepers and sponsors can fill both obstructionist and facilitative roles, not only in relation to access but also in terms of choice of theoretical orientation and methods, and with matters of disclosure and publication. Hidden agendas can emerge as fieldwork gets under way, or agendas may change as relationships between the researcher and various parties develop. There may be 'obligations to colleagues' in team research to consider. Power relationships between team members can be linked to differences of discipline and method, gender differences and expectations over career devopment. To whom does the fieldworker owe first loyalty: to supervisors and other academic staff who belong to the discipline and the university; to gatekeepers and sponsors; to employers; to individuals who participate in the research; to citizens of the wider community?

A 'conflict of interests' can arise between the researcher and one or more parties. There may be no course of action that seems satisfactory, only one that seems more 'right' than another; the researcher could be faced with an ethical and practical dilemma (Hill, Glaser and Harden, 1995). The self-negotiation which researchers undertake on a piece of research is to define their own position within the bounds of pro- fessional, ethical and moral practice, personal values and feelings. Cross- ing boundaries from conventional to dubious research topics, conventional to sensitive fieldwork sites, research methods and role relationships would seem to add to the complexity of contemporary qualitative fieldwork practice.

Various expectations and demands

In psychological inquiry, researchers are advised to weigh up the poten- tial contribution of the proposed research against the costs to participants exposed to questionable practices (Kidder and Judd, 1986: 461). When research is carried out on employers, students, prisoners and members of any institution, administrative personnel of that organization may want the information to supplement personal files (Kidder and Judd, 1986: 502). A researcher who is a staff member may come under pressure to release research information and could face the difficult decision of whether to maintain confidentiality or suffer the consequences of defying the institution's request (which could mean termination of the research enterprise). Maintaining confidentiality might be complicated by requests for access to information by third parties, such as institutional administrators, school principals, professional associates, other research- ers, and the like. The more prudent resolution to take might be to meet the requests and demands of administrators and work out in advance arrangements for maintaining confidentiality (Kidder and Judd, 1986).

It may be unwise for fieldworkers to conduct research in a setting where they are already employed and established in a work role. The expectations and demands of dual roles could be incompatible and place the researcher in an untenable position (Morse, 1994: 27). Apart from the practical issues of doing participant-observation, which require inter-viewing people in the workplace, that could interfere with continuity of tasks and the expectations and demands of other co-workers (note taking could be delayed until immediately after leaving the field), the field-worker might learn confidential information which should be reported to management as a loyal employee, but as an ethical researcher should be kept confidential (Morse, 1994). The special ethical problems with doing research that engages the investigator with a relatively small group with whom they have worked for a long period of time is acknowledged. Risks that are not always foreseen arise from close personal relationships created by long-term, face-to-face interaction and the possibility of violation of trust with disclosure of confidences.

Alternatively, the researcher who carries out participant-observation in the setting where they have no prior status as employee could find co-workers relate to them as a participant and a fellow worker who really belongs to that community and who only happens to be an observer. Demonstrating loyalty and allegiance to workers' ideals and ideas and engaging in informal practices approved by the group, but not neces-sarily by upper management, could strengthen the trust between the researcher and subjects, but make problematic the disclosure of findings to an academic audience. The expectations of subjects may insert a powerful moral pressure on the researcher to maintain confidences and ensure relationships are treated in print in a manner which accords with face-to-face interaction among friends (Hornstein, 1996).

Whose side are you on?

Fabian (1991) studied the Jamaa religious movement in south-eastern Zaïre over a period of twenty years, extending from a PhD project. His fieldwork was aimed at understanding how a religious movement among African workers copes with its world. Other parties considered this group to be a threat. They were interested in repressing their ideas and actions and to this end appropriated Fabian's ethnographic writ-ings.

The Jamaa movement had been steering a course of confrontion with the Catholic mission church; the confrontation occurred early in the 1970s at a time when Fabian was in Zaïre. Fabian was confronted with preparations being made for a case against the Jamaa by church officials (aided by occasional help from the police and the military). Although he refused an invitation to testify as an expert before the assembled prelates, he was unable to prevent use of some of his ethnographic writings by the church officials to foster their political agenda to excommunicate and generally harass the Jamaa. His refusal to engage in complicit arrangements was not based on clear-cut partisanship; those he studied were not exempt from critique. The fieldworker was caught up in complex power relationships that exert a pressure to 'take sides'.

Third party factionalism in the field and disputes about publication are not uncommon predicaments of fieldwork. They cannot be adequately anticipated and planned for and are not often written about in textbooks on qualitative methods, despite the capacity fundamentally to alter the nature and purpose of research (Fine and Martin, 1995). In the past fieldworkers have shown a reluctance to own up to personal and anecdotal accounts of fieldwork experiences and inform others on how they solved ethical problems and dilemmas during and after fieldwork (Fine and Martin, 1995). Fabian acknowledges that the general tendency in academia to criticize those who write confessionals has perpetuated the general resistance to describe the ethical and moral dilemmas of fieldwork (1991). While there has been a tendency to criticize 'confessionals' and 'cookbook' style publications, feminist scholars have attempted to rescue the personal and emotional from its discarded place in the creation of knowledge; with publications like *Reflecting on research practice*, Shakespeare (in Shakespeare et al., 1993) and Ruth Behar's works, *The vulnerable observer* (1996) and the edited collection *Women writing culture* (Behar and Gordon, 1995).

Responsibilities to gatekeepers and sponsors

When a researcher embarks upon a piece of research they may need to define their own position within the bounds of professional practices. Negotiation within a research process is about relationships between parties with vested interests and unequal power (Peace, 1993). The researcher may have to negotiate their time, aims and objectives of the study, methodological orientations and fieldwork sites, as well as details of disclosure, publication and seminar presentations and, most importantly, their obligations to others (Pearce, 1993). Gatekeepers in the academic community (editors, advisers, reviewers, journal committees who decide which articles to accept for publication) have a powerful role in knowledge production and dissemination, and the making or breaking of reputations and careers. The knowledge that is produced is 'selected' and 'shaped' by those in power (French, 1993: 121).

When a 'gatekeeper' takes the role of director away from the actor, we might say that power has become an issue in fieldwork. We might say the powerless could refuse to perform, but refusing to perform to the directing request of a supervisor or assessor could be a powerful overall disruption of the entire research enterprise. Gatekeepers have been defined as 'those individuals in an organisation that have the power to withhold access to people or situations for the purposes of research'

(Miniechello et al., 1997: 171); gatekeepers and sponsors fill both obstructive and facilitative roles. Methodological preferences, writing formulations and financial considerations may be open to negotiation with editors and reviewers. Authors and researchers may be under pressure to acknowledge 'significant others' and be unfavourably considered if they do not. While reviewers' comments may be critical but constructively helpful, or destructive, the reviewers are not required to give their names whereas the author is, along with the relevant details about professional background and affiliations to establish social placement in political terms. A book may be poorly reviewed, methodological content may be defined as 'outdated' or of a differing methodological preference to one who fills the role of 'gatekeeper', and a researcher who is not favourably accepted in a particular clique may be unable to do anything about it.

Gatekeepers can be found in government agencies, funding bodies, and within publishing and academic circles. Often they are the first social contact an ethnographer has with the research setting. Gatekeepers in academia control the allocation of resources (research assistance, travel money, typing support), and may provide patronage. Scientific gatekeepers engage in back-stage bargaining in university departments and can make it virtually impossible for some postgraduate students to pursue a project or promote continuity; patronage may be necessary. In ethnographic settings, gatekeepers can refuse access to populations for observation or permission to access written documentation, despite the researcher's superb research and publication credentials and high quality research experience. Gatekeepers can limit freedom of speech in democratic societies, stifle debate and erect barriers to protect oppressive regimes. Gatekeepers are not unknown within action and participatory research practice, where the obstructionist role seems more pronounced. Researchers have sometimes assumed covert roles to gain access to information which gatekeepers would rather have kept secret.

Gatekeepers who control access to research settings, participants and information, have a right to be informed of the research topic, aims and methods. They may try to influence and exert control over the research data, and the activities of the researcher (Ellen, 1984: 140). Researchers have responsibilities to sponsors and gatekeepers. Sometimes these responsibilities collide with the expectations participants anticipate being upheld and lead to compromising circumstances. Access to a setting and to interactional data will need negotiating and renegotiating with gatekeepers in the ongoing research process. Early in the research process the researcher could be faced with the question 'Whose side are you on?' Being a neutral observer is virtually impossible in long- and short-term participant-observation studies. Gatekeepers may ensure their interests are safeguarded. They might exercise a degree of surveillance and control over the fieldworker, either by closing off certain lines of inquiry they consider threatening to their practical and legitimate interests, or by suggesting one direction for observation or another (Hammersley and

Atkinson, 1995: 66). The opportunities to speak to certain individuals and to access written documentation might be monitored and limited by gatekeepers (Lee, 1993: 125) and explicit conditions imposed on the choice of methodology.

The researcher might resort to covert participant-observation because of unrealistic conditions of access bordering on the unethical (informed consent from high officials only), where refusal of access is implied, or there is a hint of future obstruction to the research progress (Hammersley and Atkinson, 1995: 68). Whether to adopt a fully covert insider role has not been a major problem in most field settings in the past, where anthropologists have been 'outsiders'. All participant-observation may contain a covert element for a variety of reasons (forgetting to inform newcomers that research is 'in progress', cross-cultural difficulties, and so on). As 'insider' research (participatory and action approaches) increases, propensities towards using the covert role might also increase. The cost of performing covert research may need to be weighed against the gains advanced to the wider community to meet the primary ethical principle of beneficence ('do the greatest good'). Covert research might be a conceivable way to obtain information about illegal or disapproved behaviour that obstructionist gatekeepers want kept secret, but of which the public 'have a right to know'.

Access might be based on a bargaining strategy, with permission granted to do research on the provision that some aspect will be studied on behalf of gatekeepers, or a report will be produced for them (Lee, 1993: 126). When seeking access, fieldworkers are usually in a weak position, which could mean accepting conditions imposed by gatekeepers. The consequences of negotiating and bargaining are not always anticipated; there could be unhappy outcomes. Gatekeepers might display more sympathy toward the use of quantitative methods or want information relevant to consumerism, whereas the researcher might want to do a qualitative study to promote understanding for needs analysis (Peace, 1993). Gatekeepers might be reluctant to grant the researcher permission to study an organization that is in transition, whereas transition might be precisely what appeals to the qualitative researcher for the opportunity of observing change. The expectations and demands of gatekeepers and researchers can clash on a range of issues, including aims and objectives, methodological orientation and methods, and 'trade-offs' may be linked with access, methods, publication details, and so on.

Sponsors

Sponsors and gatekeepers can enter facilitative and obstructionist relationships with the researcher. A sponsor might fill a number of roles, 'as a bridge, as a guide, or as a patron' (Lee, 1993: 131). A sponsor might provide a researcher with a link into a new social world, or act as guide to point out what is going on in an unfamiliar setting, and explain features of the setting which might be puzzling. A sponsor may provide warnings against possible faux pas, and, as a patron, secure the trust of others in a research setting. Being in a relationship of friendship with a sponsor might facilitate the confidence of others also to accept a stranger as a friend. A sponsor who performs either a bridging or guiding role may assist the researcher's movement into a new social world (especially if that social world is a deviant one).

Sponsors and gatekeepers have expectations about the researcher's identity and intentions, but the expectations can be inaccurate. The researcher could be identified as an 'expert', a 'critic', or one who is well-informed as to 'problems' and their 'solutions', one who aims to sort out the organization (Hammersley and Atkinson, 1995: 77). The definitions that others project onto the researcher might exert a pressure on him or her to act as a 'critic' and evaluate the situation, despite such activity being at some remove from the ethnographer's expectation of what interpretive inquiry is about. Fieldwork is about negotiation, which includes manoeuvring oneself into a position from where best to collect data, within a context of unequal power relations, and professional and ethical conduct.

The decision to engage in questionable activities might be weighed up against the actions of obstructionist gatekeepers, who can make access difficult through unrealistic demands, bordering on being unethical (like permission will be granted provided the rank and file are not informed). The researcher might decide not to inform those in the higher echelons of an organization, and inform only participants with whom they directly interact. This way, the questionable practice of not informing everyone about the research is advanced. It might be considered appropriate to seek the permission of the rank and file, with a view to later requesting more formal acceptance from senior officers (Hammersley and Atkinson, 1995: 68). Withholding from participants or gatekeepers the true nature of the research is not as dishonest as covert observations, since intent to deceive individuals is not inherent.

Gatekeepers might grant permission for research without the knowledge of people considered not in control (mental patients), or only those in positions of control, who have a right to speak on their behalf. The notion that research participants are to be treated as autonomous and self-determining, who ought not to be deceived for the benefit of others, reflects norms embodied in ethical codes and values familiar to the society's moral traditions (Saks and Melton, 1996). Third parties, with vested interests and hidden agendas, who wield power over researchers may breach ethical codes and community values and exert a pressure on the researcher to do the same.

Goffman's famous ethnography *Asylums* (1961a) was based on participant-observation research in which the inmates were not aware they were being observed, but staff were. Not everyone was informed and this constitutes ethically questionable research. The ethnographer conducted observations without knowing the expectations, concerns and beliefs of the participants and with disregard for privacies which may have been important to them. Perhaps decision making was based on the assumption that communicating with mental patients on matters of research would be problematic; that inmates lacked understanding of such matters; or the ethnographer could not relate ethical issues to research that did not harm participants. A variety of rationalizations for questionable practice is possible and could mirror the researcher's beliefs and attitudes about reality, and perceptions of the socially situated self. Perhaps Goffman saw deception in social research as an extension of deception in everyday life (as a cynic would), with the masked researcher performing impression management to secure the receptivity of an academic audience for a polished performance. Defining the situation, and acting towards it in terms of the meaning it has for them, is an interactionist assumption which might be applied to research practice.

A supervisor who is sympathetic toward an interactionist perspective at some phase in the academic career might justify on philosophical and theoretical grounds the advice given to students to adopt a relativistic ethical perspective toward consent. A logical extension of the constructivist argument would be that of trusting one's own conscience to deal with ethical problems that are situational and contextual rather than absolute and general. For some researchers, the dramaturgical approach to the world as theatre might favour a relativist ethical model, with the performer wearing a mask to bust 'fronts' and get 'behind the scenes', and tap into back-stage information. The spur to social interaction is reputation and 'impression management' is a tool which may be used to that end.

Academic gatekeepers

Students have not always been socialized by their training and other experiences to the ethics of fieldwork. Academic departments and other research institutions can create a barrier to getting research done ethically (Saks and Melton, 1996). In the past, social research was not generally considered for the subjects' own benefit. The interpretive approach was accepted as the norm in some anthropology before the emergence of more critical, participatory and applied approaches in the 1980s, which had some effect on the ethics of research and neophyte fieldworkers. Modelling oneself on the actions of other ethnographers (the foundation fathers) was not something students could rely on to promote ethical conduct in the field. There is evidence to suggest that early ethnographers exploited situations and appropriated people's ideas without so much as being concerned with the intrusion into the lives of others (Barrett, 1996).

The notion of the self-directing, autonomous researcher is not borne out by the circumstances of social research and the power differential between the supervisor and student would in some cases seem to underscore a potential for ethical dilemma in the educational setting. Students lower in the bureaucratic structure and with less power can be located within a relationship of oppression and potential exploitation (students' work has been appropriated to advance career opportunities and reputation by aspiring professors). The political implications of the supervisor–student relationship and the postgraduate's lack of support can contribute to dropout rates and long completion times. Where funding has been provided and publications are anticipated, delays and discontinuities could be seen as ethical problems.

Few graduate departments have courses on ethical dilemmas in research and their solution (Saks and Melton, 1996: 230). The education of neophyte researchers has not focused on the common pitfalls and dangers of fieldwork and how these might be avoided. Where the norm for teaching ethics is low-key in a department, an ethical challenge may be unlikely to occur; but should this happen the power structure of academe is such as to provide a force to dampen any opposition. The social organization of British and American social anthropology continues to be organized as a mentor system. Favourable relations with mentors (usually expressed through acknowledgements in texts), is a career strategy related to debt and obligations that binds inferiors in reciprocal bonds to superiors. The ties between anthropological teachers and 'juniors' are hierarchical, and subject to strain within the intellectual settings. Twin tensions manifested in the structuring of intellectual settings may work to dampen deviations to that which 'juniors' are conditioned to accept. These are, 'the inequality of hierarchical positions (and the resources at their disposal) and the normative equality of members to voice their ideas, and the other between guidance and continuity in intellectual traditions and an emphasis on creativity and innovation' (Ben-Ari, 1995: 141). The inequality stemming from hierarchy is removed once the researcher is no longer part of the intellectual setting and the relationship is on a different footing. The more autonomous author may be freer to assert a challenge, but voicing her or his own ideas continues to be shaped by conventions and power relationships (publishers and editors) and audience receptivity enters the juncture between researcher and publisher.

The local enclaves, as the academic departments are sometimes called, support the activity of research, not the creation of barriers in getting research done and disseminated (Saks and Melton, 1996: 234); and a number of group processes work to enforce existing practices. The fact that interpretive research is not generally for participants, and no discernible harm can be envisaged from disclosure, may exert a subtle force against a postgraduate's desire for partial self-censorship, and restricting access to protect subjects' privacy rights. Challenge to the norm of 'no barriers to research' presents the student with immediate psychological costs as well as potential social and material costs. Academic gatekeepers control access to markers, qualifications and subsequent career opportunities, and are in a position of considerable power to have their expectations met.

The researcher is part of a team that works together in rehearsals; 'behind the scene' they jointly construct the report or book. The 'team' may be the student and her or his supervisor/s, and include other members of a university department. Should the neophyte ethnographer attempt to become a 'one-person show' and break rank by wanting to conceal information 'assumed' embarrassing to the subject audience, other members of the team may decide to play a minor role in a scenario that is emotionally charged. They are unlikely to break rank to support a lone dissenter who is a junior in the university hierarchy, and the researcher could find herself somewhat alienated should she be brave enough to challenge ranked authority. Most students would not feel great comfort in disagreeing with staff members in the department of a university, especially over something as important as research, which is central to the academic work life. They would probably prefer to avoid conflict and acquiesce to the expectations of superiors.

The scenario may end with the researcher being forced to the realization that the report or book is a joint construction; that the researcher's representation is mediated not only by the subject's interpretation of the researcher's representation, but of the supervisor's interpretation of both parties' interpretations. At the end of the day the researcher may have few doubts about the potency of the supervisor's director role, and his or her ability in getting actors they support to perform to scripts they had largely written. The receptivity of the subject audience may be ceded to that of the academic audience, and the researcher's vulnerability not considered an issue. Protestations for partial concealment may be headed off by assertions of the academic community's 'right to knowledge'. Academic gatekeepers can exert a powerful moral force that has compromising consequences for both the researcher and subjects.

Gatekeepers may assert a stronger directive role and pre-empt student problems with fieldwork. Lincoln (1998) claims to offer support in whatever kind of dissertation a student might wish to do, as long as the overall design and method choices exhibit a good fit with the problem, but ironically some students are excluded from her support to do fieldwork. Lincoln asserts the right to differentiate between which students should and should not be allowed to do a phenomenological study that requires work in the field. There is acknowledgement that 'sensitive' fieldwork 'mandates a powerful sense of confidentiality and an understanding of how identities and information must be safe-guarded' and that some students are 'simply too young or immature to handle the

rigors of fieldwork' (Lincoln, 1998: 324). She will not approve a dissertation proposal that is considered over the head of the student; where she
believes a student might create ethical problems of access or believ-
ability; or where she believes a student may embarrass or create problems for the institute or university department. Doing fieldwork,
especially in sensitive sites, 'requires maturity, high self-awareness, and
high personal authenticity' (Lincoln, 1998) and some students are not
perceived ready for the task ahead. This is an ethical pedagogical
concern, underpinned by a desire for the best and most judicious
advising, that illustrates the supervisor's belief that laissez-faire may not
be in the best interests of the student, the teacher or the institute.

Lincoln (1998) claims the teacher and professional has an ethical
responsibility to make certain ethical choices satisfy everyone concerned.
She is aware that other professionals may believe she has crossed the
boundaries of professional ethics in qualitative research, but however
awkward the expression of her teaching concerns, she hopes they
stimulate a dialogue about the ethics of fieldwork and other issues. The
maturity required of a new postmodern ethnographer introduces fresh
responsibilities for the teacher and advisor to ensure that the choices
students make about the kinds of relations they want with respondents,
and their involvement with taboo topics and sites, are the best for
everyone concerned (1998: 324). Teachers and advisors are concerned
with the 'closeness' and familiarity being promoted in contemporary
social science and the potential for more ethical problems being created
than previously experienced, or in relation to positivistic quantitative
research.

While some scholars recognize that supervisors have responsibilities
for their students' choices, other scholars say responsibility lies clearly in
the hands of the individual student; that they must be responsible for the
topics chosen, their conduct in the field and what is done with research
(Bernard, 1994; Partridge, 1979). It would seem that academics have a
responsibility to 'sensitise the student to ethical problems and dilemmas,
and set an appropriate example of research behavior' (Johnson, 1982: 79).
It is debatable whether the supervisor has violated an ethical responsibility by failing to teach the student effectively and appropriately in matters
relating to ethics. While there is recognition in the literature on research
ethics that 'an ethical problem may be unforeseen by the investigator',
and that ethical consequences 'may be inadequately anticipated' Sieber
(1996: 15), there is also recognition that the validity of the research design
(recognized by some ethical committees as an ethical issue), reflects on
'adequate supervision' (1996: 13). Ethical problems facing social researchers have changed over time, and will probably be more difficult to
resolve in the future. The intimate role relationships, which put people in
closer contact than in previous moments of social science, demand
greater sensitivity, authenticity and discretion from researchers, and
create problems with the management of *confidentiality* and *anonymity*

(Lincoln, 1995). The traditional ethical model for maintaining rational, unequal and impersonal relationships between the researcher and researched is being challenged by the new ethic or moral imperative, yet to be well codified, possibly because the new form of research is not yet advanced enough.

It is the norm for the supervisor to raise with students the issue of compatibility of personalities, and provide the option of changing supervisors should differences arise. The supervisor might go beyond differences of personality to include an active, sympathetic handling of postgraduates in the induction process, advise on pre-existing departmental politics, and provide mentoring and encouragement to disseminate research in a manner, which accommodates ethical and moral dilemmas.

A conflict between researchers' needs and interests and those of women participants can be created through membership of an academic or disciplinary community. When interviewing individuals one enters another person's social world, and sometimes establishes friendships characterized by caring, sharing and nurturance. A contradiction can arise when accounts of personal experiences are represented in the text as abstract, theoretical and sociological. The representational style of modernist texts differs from lay modes of storytelling, and an academic audience has different expectations to that of a lay audience. Differences in representational style that have emerged in academe in recent years, between modernists, postmodernists and feminists, raise the question, 'For whom is the research being done?' There are segments of the academic audience that do not consider research is for participants. The researcher writes for a particular audience and the modern doctoral student style does not square with accountability to those outside the academic establishment (Skeggs, 1994: 86). Social science research has traditionally been written for a relatively powerful audience of academics and a patriarchal representation of the participant's accounts might be all that can be achieved (Skeggs, 1994).

Some practical solutions

An all too familiar relationship may develop between the student and staff members from having got to know each other more informally, which incites peers to express criticism. Abuses of power can arise when a staff member gets to know a student too well, and sets the stage for mixed messages. The issue of power and the responsibility to intervene or assist students when support is needed requires some practical means of being addressed. A practical solution to the elimination of ethical problems of the departmental situation might be to seek additional consultation from other senior members (Biaggio and Greene, 1995: 115).

Should a vulnerable student approach another member of the department to assist in mediating some difference with a superior in the hierarchy, support may not be forthcoming since the student could also implicate that member. Failure of another academic to intervene on behalf of the student, and provide support to deal with an ethical problem with 'overlapping relations', or an issue like 'closure', might be understandable should the staff member be a female, in a position of relative powerlessness in a male-dominated university department, who is not wanting to experience further struggle with powerlessness. Retreat from an opportunity to use greater power as a faculty member to intervene on behalf of the student may be related to pre-existing departmental politics. Outside the staff member might seek help for herself and the student in the form of consultation with a profeminist faculty member in another department, to put the brakes on abuses of power within departments (Biaggio and Green, 1995: 102).

Responsibilities to colleagues

The value of team research is well recognized, with representation of multiple disciplines which contribute individuals trained in different fields, such as education, psychology and sociology (Lincoln and Guba, 1986). In team research there are those responsible for training members of the team and others who co-ordinate activities. Different individuals bring to the situation their specialized skills for the job, expectations about role, status, remuneration, and so on, as well as methodological preferences and biases. Team members can accommodate multiple tasks (data collection by means of participant-observation, interviewing and focus groups, analysis, interpretation and written reports). A division of academic labour has the advantage of strengthening a research design.

In multi-disciplinary teams, questions can arise over seniority, experience and skill, the allocation of tasks to be performed, collecting data, analysis and interpretation, as the aims of research (Peace, 1993: 34). In team research, leadership, supervision and the intellectual division of labour can promote unexpected tensions in the field and lead to disputes about publications (Punch, 1994: 87). Power relationships between team members may develop and differences between members of discipline may be elaborated (those with statistical skills versus those without; quantitative researchers versus those seen as qualitative). Role-expectations and appropriate recognition of actors may be a cause for conflict (Peace, 1993).

Feminist concerns to avoid conduct in research deemed 'exploitative' rarely refer to the conditions and relationships in which feminist research is sometimes produced (the division of academic labour in team research). Researchers in higher echelons might rely on interviewing and analysis by juniors and research assistants, but show a reluctance to give due recognition with acknowledgements in the text or with articles, and even consciously 'exploit' the situation. I once overheard a principal investigator and self-professed feminist scholar, advising another team member in charge of recruiting staff to a team project, say, 'make sure they're not highly qualified, undergraduates are easier to exploit'. Those with first degrees are often employed as research assistants, to do the hackwork or behind-the-scenes activity that rarely gets the formal recognition when the accolades are handed out.

Researchers have drawn on the services of such individuals to do analysis and interpretation; their work has been absorbed in producing reports and research articles on which the principal researcher's name has priority. Sometimes recognition is given to other principal researchers who may have had very little if any practical input to the research project, but whose name as co-author adds prestige to the report. When knowledge, experience and confidences are not equal among team members, the issue of 'power' and 'empowerment' is raised. Research assistants who are part of a team are well advised to know their role and the credit which will be accorded to their work (Kellehear, 1993: 29). A major role in team research should entitle the principal researcher credit as an author of the report; but co-authorship should be accorded where specialized skill and expertise have been put into analysis and interpretation, and with writing a report or research article/s. When a principal researcher is using team research as a base for a doctoral thesis and draws on specialized analytical and theoretical skills of a highly qualified research officer, it becomes difficult to avoid perceptions of 'exploitation', especially where the findings are used to produce articles which count toward the final doctoral assessment. The research officer may assume a major role in the preparation and presentation of articles, but have any claim to co-authorship overruled because the principal researcher, as PhD student, 'owns' the materials. Should the assistant challenge the principal researcher she could risk having to face the supervisor; supervisors do collude with postgraduates in some situations. To avoid any confusion over co-authorship, get such matters clarified in writing before ethical dilemmas develop. Settle your expectations of co-authorship at the beginning of the research. Such matters should not be left unclear (Kellehear, 1993: 29).

As a result of being a team member employed to analyse data and write up findings, the assistant could find herself subjected to much criticism from 'outsiders', who have grievances with the leading figure and see the supporting role of the assistant in advancing her career as an ethical matter. The team member of a multi-disciplinary project could have her contribution and personal worth made questionable by adversaries of the principal researcher. Individual team members need to have their roles and rights clarified within the boundaries of professional and ethical practice. They should take care that others in positions of power do not unfairly assume responsibility for results that advance their career opportunities. It is critical that the obligations owed to the various parties are negotiated and that resources used in team research (expert knowledge, skills and experience) be adequately and appropriately acknowledged. Negotiations in collaborative team research are about relationships between parties with vested interests and unequal power.

Responsibilities to informants and participants

Psychologists and oral historians have fostered an understanding of how overlapping and dual relationships present therapists with a range of complex but unavoidable ethical and practical dilemmas (Biaggio and Greene, 1995: 88–123). Anthropologists, too, have directed a focus on the ethical and practical problems with dual roles of friend and practitioner (Hansen, 1976; Stacey, 1988). Where multiple roles and relationships are developed during fieldwork, there are ethical and moral obligations owed informants and other participants, which have to do with confidentiality and professional practice. The ethnographer is ethically and morally obligated to ensure that the expectations of participants are compatible with their own, and that any misunderstanding about roles and relationships do not occur.

The formation of friendships with subjects functions to balance the power differential between the researcher and subjects, but the more equal relations create a potential for ethical or moral dilemma. Feminist researchers are conscious of the need to develop methods for listening during interviews which are personal, disciplined and sensitive to differences. Noticing ambiguity and problems of expression, then drawing on the researcher's experience to provide clues to elicit future responses, are part of a disciplined method of listening being suggested for feminist interviewing (Devault, 1990: 105). The researcher's experience as a woman becomes a resource for focusing attention on the unsaid and producing information on a topic that is not commonly spoken about. With the feminist sharing and caring approach to interviewing, parties to the encounter could become locked together in emotionally charged scenarios. The researcher must ensure subjects are comfortable in the knowledge their lives may be opened up to an uncensored public viewing by having talked with the researcher.

Appropriate boundaries between the researcher and subjects may need to be maintained when in the professional role, to avoid ethical problems arising from differing loyalties and expectations that have to do with the management of *anonymity* and *confidentiality*. Biaggio and Greene (1995: 99–118) provide examples of ethical and moral dilemmas in therapy that have relevance for qualitative social science. Overlapping roles and relationships (researcher/therapist/friend) present the potential hazards of boundary violations – ethical dilemmas. There is acknowledgement that multiple/overlapping roles carry mixed messages to subjects; that unclear and vacillating boundaries can be eroded and ethical, moral and practical problems created. Therapists and researchers alike understand the importance of the power differential in the professional relationship, and the need to develop conscious strategies to avoid misusing their power. In addition to continued need for self-examination of the power imbalances in the professional relationship, consulting with ethically informed colleagues for guidance in the management of possible boundary violations is advised (Biaggio and Greene, 1995: 119).

Consultation may focus on acknowledging that boundary crossing occurs with multiple roles, that role performances can be flawed, and with anticipating the potential of this and of validating relationships. The researcher who crosses the boundary into therapy and assumes a counsellor role may, by virtue of evoking emotional displays for which they are not professionally trained to handle, be labelled irresponsible and find her research agenda adversely affected by role performance (Skeggs, 1994). Interviewing is the main method used in feminist research and psychotherapy interviewers are researchers who deal with the same issues as researchers in other disciplines (human behaviour). Highly personal and emotionally charged issues such as rape, child abuse, violence in the home, drug abuse, and so on are issues addressed by professional feminist practitioners in therapy and by researchers in the social sciences. Researchers in interviews can create emotional trauma by virtue of the topics and issues addressed, and the concern expressed with emotional responses of subjects. Being overtly concerned with emotional responses could lead some subjects to assume that the interviewer is providing a resource which counsellors or therapists customarily provide. The sympathetic, supportive good listener may create unanticipated and problematic consequences of an ethical and moral nature that have to be weighed against the traditional normative practice to ensure positive outcomes from social research are promoted.

Researchers who engage in closer, more intimate relations in social research may inevitably formulate problems that could be harmful to themselves as well as subjects. A researcher, not unlike a therapist, could be traumatized through the professional practice but, unlike a therapist, who has access to professional assistance through peer debriefing sessions and consultation, may be without professional assistance. In anthropology and sociology the personal has traditionally been sifted out from the research experience and relegated to the private sphere. The growing interest with inserting more of the self into the interview and participant-observation relationships would seem to be creating a context that requires additional assistance with handling the self.

With contemporary social research there is extension and revision of ethical codes and moral imperative. Many researchers proceed with a belief that informed consent and other ethical principles are adequate to enable them to meet the ethical and moral requirements of social research. The gap between the rational mode and situational demands leaves much that requires negotiation on the spot. Ethical and moral dilemma may force the researcher to weigh up costs against notions of non-malificence ('do no harm') and beneficence (do 'the greater good') (Hill, Glaser and Harden, 1995: 30), or draw on their own intuition and feelings which ask, 'Would I like this done to me?'

Researchers have a responsibility not to cause participants to become embarrassed and upset from having spoken to them. One may become aware of a faux pas because it is customary for both parties to a conversation or interview jointly to work to remedy what has gone wrong and to 'save face' (Goffman, 1967). The problem of differences in purpose and interpretation needs to be incorporated into the field-worker's agenda, and taking the 'role of the other' incorporated into interviewing and participant-observation. Anyone who has been inter-viewed knows what it is like to search for answers to questions, hearing your own voice speak out loud your thoughts, and being surprised at what you hear, and sometimes embarrassed and anxious about what might happen to your words, if they might be repeated to others, out of context, and perhaps even used to intimidate others (Shakespeare, 1993).

When interviewing there may be some dissonance between the roles of researcher and friend which the researcher is simultaneously attempting to perform. The actor may underplay the research role and empathize more with the ordinary person as friend as a compromise to cope with the dissonance (1993: 98). Self-disclosure, in response to the direction the conversation is taking, is an ethical and moral issue. The researcher is obligated to ensure that people know the information they convey could become data for uncensored public disclosure. There may be a need to remind subjects which role is currently the master and controlling one and which is to have a subsidiary and supportive function. Self-disclosures are ways of establishing equal relations between the researcher and researched. The ethnographer may share personal infor-mation with subjects and open windows to their shared interests and expectations, but caution is needed to ensure the participants are not too 'open' and the researcher is not subsequently cast in the role of 'exploiter' or 'betrayer' of trust.

Case one

Atkinson's (1993) project had as its primary aim an exploration of the use of oral history techniques with people with learning difficulties. The researcher established a group in a residential home. Themes were deliberately chosen and attention was directed to 'safe topics' to avoid upsetting the individuals. The researcher was mindful of the need to project an image of a friendly and interested person to combat a 'powerful personal image' and establish a relationship between 'equals'.

Atkinson failed to realize that people with learning difficulties found family memories and accounts of childhood experiences more painful than experiences in adulthood, which feature long-term hospitalization (1993: 62). Revisiting childhood experiences caused participants to reflect upon unhappy past lives that were filled with earlier loss, separation and rejection, and created for the researcher a welfare function. Atkinson felt greater responsibility for the welfare of the individuals who had been formed into a group in a residential home at her instigation, to foster research that reflected her aims, agenda and assumptions. She felt duty-bound to fill the group's therapeutic function and ensure that people were not overwhelmed by sadness and regret. The researcher's perception of role initially was at odds with other people's perception, which is not uncommon in social research where multiple definitions of the situation apply. A therapeutic role for the researcher to fill was created by participants who tried to introduce a range of 'unsafe' areas into group meetings (like being put away as children, child abuse, separation and loss, deaths and admission to hostels and hospitals).

The subjects attempted to use the interview setting as a means to talk about and make sense of their personal pasts and histories, which was just what the researcher wanted to avoid. Staff members usually reinforced the researcher's agenda, but subjects had a *personal agenda* that included topics they wanted to pursue, *areas of privacy* they were not prepared to talk about, and an *extended personal mandate*, which gave them an opportunity to hold the floor, often on rival themes. At mid-point in the project a change in research ownership took place. The researcher's agenda was being replaced by the group members' and priority was given the production of the Book. There was a coming together of the two agendas: the researcher's agenda to build a collective account or oral history; and the members' agenda for an opportunity to tell personal stories and relive individual histories. Atkinson perceived the compilation of oral historians' stories in a book would be a by-product of joint participation between herself and participants in group interviews, but with the competing agendas and expectations of the researcher, other staff members and the group, priority was given the production of the Book.

Relationships of trust between 'equals' had been developed. With the blurring of distinction between the key actor and subjects fostered by strategic action, people had benefited from relating their own accounts of past experiences and events. What had been created in the minds of the participants was an expectation of continuing involvement in the development of research, but the researcher had to move on. Atkinson reflected on members being left with a strong sense of loss or betrayal that reflects on a number of ethical questions: 'What obligations do fieldworkers have to people?' 'To whom is first loyalty owed?' Ethnographers and oral historians might develop relations of friendship and intimacy through group sessions they initiate for research ends, but the test of 'real' friendship comes when fieldwork ends. The question of whether friendships formed in the field are 'real' or only 'friend-like' and contrived lies at the heart of feminist debate about intimacy and friendship within the context of professional practice.

In the chapter written by Atkinson (1993) a focus is on how the actors related to each other and, importantly, how the researcher related to the self – recalling and reflecting to make sense of the experience and assessing personal achievement. The group meetings had provided a forum in which people were able to recall and relate events and experiences from their past lives. The group was terminated by the researcher, despite the protests and pleas of group members. The fact that responsibility for research continued up to and included the ending of research proved a painful conclusion to reflect upon for Atkinson (1993). Atkinson questions whether the personal revelations of participants and context-specific findings would be relevant to a wider audience.

With the book *Past Times* there was the question: 'Does this outcome represent a universally good outcome for this project?' The fact that the book remained unpublished meant a wider audience was deprived of the rich account of people's individual and shared experiences; the ethical issue of the public's right to know was raised. Atkinson was unable to meet her certain ethical standards, which raises the question: 'What obligations do fieldworkers have to people who bare their souls so that an article, or book can be produced?'

The interactive rather than the object/subject model of interviewer–interviewee relations has become the preferred model for some feminist scholars since the release of Oakley's work (1981). Feminist ethnographic methods are presumed to offer a corrective to the standardized impersonal survey interview, with its closed ended and pre-specified question/answer format. Attempts have been made to break down the inequitable power relationships inherent in the interviewer–interviewee relationship of quantitative research, by replacing the 'stimulus/response model' with 'interviewee-guided' interviews and phenomenological interviewing (Reinharz, 1992). The conventional value-neutral observer might have no problem with having a different agenda to participants and with impersonal relationships, but feminist researchers have found this much more difficult to accept.

Accountability in feminist research manifests itself in a readiness to ensure that participants remain active when fieldwork ends. Incorporating more of the self in the relationship with participants rather than denying personal involvement (as defined by the traditional model of quantitative research) has been argued for by Skeggs (1994) and against by Stacey (1988) and Patai (1991). At the heart of the debate about friendships and intimacy in fieldwork and observational studies is authenticity and personal integrity, and whether friendships developed in the field are 'real' or only 'friend-like' and 'impression management' carried over to social science research. 'Are power relations and exploitation of subjects as resources, being perpetuated in fieldwork under the guise of friendships?' Continued relations and social contact when fieldwork ends hold some answers to this question.

Case two

Glucksmann (1994) wanted to understand the occupational structure and the labour force in Britain during World War II. She took an assembly-line job that would bring her into close contact with workers from whom she might learn more. Glucksmann found the workers took an assembly-line job to earn a living. The work processes she wanted to learn more about were strategies they had primarily developed in order to deal with the pace and tedium of the job. Glucksmann recounts how she had to learn from a collective enterprise through participating and observing and how the assembly-line workers had no interest in producing anything written for external consumption from what they knew of the set-up. Following the early participant-observation experience, a series of oral history interviews took place.

Glucksmann's (1994) account corroborates that of Atkinson (1993). Participants placed limitations on developing collective knowledge and their different interests were at variance with those the researcher treated as significant. What they hoped to get out of the research was not the same as the researcher. Those interviewed about mass production during the inter-war period were fixed on talking about World War II once they started discussing this. In particular, the blitz and evacuation took the centre stage, with personal and emotional experiences far more memorable than 'boring' assembly-line work. As the research project was not about the war, so their accounts were of little relevance to the researcher at the time. While Glucksmann was mindful of the need to avoid treating people as 'objects' and of doing 'good' research, the pursuit of her own agenda seems to have made questionable the feminist ideal of completely getting away from treating participants as 'subjects'.

Juggling audiences' expectations and demands

Staging and performing are processes in fieldwork complicated by multiple audiences made up of sponsors, academic gatekeepers, participants and the wider community, each with expectations of what constitutes a 'good' performance. Expectations about role and identity could differ between the researcher and subjects, depending on which of the two major audiences (academic and member group) the researcher was performing for. The bipartisan nature of the fieldworker role raises the question: 'To whom does the researcher owe first loyalty, the academic community (comprised of supervisor/s, other staff members, fellow researchers of the postgraduate body), or the observed group?'

Modern fieldworkers have found the competing demands of allegiance and loyalty made by the two main audiences problematic. With
the physical and social separation of the two main audiences (the
members of each party are unlikely to be in contact with each other), one
would assume the opportunity for information to infiltrate one group
from another and spoil the identity of the researcher or halt the research
performance would be unlikely. Not so! Physical and social separation of
the two major audiences is no guarantee of information control. Gatekeepers can withhold funding and make progress difficult and research
subjects can eject the researcher from the field setting because she or he
has failed to meet the strandards of group behaviour. The researcher
must mobilize the support of both academic and membership audiences
to ensure fieldwork moves beyond the planning stage.

Some modern interpretive inquirers have done their fieldwork at
home, where an academic audience was in close physical proximity.
They performed with peers and supervisors on a regular weekly basis,
with analytical and theoretical displays rather than descriptive accounts.
Anything 'personal', 'idiosyncratic' or 'impressionistic' was likely to be
avoided. Avoidance was based on implicit understanding rather than
any explicit or verbally professed announcement about the inappro-
priateness of addressing the 'personal'. The student was socialized into
being first and foremost an observer who happened to be a participant,
with loyalties and allegiances owed to others who resided outside the
department. Personal affairs were part of another story, part of the 'story
behind the story' yet to be told to an academic audience or readership.
The role of participant facilitated movement to back regions and behind
'fronts', to extract the meaning of customs, rituals and the like from the
perspective of the members which otherwise may have not been available to ordinary members. Performing as an impersonal, analytical,
observer in the field was the norm in my postgraduate days. In the
seminar situation a 'good' performance was deemed 'theoretical' or
'analytical', but not 'descriptive'.

The roles of participant and observer form part of the bundle of roles
that make up the actor's repertoire of roles and face-saving devices; such
roles need to be activated in order to become a 'reality'. When
'immersed' in the field in some far-off land, and not interacting on a
regular basis with faculty members and peers in the department, the
participant role could become the master and controlling status and the
observer role be accorded less significance. It has sometimes been
considered necessary to introduce periods of remission from the field to
ensure that ethnographers have the distance required for self-
conceptualization, and to avoid 'going native'. Close and regular contact
with the academic audience protected the neophyte against over-
involvement and served to reinforce the definition of self as researcher
(Hunt and Benford, 1997: 114).

Additional precautions were sometimes thought necessary to guard against too much embracement of the group's values, ideals and shared sentiments, and 'going native'. Separating the analytical and theoretical from the personal and private, and the cognitive and rational from intuition, feelings and emotions, with different types of field notes, captures something of the analytical and emotional compartmentaliza- tion characteristics of the modern fieldwork experience.

Leaving the field

Stories of the ethnographer's experiences when leaving the field provide insight to ethical and moral dilemmas with relationships, since leaving the field is a time when personal relationships with key informants and other participants must be managed. When fieldwork ends and contact is termi- nated with people to whom the ethnographer may have become attached, we are concerned with the social, political and ethical implications of ethnography and fieldwork (Taylor, 1991: 238). Taylor (1991) suggests in some cases the most moral and ethical course of action would have been to leave the field before data was saturated and the researcher's data collection goal was achieved.

Taylor observed attendants or 'direct-care staff' in institutions who looked after mentally retarded people and regularly abused the resi- dents. He was morally offended by what he saw of conditions on the ward and the treatment of residents under their care. But he came to like the attendants personally and was grateful to them for how they 'opened up' to him; he allowed his personal likes to override professional and ethical imperatives. In retrospect, Taylor admits he should have stopped observing the regular abuse and dehumanization on mentally retarded people under the care of the attendants, and that his failure to do this could be considered tantamount to condoning and supporting abuse (1991: 246). The decision not to observe needs to be balanced with acknowledgement that there are certain settings, people and situations which are important to study, and to understand that even if observa- tions offend the ethnographer there is a need for research.

When leaving the field, the responsibility of ongoing relations to informants with whom close relationships have been developed become apparent, and so too does the authenticity of the researcher as a friend. Atkinson (1993) reflects upon leaving the field against the wishes and protests of the participants who related to the researcher as a friend. Taylor says 'a common problem among researchers studying people with mental retardation is that they become their subjects' best and only friends' (1991: 246). He based the claim on experiences of three doctoral students under his supervision. Taylor (1991), like other researchers, believes the researcher is indebted to vulnerable and lonely people who have been encouraged to become close to the researcher, and depend on them for the opportunities which research makes possible. How one leaves the field is a personal decision that depends upon the people and the relationships developed with them. Some people neither want nor need to continue relations with the researcher, while others might desire continued contact. In such cases breaking ties can create feelings of disappointment and even feelings of betrayal and exploitation.

The ethnographer's exit from the field has not traditionally been considered data worthy of inclusion in the text, as the aftermath of relationships between the researcher and informants and other participants. Such matters have traditionally formed part of the ethnographer's personal experience, to be resolved privately. Taylor says as a general principle we have a responsibility to make sure that people are not worse off for having let us study them, even if we cannot guarantee that their lives will be improved (1991: 246). Pains to ensure no one comes to harm from research must underpin reportage.

Responsibilities to self

The social analyst is at once a cognitive, emotional and ethical individual, who constructs knowledge through contexts of shifting power relations and varying degrees of distance and intimacy. With subjects, the knowing person blends a range of cognitive, emotional and ethical capabilities into the roles (participant, observer, analyst, academic, friend) which they perform before different audiences (academic, subject group, wider community). Overlapping of roles and relationships is unavoidable with audiences in everyday life. People operate with 'multiplex relationships' (they enjoy the company of the same people across a range of social activities). In the context of professional practice and social research, such overlapping of roles and relationships may become problematic. The different interests and expectations of groups have the potential to create a 'conflict of interests' (Stacey, 1988).

During fieldwork, the identity of the fieldworker might fluctuate between value-free impersonal analysts to morally conscious participants of a group, and the duality may be dramatically impressed upon the researcher who witnesses a 'degradation ceremony' that arouses empathy and sympathy. The social identity of the researcher can be shaped by the experience of having been intimate and close with friends in the field, of having been 'one of them'. Fieldwork may include behaviour that runs counter to the researcher's moral code, values and personal integrity. Intrusion into private spheres can create ethical dilemmas and exacerbate field-related stress (Ellen, 1984: 144). Participating in, recording about and publishing on such activities may place the subjects and fieldworker at risk of threat to reputation and damage their sense of well-being. The general trend has been to treat ethics in terms of what the researcher might do to others, and to neglect or downplay the risk of threat from research for the researcher.

The minidramas of ethnography, the degradation ceremonies and epiphanies, where the social actor is made to feel estranged from others, are dramatic events when the researcher could become aware of the audience's interpretations of their roles and performances. Dramatic scenarios or epiphanic episodes, commented upon in the next chapter, have the potential to mobilize forces to establish moral order and may capture the dilemma of the social actor who is forced to a realization that they are no longer 'acting' a part but caught up in a real life drama that features competing interests and expectations. In normative fieldwork the actor performs before a relatively unknown audience; approval is a contingency of ongoing research. The researcher must initially perform without being familiar with a script, without rehearsals, and in a manner to establish rapport with subjects when struggling to come to terms with being an actor. Indiscretions and incompetencies, combined with the paradoxes, ambiguities and dilemmas of fieldwork, can make performing a daunting and personally threatening affair.

The novice ethnographer, less dependent on time spent in an establishment and the internalization of its moral values, may demonstrate an inability adequately to read the script for the cues for corrective behaviour. They may be without enough cultural sophistication to respond to the immediate situation in a manner to convey respect for the interests and expectations of others, and not overstep the boundaries of acceptable practice. There is a need to realize the differences in purpose and interpretation between 'insiders' and 'outsiders' and attend to the expectations of group members. Organizations, as groups of interacting people, evolve their own cultures and interpersonal scripts for members to perform. Knowledge of such matters is an indicator of 'insider' status and crucial to establishing a working arrangement that satisfies both the major audiences (academic and member).

The problems with conducting sensitive research go further than funding, sponsorship, access and establishing rapport. They relate importantly to ensuring that fieldwork does not cause the researcher to undergo change that is negative. The general message in the literature has been to establish as far as possible the pitfalls that may be anticipated, and where possible to plan at the outset ways to get around problematic areas before things get out of hand. When researching sensitive topics which may pose problems with disclosure and publication, there are a number of options available to the researcher which include planning another project, proceeding with caution, or publishing and taking the consequences (Alty and Rodham, 1998). The nature of fieldwork, however, makes problematic a capacity to provide a set of prescriptive guidelines to avoid pitfalls and harms of fieldwork. Many of the ethical and moral dilemmas cannot be adequately anticipated because of their futuristic and potential or emergent nature that require on the spot solutions.

Conclusion

Ethics committees are concerned to ensure participants do not suffer harm from research. The protection of subjects is promoted by informed consent (and modifications to informed consent) and the maintenance of privacy and confidentiality. Codes and guidelines can give the impression that ethics is 'what we do to others rather than the wider moral and social responsibilities of *simply being a researcher*' (Kellehear, 1993: 14). Codes and guidelines remind researchers of values they already share by virtue of being members of the wider community. Taken alone, codes are not adequate to deal with ethical dilemmas of fieldwork, because decision making in such matters involves more than cognitive or rational reasoning; decision making draws on intuition, emotions and feelings. Codes and guidelines are rationalized, impersonal bureaucratic constructions that are not conducive to handling context-specific, value and emotion-laden decisions of individuals and groups at a particular time and place. To their many decision-making encounters in the field, contemporary researchers bring an awareness of ethical codes and guidelines and a familiarity with society's moral traditions, which underscore traditional ethical models (Saks and Melton, 1996: 231).

Many ethnographers reject the medical or positivist model of ethics as not fine-grained enough to deal with the actualities of fieldwork. Instead they prefer to work with guidelines established for the discipline to which they belong and into which they were most probably socialized as neophyte fieldworkers. The traditional impersonal ethical model assumes there is some common and agreed upon sense of what constitutes consent, harm, privacy and confidentiality; more to the point, one's judgement about these principles is assumed to be distanced from one's political and personal experiences. One's position in the culture, however, particularly in relation to power, 'deeply affects how one defines each of these principles and thus is at the very heart of one's ethical decision making' (Hill, Glaser and Harden, 1995: 21). Ethical codes and the general moral principles underlying them and various models based on one or both, provide guidelines but lack specificity (1995: 24). 'Situational and contextual elements in the particular ethical dilemma are missing from most ethical guidelines' (1995).

In an attempt to integrate the personal, social and political into ethical and moral practices, the focus of this chapter has been on power relations and the expectations and demands of various parties with an interest in research that can create ethical dilemmas. Ethical dilemmas are defined as situations in which there is no 'right' decision, only a decision that is 'more right' (Hill, Glaser and Harden, 1995: 19). When confronted with an ethical dilemma, the researcher needs more than a code of ethics or formal guidelines for guidance. There is a need to understand how to use ethical codes and guidelines in ethical dilemmas with other resources to come to a decision that is 'more right'. When the researcher experiences 'a conflict of interest' from dual or overlapping roles, one's personal and professional loyalties and feelings are likely to be drawn together and reflections made on society's traditional moral norms. Solutions might be found by drawing on personal values and ideals, professional and personal standards, intuition and emotions as well as rational ethical models. What feels 'right' and 'good' might need to be taken into consideration with other professional ethical criteria since one has to live with the self when fieldwork ends.

Feminist researchers have commented on a 'conflict of interests' arising from co-operative and collaborative relations with participants in the field (Stacey, 1988). Dual or overlapping roles and relationships create a context for ethical and moral dilemmas, since they bring together sets of interests and expectations that may be incompatible. Friendships developed in the field can create or alter researcher allegiance and loyalty or, conversely, the researcher's commitment to the research goal can undermine friendships when fieldwork ends, making questionable the authenticity of intimate relationships in fieldwork. During fieldwork, ethnographers may be drawn into political arrangements and intrigues with members in higher echelons as an organization or community. A powerful moral pressure may be exerted upon the researcher to conform to their expectations and demands, despite these being at variance with researcher goals. Such matters are part of the unanticipated consequences of qualitative research that requires fieldworkers to form relationships with people in the field. They are subject to the same sorts of political machinations that occur in everyday life. One's loyalty to friends can be compromised by obligations owed to more powerful others with hidden or emergent agendas that require allegiance.

Given the actualities of fieldwork that involve researchers in relationships with people at various levels, with gatekeepers and funders, colleagues in team research, subjects and the self, each with interests and expectations some of which may clash, it is not difficult to appreciate that fieldwork is about negotiation and relationships; and the potential for ethical dilemma. Each ethical dilemma is different, being located within shifting relations of power and powerlessness, professional and personal standards. One must be guided in decision making by codes and guidelines, but not forget the part played by other values, ideals and interests, including theoretical and philosophical preferences, intuition and emotions.

CHAPTER 7

Field notes: ethics and the emotional self

M ost fieldworkers create material records like field notes, which are basic for analysis when integrated with materials from other sources (official documents, photography and video tapes). Field notes as data combine bits of information that must be organized into categories to have significance in the text. Much information recorded in field notes and other records directly relates to individual persons, their social interactions, personal relationships, behaviours, beliefs and opinions (Akeroyd, 1991). A record of illicit activities, dubious methods and 'guilty knowledge' might combine with negative images of insecurity, guilt, confusion and resentment in field notes, to represent the 'darker side' of fieldwork (Wolcott, 1995).

Participants may be named, often without pseudonyms, and described in personal status/role terms, and references may include various 'identifying particulars' they would not want. Participation in activities with the researcher might portray identities in a not too positive light. Participants are sometimes disparaged in descriptive and explanatory notes and in methodological commentaries. Field notes often contain information that has been obtained without permission and not verified. Much information may have been 'known' to all in the setting, some confidential and private, and some 'known' but not openly acknowledged (Akeroyd, 1991). Verbatim data are gathered during informal discussions or during 'time out', when actors relax in the back region form part of the informal interactive scene of field notes. The ethnographer is never 'off duty' and much information recorded that is inadvertently divulged is best kept 'off the record'.

Field notes may record the researcher's struggle with balancing a feminist 'ethic of care' with masculine principles of justice, determined by ethical codes and guidelines, or the researcher's failure and successes, fears and insecurities, likes and dislikes (Lehnerer, 1996). Field notes are more than 'records'; they are personal property. They are usually kept in a safe place, and brought out for use according to the purposes of the analyst at a given point in time, which can be a number of years after fieldwork is completed. Despite their often personalized content, field notes are probably not perceived by their owners as a compilation of personal data pertaining to individuals in the sense that data protection laws conceive of records (Akeroyd, 1991).

Field notes contain sensory details that usually show rather than tell about other people's behaviour. How others express their feelings in the field might be conveyed in field notes by direct quotations of the speaker's own words, supplemented with non-verbal expressions (facial gestures, bodily postures and the like). The significant characteristics of a setting and of people might be gleaned both from the observations made and recorded in field notes and from the personal reactions felt by the researcher. The two orientations, observations and personal reactions, are balanced in field notes (Emerson, Fretz and Shaw, 1995).

Ethnographers are concerned with collectivities rather than individuals and tend to have a diminished awareness of the relevance of personal notes in relation to rights and interests, and the need to safeguard them (Akeroyd, 1991). Akeroyd (1991) acknowledges it has been held that data in field notes are not necessarily sensitive, damaging or harmful; the possibility arises from their use/s and the contexts in which they are transformed into information (Sieghart, 1982: 103). Field notes have been used for purposes other than the researcher intended and what they wanted (Fabian, 1991). It is easy to exaggerate the risk of threat that data in field notes pose for the researcher, but the risk of threat must not be underestimated. Researchers should consider what elements of their data they consider confidential and/or private, and organize data in field notes with this in mind with use of pseudonyms and/or indicators to suggest materials are 'off the record'.

Identities can be deduced from descriptions of people's roles and their relations to others, and from the overall impression of a setting (the description of events, people or places, the surrounding environment in terms of physical proportions, and tone). The accumulation of incidental material or background detail can lead to a deductive disclosure (Lee, 1993: 186). A researcher might take great pains to maintain anonymity of data, with use of pseudonyms for people and places, but provide a description of the setting which is so detailed and precise that it is virtually impossible for someone not to identify the environment with specific individuals or a group. There might be a need for sufficient ambiguity in field notes to disguise or misguide, even when pseudonyms are used.

Social science disciplines and individual researchers differ markedly in techniques used in field notes to hinder identification of participants and protect privacy and confidentiality (Akeroyd, 1991: 89). Omissions of personal identifying information from field notes can affect features critical for analysis. The fieldworker can find the depersonalizing effect of pseudonyms in field notes a barrier to relating with people they are writing about. There are difficulties with 'losing' individuals in the usually small 'qualitative crowd', and adequate non-identification in field notes and the text is an ideal worth working toward, for ethical purposes (1991).

Just as knowledge in the social world is layered and differentiated into scientific and everyday understandings, so too in field notes knowledge might be separated into theoretical, analytical and methodological notes, and descriptive and personal categories. The personal and the private have traditionally been relegated to the diary, to be used as a base for footnotes and the appendix. Field notes are sifted and sorted in a selective process assisted by the analyst's theoretical preferences and sociological concepts. Much that remained hidden in field notes in the past is now being made public in attempts to tell the 'story behind the story'. The same data used to establish a claim to validity and establish 'truth' are now being used as base to mount a critique of past ethnographic practices. Field notes assist with an examination of our own prejudices and biases (personal and professional). They can depict the flesh-and-blood human being who is vulnerable and confused by the 'messiness' of methods in the contemporary moment of social science.

Adopting a critical attitude toward field notes might enable the analyst to explore questions like 'What do field notes convey about the cultural climate of the day?' 'Are ethical and moral concerns obvious?' 'Are there difficulties with describing accounts of actual emotions?' 'Does this reflect confusion over feeling "rules"?' 'Are the notes scholarly, personal, or cynical?' 'Can embarrassed self-consciousness be detected?' 'What can field notes tell about traditional forces working on the researcher?' 'Can the ambivalences inherent in the role of participant-observation be detected in field notes?' 'Scientific' or 'objective' knowledge is given priority within anthropology and sociology and distance has been linked with the prevention of bias. Impersonal methods are advocated for preventing bias and evidence of this might be detected in field notes.

Field notes and the construction of social reality

Field notes are developed and created by the fieldworker, who is in the unique position of bringing personal meaning to the created account. Field notes then are not 'raw' data, since they come 'encoded with the author's conscience, understandings and interpretations' (Coffey, 1996: 66). The 'reality' of a social world that is created in field notes, with actors fitted into leading and supporting roles, is the work of the ethnographer who exists in that world known as the 'field'. The ethnographer's work is intertwined with social processes of routine everyday life given in setting, via field notes. The fieldworker is a 'doer', a 'sufferer' and an 'enjoyer' (Rosaldo, 1994), whose work of doing ethnography involves a bundle of prejudices and biases, pleasures and fears.

The reality of fieldwork is that involvement covers not only being an observer, but also being an actor, author, teller and writer (Coffey, 1996). Field notes may provide evidence of the multiple roles performed by the researcher in the field and the difficulties of infusing roles with personal creativity and personal style.

Re-entering the 'field' for a pre-arranged second phase of a research project made Coffey (1996) aware of the socially constructed nature of her initial fieldwork and sensitive to the version of reality she had created in field notes. Between the two periods of observation, she read and reread field notes, analysing and writing about the data. With this process came the realization that the researcher was a sieve for all the possible data, who exercised authority over what was recorded and written about in field notes. The researcher selected incidents to record and certain conversations to note or copy down verbatim. The themes and ideas worked up differed from what the members probably considered important or significant (1996: 64). Writing field notes was likened to writing a novel; the roles the researcher wanted to capture were constructed from data selected by the researcher. The individuals in the 'story behind the story' would not be quite the same as the 'real' people the researcher had observed, as they were constructs like characters in a novel. Drawing on a combination of field notes and 'headnotes' enabled the researcher to 'people' the world of an accountancy firm under inquiry and give to the accountancy graduates characters which were plausible for that reality; the author would 'allow' the characters to develop as the story progressed.

Every social situation includes people who are considered to be particular kinds. For example, all people might be customers for the period of time they are in the social situation of a large departmental store or second-hand clothing shop. The fieldworker might approach a social situation for doing participant observation with a notion of the kinds of actors that customers become when located within certain types of stores. From preliminary observation of one store and through discussions with friends, I was furnished with an impression of customers who frequented budget shops; the most controversial types were 'bargain-hunters'. With repeated observations, differences between regular customers were noticed in terms of clothing, behaviour, demeanour, terms of reference and other features that women with whom I worked used to identify specific customers in the situation.

Within the second-hand clothing store women watched who bought what and when, and the arrangements they made for payment (cash or lay buy). Non-verbal symbolism supplemented verbal expressions to give a more rounded definition of the situation. Through conversations the salesladies learnt the marital status of regular customers, residential address, transport arrangements and the like. Gradually a dossier was built up of identities of certain regular clients, who were identified in field notes under a 'cover term' (Spradley, 1980). The customers who engaged in sales encounters in the shop were identifiable as cultural categories ('customers' or 'clients').

Social types were developed in the field notes (Spradley, 1980: 89). Social types are constructs that fall conceptually 'somewhere between individual, idiosyncratic behaviour on the one side and formal and informal role behavior on the other' (Lofland and Lofland, 1995: 106). One dealer was defined 'good' and the other 'bad'. In field notes specified customers were linked with certain characteristics, propensities and activities, and moral evaluations were sometimes made. Women referred to the 'bad' dealer as 'the witch from hell', a label she had helped create from a regular practice of 'beating you down and treating you like a silly little shop girl'. By way of contrast, the 'good' dealer paid the marked price and never haggled. Finer discrimination than available with formal role was recorded in field notes. As fieldwork progressed the characters in field notes consciously or unconsciously became stronger and more pronounced.

Usually field notes contain page after page of descriptive notes, most of it in the fieldworker's own words. 'Cover terms' (Spradley, 1980) or 'in vivo codes' (lay terms) may be used to depict categories of clients (Strauss and Corbin, 1990), or to name different kinds of individuals in field notes which the analyst may choose as characters of the story. In field notes I created characters to 'people' the social world of the second-hand clothing store, give the text its interest and meaning and establish my authorial authority from having 'been there'. The researcher, as actor, writer and teller of the story which would be unfolded in the text, needed to be mindful when searching field notes for characters to fill the leading roles in cultural scenarios that identities behind the roles (dealers) and relationships with other participants in the 'plot' (notably the author) could not be deduced and result in identification. People could be humiliated, embarrassed, angered and hurt by 'deductive disclosure' of social types. 'What should be disclosed?' is a central anticipatory ethical and moral issue when considering crossing the boundary of field notes to the text (Lee, 1993: 185).

A number of ethnographers have returned to the circumstances of their doctoral fieldwork and to the events and moods of fieldwork by re-reading field notes. They provide memories and recapture what it was like, which can sometimes be embarrassing and uncomfortable. Coffey (1996) used the experience of 'going back' to explore how ethnographers as writers and authors socially construct a social world in which they have a part (albeit a de facto one). Other researchers have revisited field notes, via interviews that yield information about emotions experienced during fieldwork (Young and Lee, 1996). Jackson (1990, 1995) used interviews to explore the liminal qualities of self, worlds and words in field notes.

Emotions and research

Emotions have been viewed as irrelevant or disruptive of the modern academic agenda and generally relegated to the personal and private realm of the diary. The intellectual mission of 'classic' anthropology was to get the 'native point of view' without actually 'going native' (Behar, 1996). The methodological tradition required the fieldworker fill participant and observer roles, with the emphasis on 'keep your eyes open' (1996: 5). The ambivalence that is characteristic of fieldwork can be traced to the work of Malinowski (1922), the founding father of anthropology, who saw the need to provide candid accounts of conditions of observations, but his accounts were to be relegated to a diary, perhaps to discipline him to objectify.

Generations of ethnographers in the 'classic' tradition have considered personal reactions inconsequential or irrelevant to analysis and establishing generalized meaning. In some segments of anthropology and sociology today, what happened to the observer in the process of doing ethnography need not to be known. The reigning paradigms traditionally called for distance, objectivity and abstraction; 'the worst sin was to be "too personal"' (Behar, 1996: 13). According to Behar emotion has only recently 'gotten a foot inside the door of the academy and we still don't know whether we want to give it a seminar room, a lecture hall, or just a closet we can air out now and again' (1996: 16). Despite the disdain toward emotions in anthropology and sociology there has been a growth of interest in fieldwork accounts that recognize emotions and morality in field notes (Lehnerer, 1996; Young and Lee, 1996).

Emotional experiences have been used to position theoretical arguments (Young and Lee, 1996). Records of emotions and emotionality in field notes have been seen as important sources for reflecting the way methodologies shape and colour research practice (Wilkins, 1993). The 'dispassionate' approach to fieldwork is under challenge from contemporary and feminist critiques of modern ethnography. Within the feminist and critical strand there is concern with more caring, sharing and nurturing relationships and an emphasis on emotionality, intuitiveness, intimacy and morality. The emotional impact that research has on the researcher is being recognized (Behar, 1996; Bochner, 1997: Lehnerer, 1996; McGettigan, 1997; Ramsay, 1996; Young and Lee, 1996).

Feminist methodological literature has challenged the notion that subjective and emotional responses are irrelevant or disruptive of epistemology, academic analysis, interpretation and theorizing. Emotional response is being linked to establishing the veracity of the text and the quality of qualitative inquiry. It is argued that the 'new' writing of sociologists should have as its main goal a capacity to evoke emotional responses in the reader, thereby producing verisimilitude and shared experience (Denzin, 1997). The private feelings and doubts of the researcher and the moral and ethical dilemmas of field may be a feature in the 'story behind the story' that is yet to be told.

With the introduction of critical methodologies in sociology and anthropology over the last couple of decades, new ways of performing have been added to the researcher's repertoire of roles and face-saving strategies. There has been a move away from observation with a preference for more participation with 'cultural members'. A new moral ethic is required that is consistent with new ways of performing. The moral imperative is yet to be formally codified and this partly explains the confusion over appropriate ethical and moral practices (Lincoln, 1995). Traditional roles are still being performed by interpretivist inquirers (Adler and Adler, 1987) and some concern with 'going native' can still be found in the sociological literature (Ram, 1996); but the changing repertoire of critical interpretivist researchers from anthropology and sociology requires a measure of control be transferred from the researcher to subjects to ensure they too become script writers, actors and directors of their own fieldwork dramas. Identifying *with* rather than *looking at* is a moral alternative to the ethnographic realist approach to fieldwork practice and textual representation that is being recognized among contemporary interpretivist inquirers.

A social constructionist view of emotions

Goffman's (1959, 1967, 1969a) many writings have played a central role in developing a relational approach to self-presentation and emotions (Gergen 1994: 217). Explorations of self-presentation have included 'face work', degradation ceremonies and epiphanies, dramatic events with a potential for highlighting social interdependency and emotions, without recourse solely to psychological explanation. The self of symbolic interactionism is constituted by its own activity and by the activity of others, working back upon it and exerting a pressure for self-awareness and self-control. By extension, feelings might be seen as situational and interactional reactions, constructed, interpreted and expressed through processes of social indication and self-indication.

The implications of the micro-social perspective for emotions are effectively drawn by Hoschild's (1983) inquiry into emotional management, where the concept of 'work' is captured in thinking through the management of emotional expressions. Social guidelines are influential to how we feel; emotion 'work' is directed by 'feeling rules'. The rules and norms underpinning emotional management, the 'feeling rules', do not merely refer to stifling or suppressing feeling, but are also about constituting feeling, bringing it into responses to awareness of social norms about what one 'should' be feeling (Lupton, 1998: 19).

Many scholars are interested in the social ordering of emotional expressions and the norms and rules underpinning emotion 'work' in various contexts (social contexts and textual representations, including field notes). It is when these rules are broken that the individual stands out as a deviant other, provoking anger and frustration in others (Lupton, 1998). Hoschild (1983) is one of the most influential writers on 'emotion work'. The concept of 'emotion work' refers to the act of trying to change in degree or quality emotion or feeling (Hoschild, 1979: 561). 'Emotion work' becomes an object of awareness most often, perhaps, when 'the individual's feelings do not fit with the situation' (1979: 563). 'Emotion work' can be accomplished by 'evocation, the attempt to create a desired feeling, or by suppression, the attempt to diminish an undesired feeling' (Young and Lee, 1996: 97).

Sociologists and therapists are beginning to recognize an acceptable way of feeling that is underpinned by 'feeling rules' (Ramsay, 1996; Young and Lee, 1996; Wiley, 1990). Hoschild's work on emotions and feelings was found pertinent to a situation where 'emotion work' was not adequately informed by the 'classic' methodological writings of mainstream sociology (Young and Lee, 1996). Hoschild's concepts 'emotion work' and 'feeling rules' have been examined to inform analysis of a first person fieldwork account (Young and Lee, 1996). It is proposed that 'emotion work' may be more problematic if the field experience posits a challenge to implicit methodological tenets held by the fieldworker (1996: 97). During fieldwork Young was concerned about what 'should' be felt relative to the topic of death and dying. There is a sense that the issue should evoke anxiety. Because she had not experienced any physical symptoms that would have mirrored the appropriate emotion, she felt hard, unsympathetic and callous. The researcher's feelings did not fit with documented expectations of fieldworker feelings in relation to interviewing, documented in symbolic interactionist and feminist methodological literature.

Young and Lee (1996) enter into a dialogue with established sociological concepts of 'emotion work' and 'feeling rules', and mainstream literature in sociology (symbolic interactionist and feminist scholarship). The expression of emotions, the attempts to evoke, diminish and suppress undesirable emotions, or what the actor 'should' be feeling, expressing or suppressing, are underpinned by feeling 'rules' (Young and Lee, 1996). The social situation of the field, field notes, and the text are various contexts in which a reviewer/s or analyst/s might identify emotion 'work', albeit mainly in terms of suppression and diminished interest.

Young and Lee's (1996) article featuring 'emotion work' and 'feeling rules' arose out of a series of discussions between the authors. In these discussions an attempt was made to identify theoretical barriers to an understanding of the role of emotions in fieldwork. The starting point for discussions was Young's fieldwork account, her diary, and a series of debriefing interviews during fieldwork which she had with her supervisor (who was not Lee). The published fieldwork account was subjected to a secondary analysis by both authors, assisted by Young's theoretical agenda. Field notes are seen as 'data' to be contextualized and analysed. Both authors acknowledge the field note account might be criticized on grounds of being selective and reconstructed. What is emphasized is the significance of returning to research accounts like the diary, as a source that makes explicit the actual processes undertaken in research writing.

The lack of fit with expectations of fieldwork feelings, derived from a reading of methodological literature of mainstream sociology, moves the discussion back to the work of early and later symbolic interactionist and forward to feminist scholarship. The early symbolic interactionists emphasized 'involvement' as central to fieldwork, with distance being linked with prevention of bias; the 'personal' was thought to be a contaminant. The later generation of interactionists (the more 'existenti-alist' sociologists) emphasized the 'comfort' of the researcher and roles (Adler and Adler, 1987). The feminist literature placed importance on 'identifying' with participants and a shared perspective as the moral and ethical ideal. The irony of classic interactionist ethnographies is exposed; the early interactionists hid a range of emotional responses in field notes, and a later generation emphasized the relevance of feelings, but were influenced by tradition in handling them. Johnson for example, (1975) failed to describe actual feelings in his field notes and there was fusion between 'thinking and feeling'. A combination of theoretical perspectives in the mainstream sociological literature failed to provide unambiguous rules or norms for 'emotion work' and this is reflected in Young's fieldwork account (Young and Lee, 1996).

Secondary analysis reflects the doubt over whether Young's comfort was an adequate indicator of 'good' interviewing. Young was unable to rely on the feminist notion of 'identifying' for establishing 'good' and 'right' interviewing either. Her own health status was not the same as the interviewees (she was not dying) and any attempt to create a shared experience, by introducing her biography into the interviews (she was pregnant), was ironical and inappropriate. The strategy of probing was made questionable by the circumstances; yet probing is the norm of 'classic' ethnography and one of the 'tricks of the trade' (Bernard, 1994; Wolcott, 1995). The authors did not fit with expectations of fieldworker feelings documented in the literature of mainstream sociology. Researchers who are undecided where their methodological preference lay can become confused by ambiguous messages disseminated from the published literature of mainstream sociology (Young and Lee, 1996). The mixed messages were indicative of ambivalences, ambiguities and inde-terminacies of theoretical perspectives and philosophies. Young searched and struggled within a context of conflicting sets of feeling 'rules', one implying your own comfort is an indicator of what is right and good and the other emphasizing 'identifying' as the moral and ethical standard for interviewing.

Wilkins (1993: 94) acknowledges her astonishment at the 'intellectual cover-up' of emotion, intuition and human relationships in the name of expert knowledge, after finding feminist methodological writing. Such writings aligned with her thoughts and feelings toward emotional practices, and she experienced a sense of 'coming home'; unfortunately this was not Young's experience. Perhaps we might say Young's field-work account captures a glimpse of the 'messiness' of ethnographic practice in the postmodern era that reflects the 'messiness' of texts. We are in a transitional phase and transitions are characterized by inade-quate structure, and the need of frames to assist people who are vulnerable and not in control of their emotions.

Modern fieldwork required the ethnographer to interact with 'cultural members' and their typical ways of thinking and feeling (Van Maanen, 1995: 6). Procedural rules for fieldwork were not clearly defined and fieldwork practice covered a variety of observational techniques and strategies, interviewing styles and relationships with members. Field notes that reflect little agreement with recording patterns, content and tone perhaps mirror more generally the lack of formal standards of fieldwork in the past. Fieldwork over the generations has developed into a highly personal and diverse activity; the 'emotional frame' that devel-oped was to be 'dispassionate'. The dispassionate approach forms the value basis on which social scientists advocate and consolidate fieldwork (with the information in field notes, assembling data on activities for analysis and drawing on other relevant studies and writings, establish-ing themes and discerning expanded domains of relevance) (Lofland and Lofland, 1995: 173).

Students learnt from participating in social practices and by becoming familiar with the lives of the people who illustrate a variety of patterns of behaviour. The illusion that the researcher is socialized into accepting as normal and 'natural' is that cognitive can be separated from emotional aspects of self in the context of social research. This distortion of reality underscores the prejudices and biases of the scientific world that other fieldworkers have exposed (Bochner, 1997; McGettigan, 1997). Only in more recent times have researchers begun to appreciate they routinely 'feel' as well as 'think', and this appreciation is being incorporated into their reports. Fieldwork roles generate emotional problems and experi-ences. The person who activates the role into reality, with personal style and individual creativity, is a person with aspirations and ambitions, doubts, fears and anxieties that need to be managed somehow.

Degradation ceremonies

Communication work that leads to the transformation of another per-son's identity from one accepted in the group to something lower in the status hierarchy of the local scheme has been referred to as a 'status degradation ceremony' (Garfinkel, 1956). Characteristics of degradation ceremonies are that they contain an act, the perpetrator of some moral infraction, a victim and a spokesperson/s who speaks in the name of a group and ultimate moral values. Characteristics of degradation ceremonies are 'techniques of neutralization' and public denunciation; they are transformative of identities and facilitate 'putting the house in order'. Such ceremonies are most clearly performed in regard to the maintenance of moral standards. A degradation ceremony may provide a framework for understanding the process of 'emotion work'. The villain of the piece who is ritually exposed is made to 'stand outside the ordinary' and made to feel 'strange'.

Groups of interacting people create their own emotional and social standards, which over time assume a degree of factiticy. Implicit meanings might underpin and script for emotional and moral practices in some organizations. Just as reality is socially constructed, so too feelings might be understood as social construction as well, that is organized by implicit rules and situational and interactional factors. Degradation ceremonies may provide a setting for the analysis of these processes. They can elicit an emotional display by members in response to the cues given by a spokesperson and bring to the surface the moral values that underpin activity in an establishment. Emotions do not just happen; they are social constructions and may form part of an unfolding dramatic scenario.

Emotional eruptions are not independent of appraisals and judgements, beliefs and conceptualizations. At the second-hand clothing store, the newcomer to the group, on her first day at the store as a worker, placed a large bundle of goods she had selected during the work process to one side, in readiness for the head lady to fix a price. She was unaware that anyone who took goods too early in their career as a worker, or before giving support to co-workers in the assembly-line-like process, could be criticized. Not only was she guilty of this offence, but also over time she was observed to take too much, too often, and without an adequate return of labour. The social actor had not spent enough time in the organization to internalize its moral values and she relied on her own feelings of comfort as an indicator of appropriate action. The recalcitrant worker ignored minor confrontations from the audience that cast aspersions on her performance. Hostility began to harden into resistance, but the actor maintained an 'intransigent line'. The line she assumed both reflected and stimulated regular and hostile responses of the audience. In my field notes I recorded how the audience dealt with the recalcitrant worker who consistently flouted moral norms and breached informal rules pertaining to privilege.

Initially mild censure took the form of joking behaviour, bantering and horseplay, with the spokesperson cast in the leading role. Emotions were part of the unfolding dramatic scenario. The recalcitrant worker, without enough cultural sophistication to abide by the conventions of the group, and unwilling or unable to read the early clues registering audience disapproval of the line she was taking, was subsequently faced with an openly critical and unrelenting audience, consumed with hostility. Like Goffman's inmate in the asylum, the 'recalcitrant' had taken an 'intransigent line' and subsequently faced the pressures of negative sanctions.

Audience members began laughing, perhaps in response to mounting pressure that caused them to feel anxiety, and this seemed to add to the spokesperson's exuberance and provocation. Motives were imputed and value judgements were openly made, which reflected on morality and provoked anger. One 'caught out of face' and unable to 'save face' was being ritually transformed to an identity lower in the local scheme of things, and she fought in her own defence, asking why the women were picking on her. The audience laughed nervously and were probably secretly wishing like me that the emotional scenario would soon end. Eventually the recalcitrant worker burst into tears and hurriedly left the scene.

A degradation ceremony has the potential to heighten a fieldworker's consciousness of being an observer of 'techniques of neutralization'. My consciousness of being an outsider looking at the ceremony was complicated by moments when I was *with* the perpetrator in spirit (sympathy), and feeling very uncomfortable with 'identifying'. Speaking from my own experience, such dramatic rituals are thankfully not common in fieldwork, but when they do occur they can leave a lasting and deep impression on the fieldworker's consciousness. This may be seen as part of the unanticipated consequences of having 'been there'. Degradation ceremonies have the potential to heighten the fieldworker's awareness of tensions between 'involvement, comfort and identitification' that are probably inherent in fieldwork (Young and Lee, 1996: 111).

The site of the degradation ceremony was laden with heavy moral reprimand, much tension, anxiety, anger and nervous laughter; degradation ceremonies arouse deeply felt emotions, requiring 'emotion work'. Distancing behaviour, displayed by observed positive emotions (laughing), is a patterned response that may be evoked in those who perceive the self is 'at risk'. Degradation ceremonies can delineate the conditions of emotionality and sensitize fieldworkers to the interconnections between emotional expressivity, morality and situationally based power/status differentials. Degradation ceremonies can provide an entry point to a discussion of the management of emotionality, morality, power and status.

The risks of threat to researchers are many and varied in fieldwork and can be linked with various phases. Access or entrée marks a phase of fieldwork that presents the threat of risk; the insecurity of being in a strange place may initially evoke feelings of anxiety and fear. Apprehension with activities one is required to perform, and what constitutes an appropriate performance, can evoke fear during first observations. The fieldworker without a script must learn on the job; mistakes are under-standable and audience receptivity is crucial to acceptance. At first mistakes are likely to be rationalized away as normative for a newcomer who is learning the roles, but should the fieldworker consistently make mistakes after the probation period is over, there could be reprimands that humiliate and arouse emotions.

The minor mishaps during first observations are likely to be relatively unimportant compared with the more dramatic moments in later phases of fieldwork. Goffman's (1959) actors may behave in a wholly calculating way in order to elicit favourable responses from others and yet not be consciously aware of it, that is, until something unexpected happens to halt the performance. So too, with the researcher who is in control of a performance and seemingly adept at 'impression management', the unexpected sometimes happens in the field that puts the self strangely at odds with the plot and disrupts the performance.

In Goffman's (1959) work the moment of exposure from the unex-pected is captured. The glamorous, luxuriously attired and frivolous actress displays the seriousness of expenditure and time invested in a lavish illusionary moment when wine is acidentally spilt on her dress and she lapses into a position of inadequate demeanour. The audience is inadvertently given a glimpse behind the scene of a performance, of the glamorous, luxurious attired and frivolous actress contemplating the disappointment of the moment, and her feelings of insecurity. The performer is captured in a difficult and treacherous task of impression management. The actress may come to feel shame, and embarrassment from realizing her feelings can be seen by an audience. She may engage in defensive manoeuvres anticipated for one who is guilty and subse-quently, 'come to experience a special kind of alienation from self' (Goffman, 1959: 229). In dramatic sequences of fieldwork the metaphor of the theatre may be useful to capture the illusory moment when the 'rational analyst', through some unexpected event, comes face to face with the breathing, living human being – behind the mask – who is neither 'actor' nor 'audience' (McGettigan, 1997).

In routine fieldwork practice, fieldworkers, not unlike Goffman's (1959) actors, may behave in a wholly calculating fashion in order to elicit responses from others. Projecting an image to evoke a specific response she or he is concerned to obtain is certainly applicable to the research process. A comparison may be made between Goffman's social actor, who is calculating and conscious of it, and the contemporary survey researcher or fieldworker, advised to draw on symbolic inter-actionism (especially the concept of 'taking the role') when constructing questionnaires and conducting interviews in order to ensure that they work the way the researcher intended (Foddy, 1993). Impression man-agement is part of presenting the self in ways best to elicit favourable responses from interviewees.

During fieldwork there will be times when researchers are calculating and aware of it and other times when they take their actions for granted. One may live their many roles in the field and not step out of them during the ongoing flow of action and interaction. Goffman's dramaturgy encourages the analyst to get beneath the surface and explore the latent meaning of human action and interaction. The theatrical metaphor reveals the actor's impressive efforts of performing precisely at the moment when they are confident of their own act/s. The unexpected forces the analyst (read ethnographer) to contemplate the subjectivity of his or her own act or activity.

Though the risk is there to overstate an actor's contrived action, it would appear Goffman makes the distinction between those with difficulty in differentiating between being 'on' (mental patients) and 'normals', which through an unexpected accident become self-aware. In Goffman's dramaturgy the ultimate aim is to uncover the hidden drama and the real actors in the secret theatre of the mind (Lyman and Scott, 1975). As Goffman (1959) has shown, we act 'out' our actions and interactions through performing various roles, shifting between front stage performances and back stage rehearsals. Our rehearsals are not limited to such physical locations as front and back regions in real life situations. 'Taking the role of the other' (either the role of a specific person or the role of a group, the 'generalized other') is about rehearsals. Actors are constantly seeking to ascertain the intentions or directions of others, imaginatively aligning with their positions before responding. Symbolic interactionists claim this communicative work for all actors in all social situations where people seek a shared definition. By taking one another's viewpoint into account and interpreting one another's responses imaginatively, before selecting subsequent lines of action, the actor calculates to elicit favourable responses (Foddy, 1993: 20).

These fundamental characteristics of human behaviour are not limited to a single episode. There are past and future elements that might be considered from a phenomenological approach. The lived experience of any one episode frequently becomes a condition of subsequent actions that are serially linked to each other, but temporally discontinuous. There are in other words present, past and future contexts to consider when dealing with 'plots', strategic action and stratagems (Hall, 1999: 89). People individually and pointedly compose 'scripts' and 'scenarios' to make sense of projects they plan to undertake in the future (1999: 90). People act on the basis of received knowledge and sometimes reconstruct 'what this means' within a text. Part of the drama of life on the ground hinges on the unfolding constructions of past, present and future.

The unexpected came for Bochner (1997) when he received the news of his father's death while attending a conference. Reflection on the relationship he had with his father is provided in the article, and also a copy of what he said at his father's funeral. The personal had intruded into the scientific world he inhabited as an academic and forced awareness of a divided self, a 'thinking' professional and an 'ordinary person'. The 'plot' promoted in the name of science was unveiled and past prejudices and biases of the scientific world were revealed. The epiphany marked a 'turning point' in the 'life project' of the researcher. He moved to a more personalized approach with the production of narratives and use of personal experience in teaching practice.

Similarly, Ruth Behar (1996) was confronted with a 'turning-point' event that impacted on her 'life project' when her beloved grandfather died. His death propelled her into trying to write in a vulnerable way. The death caused intense regret and 'self-loathing'. She knew her grandfather was dying but she had gone to Spain on a mission to gather material for an academic paper, ironically about death. Talking about death at a conference proved a most distressing empathy charged experience for the suffering of others from which Behar emerged shaken and confused. Anthropology had been influential to her intellectualizing death and created intellectual complacency. Her 'life project' was changed by the epiphany. The essay 'Death and Memory' (1996) is in memory of her grandfather and sorrow for the dead.

Epiphanies

Definition

Epiphanies are existential moments in the lives of individuals that rupture routines and lives, and provoke radical redefinitions of self and perhaps one's 'life project' (Denzin, 1992a: 26). Such turning-point events, when people redefine themselves, the personal and the structural might be mediated through a process of communication (1992a: 27). The narrative has emerged in social science as the genre for addressing epiphanies, with field notes sometimes providing concrete evidence of problematic relationships (Johnson, 1975; Lehnerer, 1996); or scientific frameworks of understanding (Bochner, 1997; McGettigan, 1997). A problematic interactional sequence can provide a glimpse of the breathing real life human being that is not commonly recognized in the scientific world, where the 'analytic psyche' is valorized and the personal is in contrast to the objective and rational ideal.

Denzin (1992a: 84) identifies four types of epiphanies:

- the *major upheaval*, which changes a life forever (e.g. a man murders his wife);
- the *cumulative*, which refers to the final build-up to a crisis in a person's life (e.g. a battered woman finally leaves home);
- the *illuminative moment*, in which the underlying existential structures of a relation or situation are revealed;

- the *relived moment*, wherein the person, after an event occurs, comes to define it in consequential terms (e.g. a widowed spouse gradually comes to feel free from a loved one's presence in their life).

An epiphany occurs in the problematic interactional sequences when the person confronts and experiences a crisis (1992a).

Any one of the four types of epiphany may build on one another. For example, an event or phase in a person's life or a social relationship might first be treated as a *major epiphany*, then a *minor epiphany*, and later be *relived*. Epiphanies of an *illuminative* type might depict the discomfort and confusion that an unanticipated 'turning-point' event creates in the fieldworker. A fieldworker might observe a major epiphany (like a custody case involving a child) and be so emotionally changed by the observation of the problematic interpersonal relationship between child, real mother and foster parents as to be sick and cry (Johnson, 1975). Johnson draws on field notes as evidence of the depth of feeling aroused by the dramatic custody case, which pre-empted breaking off long-term links with human rights groups and permanent change to values about bureaucratic based welfare.

The death of Bochner's father, on the other hand, caused him (1997) to reflect upon the knowledge frameworks that had impeded appreciation of the ordinary person who stands behind the 'professional'. The illusion that a divided self can be perpetuated in the production of knowledge was shattered by an epiphany that brought forth the 'inner voice' of the ordinary person; wanting to be recognized. The epiphany was perceived as a 'turning-point' event in the conversation between Bochner's academic self and his ordinary self that had unintentionally intruded on his public, professional life (1997: 430).

Case one

McGettigan (1997) provides an optimistic view of critical postmodernism by focusing on the modest effort of the researcher grappling with the subtle influences of knowledge that influence the way fieldworkers think and act. Cultural scripts or frameworks of knowledge are shown to exert a significant unconscious control on researchers as they go about their work in the field.

McGettigan (1997) elaborates upon an epiphany, or 'turning-point' event that caused him to be redefined by others in the field, and to reflect upon the knowledge framework of his profession. He went into the field armed with a script that predisposed him to perform the 'peripheral-member-researcher' role in the field (Adler and Adler, 1987: 36), to provide valid results. During the process of fieldwork, however, the researcher was forced to confront the misconception that while he was physically present in the fieldworker role part of his being was removed from the events.

The site of McGettigan's (1997) fieldwork was an adventure trip by bus, scheduled to take two weeks, and referred to as The Green Tortoise. He anticipated observing participants enjoying their escape from mainstream society, but instead came to a realization that the adventure trip was a metaphor for liminality. The Green Tortoise became a vehicle within which the riders could redefine relationships to social norms, or 'bend the rules' for a limited period of time. The river crossing represented a major turning point in the way McGettigan rationalized and framed understandings of his fieldwork experience.

A struggle broke out at the river crossing, between a male bus passenger, a female passenger and a Mexican rowboat operator. As a result the female faced difficulties in the river and the researcher felt obliged to intervene in events on behalf of the bus passengers. He subsequently dived into the river to help the female passenger. At this moment his theatrical gaze was shattered. He was not an 'actor' or a member of the 'audience'. It was a 'real' life drama, a matter of life or death with 'real' people, and he had to move quickly. The fieldworker's awareness of the fantasy about the 'analytical psyche', detached from the ordinary person, was shattered. The performance was halted and the actor forced to contemplate the cultural baggage he carried into the field with him. The actor, previously calculating but relatively unaware of it, was made self-aware by the unexpected event. The performance was halted and confusion followed. Like the actress on the stage, whose illusionary and lavish display was shattered by an unexpected event that halts the performance (Goffman, 1959), the fieldworker was confronted with the illusory moment when caught 'acting' how he was trained. He was subsequently forced to cast a reflective gaze over the script.

After the event McGettigan became an object for himself. There was an ordinary person behind the illusion who was no longer 'acting', or a member of an 'audience' who looked at a 'drama' unfolding (1997: 377). He was disgusted with the 'detached from reality orientation' that had precipitated his naïve orientation toward 'good' science, which had underscored his thinking and acting prior to the river crossing. Discontinuities with what he had 'planned' to see and what 'actually' transpired emerge from a reading of the story. McGettigan redefined his 'membership' relations to other bus passengers. He became critical of the assumptions that had framed his understanding of the field site, and negative feelings threw him into a quandary. No longer could he tolerate further participation as a 'good' scientist (detached), nor could he be an actor who was performing in some postmodern 'drama'. He was no longer oriented in the field as a scientist or as a passenger who was an 'actor' and was confused by the indeterminacy. By rejecting the 'detached orientation' he was cut adrift from the 'scientific fantasy' and left to float into liminality. The barriers posed by the scientific/artificial orientation that had structured the analyst's perception were demolished by the event and the researcher no longer felt in control.

After the river crossing, the passengers redefined him in response to the concern shown to others. He was associated with a father figure and a protector. Subsequent leisure activities were wholeheartedly participated in and enjoyed by the researcher. Rather than contaminating the social environment of the field site (as his original research orientation had caused him to fear), the morally involved and relaxed bus passenger now experienced the field site more realistically. The 'power' of the adventure bus trip was its capacity to bring about a reorientation in the relationship that the researcher had towards the social environment. Being dislocated from frameworks of understanding was tantamount to releasing the researcher from impediments to appreciation and opened up possibilities for alternatives.

An epiphany has the potential to reorient worldviews and ways of thinking and doing ethnography. The narrative of the researcher's lived experience is aimed at developing an appreciation of new ways of comprehension to those which have traditionally shaped and coloured what we see and how we act in the field (McGettigan, 1997). To think *with* the unfolding experiences in the field and *with* the recording of experiences is to reject the *looking at* perspective of the 'detached' observer and the omniscient authorial author. One needs to bring together in each set of ethnographic processes (fieldwork practice and textual representation) the 'professional' and the ordinary person who faces contingencies of a moral, ethical and emotional nature in the course of her or his work, for a realistic rendition of the lived experience.

For critical postmodernists, establishing validity and 'truth' has been superseded by the concept of verisimilitude, which connotes having an appearance with truth, being likely or probable or modelled on, and with an ability to reproduce (simulate) and map the real (Denzin, 1997: 10). What feels truthful and real for the reader is what counts as criterion for contemporary researchers establishing the plausibility of the text. The reader brings the meaning of truths or verisimilitude to the text. The subjective experiences of the ethnographer provoke opportunity for vicarious experience of the reader, who 'comes to know something told, as if she or he had experienced them' (Denzin, 1997).

McGettigan (1997) believes it is through the modest efforts of people grappling with the subtle influences of power over knowledge that insight is produced and a worldview can be changed. The narrative of the epiphany might have vicarious properties for students who are grappling with postmodern research. The privileging of the welfare of people from whom one seeks to gain knowledge over the pursuit of knowledge might be advanced (McGettigan, 1997). The moral of the narrative seems to be that one might not be able to produce large-scale change through critical postmodernism, but there is something to be gained at the very least from not, through research, exacerbating the problems people already have.

Case two

An epiphany or turning point in a 'life project' might take the form of a series of events performed by the researcher that feature a variety of work roles carried out during fieldwork. The trials and tribulations with performing such roles can have a cumulative effect and result in altering the perception the researcher had of his 'life project'.

A *cumulative* epiphany (Denzin, 1992a) perhaps defines the lived experience of Melodye Lehnerer at the fieldwork location defined as Halfway House. A narrative of the lived experience depicts many minor eruptions and reactions on the way to a 'turning-point' event. Eventually a letter was written to the dissertation chair conveying a belief that her methods might be 'a little too subjective' and 'more existentialist' than previously realized, or in terms of her previous theoretical leanings (a mixture of Marxism, symbolic interactionism and variants of 'underdog sociology' and phenomeology). From fieldwork experience a decision was made to use the methods section on 'becoming involved' as the dissertation. The narrative provides an insider view of phases of fieldwork, depicted as episodes of an epiphany.

Lehnerer (1996) reflects on the importance that personal likes and dislikes had with formation of policy, decision making, information control, emotions and ethical decision making. Frustration and simple fatigue were experienced as outcomes of the pressures of work and mood swings are linked with the attitudes of residents toward programmes she ran, and her responses to their personal appearance. In the narrative her inability to perform in a detached impersonal way comes through. Her definition of the situation played a significant part in subsequent action toward others. Promoting a 'feminist ethic of care' (Noddings, 1984) rather than a masculine-inspired notion of justice was problematic because it made the researcher feel vulnerable. The fieldworker perceived being liked as a much more emotionally charged state than simply having rapport with others (Lehnerer, 1996: 345) and ethics was influenced by feelings.

Emotionality is part of the 'story behind the story', usually hidden in field notes, but occasionally allowed to become public when they are published. Field notes written ten or more years prior to publication depict Lehnerer's (1996) struggles with ethics, information control, involvement and emotions. With regard to emotions, field notes capture her insecurity when first in the field because of lack of practical experience. Later she was 'hurt', 'embarrassed' and 'humiliated' by the betrayal of a man she trusted and supported in her role as caseworker. He subsequently admitted guilt over alcohol abuse under heavy questioning. Field notes depict her lack of control and mention is made of being 'on the verge of tears' at one stage, and trying to 'rationalize what to do next' after being rejected for a caseworker job. The 'hurt' felt at not being considered a serious candidate and being 'desperate' over the implications for her dissertation find expression in published field notes. Also included in field notes are the pleas, threats, perks and bribes applied to appease residents who were angered over the timing of programmes she taught on life skills at the Halfway House.

The author realizes that the narrative of unfolding events and personal experiences in the field would probably lead social scientist readers to dismiss her entire work as self-indulgent (Lehnerer, 1996: 349). She is familiar with the debates surrounding the 'ethic of care' (Noddings, 1984) and 'new' forms of writing (Richardson, 1990), and aligns herself with those field researchers who are familiar with the practice of fieldwork and inherent problems, and with the writing traditions of feminist ethnographers. Her narrative on fieldworker experiences is meant to have significance to this readership.

Denzin (1997) emphasizes the need to do more than put the self of the writer on the line in emotional stories. The tale being told 'should reflect back, and be enlarged in, and critical of, this current historical moment and its discontents' (1997: 200). The narratives of both Bochner (1997) and McGettigan (1997) underscore this project, by revealing past biases and prejudices promoted by knowledge frameworks. Ribbens (1993), while acknowledging the potential usefulness of the self as a source of sociological analysis, reinforces the belief that the private must be linked with the public to have sociological importance and to avoid charges of self-indulgence.

The liminal qualities of field notes

The liminal qualities of anthropological field notes have been commented upon (Jackson, 1990, 1995). In anthropological terms, liminality relates to the 'betwixt and between' state of being within rituals, be they of conversion, rebellion or reversal (Turner, 1969). The liminal phase of rituals are qualified by 'normlessness'. This is not to say there is no structure but that the normative arrangements which apply in everyday life are not present. Being 'betwixt and between' means the actor is without a conceptual scheme to order patterned action, and the unknown creates confusion and anxiety (Jackson, 1995: 38).

Field notes, possessing the liminal qualities of being 'betwixt and between', might display strong, ambivalent and unruly feelings from being without adequate 'feeling rules'. Jackson (1995) suggests a clue to understanding the strong feelings which people she interviewed expressed in field notes lies with their striking liminality. The liminality of field notes has been divided into three overarching categories:

- betwixt and between worlds;
- betwixt and between selves;
- betwixt and between words (Jackson, 1995).

Betwixt and between worlds

A functionalist social-structural explanation of the relationship between liminality, highlighted in field notes and debated in sociological literature, would suggest liminality reveals a confusion of rules and classification that creates a loss of constraint to order reality (Jackson, 1995).

The liminal phase might be linked with Young's fieldwork experience (Young and Lee, 1996). Young knew the technical properties of 'good' interviewing but she was unsure of what 'good' interviewing was in the context of interviewing dying women. Was it appropriate to probe? Was it appropriate to ask 'What does dying mean to you?' She was thrown back on her own sensibility as to what was proper for the situation. Young's field notes suggest that judgement of her own sensibility was put on the line, since she experienced discomfort. Ethical committee members had wanted reassurances that she would not ask the question 'What does death mean to you?' unless she thought it appropriate; but there was no explicit indicator from a reading of the methodological literature of mainstream sociology to provide explicit information on how to proceed. In a situation where 'sensitive' interviews are being carried out, it was crucial the interviewer perform in a morally acceptable way, but the model of 'good' interview was illusory and this was a major source of anxiety (1996: 105).

From my own experience, it seems supervisors are not interested in looking at students' field notes or in providing clearly defined rules for producing them, other than a few basic directives. Observations had to be recorded in field notes as soon as possible after leaving the field; otherwise valuable information could be lost forever 'like water under the bridge'. There are contradictory and ambivalent meanings attached to field notes. They are important enough to warrant being recorded as soon as possible and in detailed form, but while much that is relevant in them is personal, that which is personal is to be recorded in a diary and not represented in the text. Field notes convey the researcher's attempts to balance two orientations: one fixed on identifying significant characteristics gleaned from impressions and the other identifying significant characteristics drawn from personal reactions (Emerson, Fretz and Shaw, 1995: 32).

Often the latter is inadequately recorded, or recorded through the lens of the detached, objective and 'dispassionate' observer (Johnson, 1975). The personal reactions, revelatory moments, unexpressed longings and wounds of regret can be swept up with the depersonalizing effect that is characteristic of the scientific world (Behar, 1996). The prejudices and biases of the academic world towards theoretical and analytical ways of knowing in anthropology and sociology have been commented upon previously with reference to epiphanies (Bochner, 1997; McGettigan, 1997).

Betwixt and between selves

In academia, a major and determining status is accorded one whose 'analytic psyche' is of commanding quality. When assessing the value of the researcher, the emotional dimension of self is detached from the total social 'me' (to use interactionist terminology). The 'analytic psyche' is prioritized and projected as the social 'me' of the scientific world, presumably devoid of the personal, that is, until an unanticipated event shatters the illusion and leads to reaggregation of all components of a negotiated self.

A variation to the divided self theme might be recorded in field notes with mention of the tension between 'involvement', 'comfort' and 'identifying' (Young and Lee, 1996). The modern approach to participation might reflect the normative role performance of the traditional researcher, *looking at* the other. Lehnerer (1996) captures in her field notes a sense in which she was moving closer to *being with* clients of Halfway House, but she carried 'guilty knowledge'. From observations recorded in field notes, there was evidence of rule-breakage, residents talked about in-house rule-breaking behaviour (drug/alcohol use; relationships with other residents, and the like) in front of her, indicating she was trusted and on relatively equal terms. She had to weigh reporting 'guilty knowledge' and staff relations with maintaining relationships with residents, and still perform as an effective caseworker.

The classic example of the divided self is that of the covert researcher, the 'spy', 'fraud' or 'infiltrator', attempting to conceal a part-time deviant self from others, and concerned that the contaminated part-time self does not interfere with the production of a total social 'me'. The covert researcher may pose a threat of risk to participants, because they carry 'guilty knowledge' that may be divulged. The threat of risk for the fieldworker from research is less often commented upon than the need to protect subjects from what the researcher might do to them. The 'spy' must ensure the 'cover' is not blown and she or he is exposed, which can cause tension at times. A dramaturgical approach to informed consent suggests a continuum where research is more or less manipulative (Hunt and Benford, 1997: 117). The indeterminacy of informed consent perhaps is favourable to accounts that are neutralizing in their outcomes since there is available a range of opportunities to evade responsibility. One seldom reads of researchers aligning the self with the negative end of the continuum, but mention has been made often enough in the literature of the indeterminacy with informed consent.

When an individual is engaged in sensitive activities (secret and private, deviant or about control), one might anticipate finding at times a heightened sensitivity toward other people's responses (Lee, 1993). The actor looks for signs that would convey favourable receptivity and any discrediting information would be closely monitored. On one occasion, when negotiating prices with a co-worker on goods she wanted to purchase, a pause in response to the price she proffered and wanted to pay prompted her to say, 'You're not a spy are you?' The silence provided a glimpse of her inner consciousness. She wanted a bargain but she also wanted to be seen doing the right thing and my response was linked with both aims (see pp. 32–33).

In similar fashion, I responded to non-verbal expressions when the shop manageress in my first placement withheld my rights to privilege. Attempts to rationalize the reasons behind the head lady's actions were recorded in field notes, including the question 'Do they think I am a spy?' What were not revealed in field notes to any degree warranted were references to my personal and emotional responses to the actions of the manageress who symbolically withdrew her support by means of non-verbal expressions. The experience of watching the head lady cut in half the price tag on the garment she knew I wanted, adjust a new price considerably higher on the remaining half and then deliberately let the original price fall to the floor to expose the margin I would have to pay should I still want it, was devastating. I literally trembled, felt the blood rush to my face and could not speak for at least an hour or more. I was made to feel an 'outsider' and not 'one of them', strange, alone and ostracized.

The fact that something as personally and professionally significant as a degradation ceremony/epiphany, which caused my hurried departure from the store in the knowledge that I would never return and influenced a decision never to do fieldwork again once the project was completed, did not hit the headlines in field notes, but was relegated to the memory or 'headnotes', was really quite amazing. Only recently has my attention been drawn to how much which was personal and distressing was left out of the notes and never spoken of to others. Reading about the epiphanies of others, Johnson (1975) alerted me to how the moral and emotional experiences of the researcher, which are worthy of discussion but 'uncomfortable' information, could be erased from what is considered 'credible' and 'public'. While the dramatic event was distressing enough to avoid writing notes that would mean reliving and prolonging the experience, there is a sociological rendering in field notes. My sociological approach to field notes is comparable to the impersonal treatment given by Johnson (1975) to the dramatic custody case that evoked deeply felt emotions. Actual feelings were not described; only feeling words like 'hurt' and 'humiliated' are used. What is captured in the field notes is an objective, analytical and rational application to an emotional experience that is disassociated from the ordinary feeling person who is not given a voice.

The personal component of fieldwork, the subjectivity of the observer, nowadays is being given more significance in narratives and field notes. Field notes are not just 'data'; they capture the subjectivity of the fieldworker. Many of the academics whom Jackson (1990: 21) interviewed were not prepared to see field notes in such an overly subjective way. They maintained that ethnography is not mainly reflective of internal states and not only an extension of someone's self, but is about the methodology of a discipline – anthropology. The traditional value of anthropological writing has been theoretical, and this quality enhances the authority of the speaker. Field notes as 'record' conjure up thoughts of 'hard' scientific and objective fact, whereas field notes as 'me' raise speculation of emotion as theory's opposition.

My field notes contain descriptive accounts of contingencies of the moral career of the interpretive researcher in the world of shops. In field notes, a step-by-step account is exhibited of the newcomer in the 'learner' role under the guidance of a mentor, being introduced to both formal procedural rules and informal practices. The insecurities and fears experienced by the researcher are relegated to the sphere of memories, or contained in 'headnotes'. Personal experiences were part of the taken-for-granted understanding of the ordinary person and generally not recorded in field notes. The emotional distress of the women I worked with, many of whom were adjusting to widowhood, loneliness and boredom, was not described since my mandate was to observe the social organization of the second-hand clothing store.

In field notes, 'betwixt and between selves' might relate to the tension structured into fieldworker roles of observer and participant. Stanley and Wise (1983: 162) advised of the need for feminist scholars to locate one's self and one's emotions and involvements in written accounts of the research process. Willliams (1990) brought a feminist reading of her field notes to elucidate constructions of 'self' and emotions. She looked for examples of how she felt about what she was doing and about people she encountered during fieldwork, and found much in her field notes pertaining to her feelings. This mirrored a belief which Williams had at the time that her own feelings would provide insight to other people's experiences. Having provided examples of field notes where feelings were comparable between the parties concerned, Williams then found examples of the indifference of an observer. Nurses engaged in practices that were in need of change and quite obviously associations with patients were not sufficient enough to warrant recording the need to rectify practices. The researcher identified with the need to report such matters, but failed to do so on grounds that she was a researcher and not primarily a nurse in the situation.

Being a 'stranger' was not far from her mind, as evidenced by the failure to report dubious findings in support of professional nursing standards. Williams identified as a fieldworker, not a nurse, for much of the time. Field notes exhibited the tension between her status as 'participant' and that of 'observer'; a difference of status experienced as problematic separations within a continuous fieldwork experience. Looking for the 'self' in field notes highlighted the tensions between wanting to be *with* others and part of the group and to understand their experiences, and to separate the self from them and be different (Williams, 1990: 260). A reading of the field notes illuminates methodological and epistemological problems in the process of doing ethnography.

Moral matters emerge from the discussion of field notes that feature 'betwixt and between selves'. Captured is the dilemma of the field-worker, through conflict between her values, ethical codes, personal and professional loyalties, clinical knowledge and feelings. Williams (1990) embarked on a contradictory and incompatible course of action. She was interested and she was not interested in being 'one of them'. We cannot assume that fieldworkers who share the same profession (nursing) as subjects in a research project will share the same values and dispositions (or moral principles) in all contexts, any more than we can assume they would share the same professional codes of ethics (Harrison and Lyon, 1993: 106). From this exercise with field notes, there arises awareness of differences in ways of being in the world, methodological orientations, ethical and moral issues and feeling states.

Betwixt and between words

The world the researcher moves within for a designated period of fieldwork, and the social world of the text they 'people' with characters drawn from field notes, captures the separation of social worlds that underscores the 'crisis of representation' debate (Clifford and Marcus, 1986). Textual representation has been favoured over actual fieldwork practice; the world of the story rather than the world of the 'field' has been favoured in the crisis of representation debate.

Whether field notes are used productively, as foundation for the story in the text, or for validity claims of text and authority of the author, the kinds of words used seem significant. Some people to whom Jackson (1990, 1995) spoke about field notes saw their notes as 'scientific' and vigorous because they were a record that helped prevent bias. Other people *contrasted* field notes, as a 'record of one's reactions' (Jackson, 1990: 7). The liminal status of field notes is given in their being 'way stations rather than an end point' (Jackson, 1995: 62). What gets recorded in field notes may be included in the text, since much is extrapolated as supportive evidence to analyses and interpretation. Jackson found in the field notes of interviewees a remarkable amount of negative feelings and images of 'exhaustion, anxiety, inadequacy, guilt, confusion, and resentment' (1990: 10).

Field notes are between the reality experienced by the fieldworker and the social world produced by the author of the text. 'Raw' data would possibly make little sense to the people being studied or a wider public. The social types or constructs used to people the social world that is produced by the author from field notes, are more like characters in a story and can infuse it with vitality (Coffey, 1996). The characters become loosened from their moorings and take on a life of their own, provided the author allows them. More abstract language and academic jargon is a kind of writing synonymous with 'profound', 'serious', 'substantial', 'scientific' and 'consequential' (Lutz, 1995: 254), and may make problematic a review by lay people not used to the technical language of a discipline.

Field notes usually come in chronological order, capturing the life-world of the fieldworker. Words are the smallest of the units of analysis, to be lifted during 'open coding' from the flow of conversation in field notes, given a name or tag and temporarily relocated on a card or a book (Strauss and Corbin, 1990). When coding data, lay words in the hands of sociologists are transformed into 'in vivo codes' (1990). Words strung together to form sentences and paragraphs become 'analysis units', 'a segment of the text that is comprehensible by itself and contains one idea, episode or piece of information' (Tesch, 1990: 116). Decontextualized analytical units have properties and dimensions to be explored by the analyst, and a dimension range can be defined in terms of frequency, extent, intensity and duration (Strauss and Corbin, 1990). The original words exhibited in field notes are betwixt and between 'raw' data and the polished text, and many get lost in the process of filtering, extrapolating and analysing.

Field notes might be seen as part of the 'territory of the self' (Lupton, 1998: 157), akin to a back-stage region at work or the home, where people can 'let off steam', relax and give way to their inhibitions. Differences in whether field notes are defined personal or subjective, by way of contrast to objective, reflects the fieldworker's notions of how anthropology contrasts with other social sciences, anthropology's weaknesses and strengths, and how ethnographers fit with or rebel against the profession's concerns and epistemological differentiation (Jackson, 1995: 64). The traditional differentiation between the personal and the objective, 'hard data' and 'soft', captures the betwixt and between nature of words in field notes. Use of the first person in the fieldwork account has exhibited awareness of deviating from the sociological norm and the professional ideal.

Young's fieldwork account, written in the first person, made her feel 'strange'; she felt uncomfortable with speaking about herself (Young and Lee, 1996: 102). There was awareness that forays into emotions and feelings were indicative of baring one's soul, which had implications for audience receptivity and for career opportunities in academia. Creating a 'professional' self was important in relation to an academic audience. A turning towards the self, and one's personal feelings, could lead others to reject one's entire 'life project' (Lehnerer, 1996). Personal dramas have to have sociological significance to avoid charges of self-indulgence (Ribbens, 1993). The self as self-indulgent person was to be differentiated from the sociologist who was in the privileged position of interviewing women who were dying (Young and Lee, 1996). Young did not want to overplay the sensitive nature of the research topic, nor hide behind sensitive interviewing, but felt the first person account of fieldwork could leave the reader with the drama of the research experience, but without methodological substance (1996: 102).

Field notes have been compared with biographies (Jackson, 1995), as evidenced in my own field notes. The socialization of the interpretive inquirer into the social world of shops features processes of induction and acclimatization to women's moral ideals, norms and values. Field notes capture the 'moral career' of the fieldworker, as this unfolds with the role of 'learner', under the tuition of a mentor, who provided the script and directed the novice through her lines. When mistakes were made with processing goods a reminder was given to 'pay more attention, and listen to what I say'. Field notes provide a preview of contents to be structured by concepts and reassembled in a form to give interest and meaning in the text. Moral issues can be extrapolated during 'writing up' and 'techniques of neutralization' applied. Field notes themselves are not harmful or damaging; it is what is done with data from them that makes them so. This awareness underscores my use of the concept 'moral career' (Goffman, 1961a) to trace the researcher's acclimatization and acculturation to the social world of the 'field'. The concept 'moral career', used to divert attention away from the actors and onto the researcher, was not indicative of moral neutrality. Rather, the strategy reflected the author's moral and value commitment to avoiding the role of 'moral entrepreneur', which a discerning audience might bring to a reading of the text.

Field notes are objects that exhibit certain characteristics; they are written and recorded under certain conditions (Jackson, 1995: 62). They are a kind of literary genre, capable of being compared to other kinds of writing. They can hide the ambivalence between thinking and feeling perpetuated by the world of science, and the struggle of the researcher with the self. Field notes differ from other kinds of writing in that they are not written for public consumption and the writing format can be extremely vague. Traditional ethnographic note taking precedes the main fieldwork goals of analysis, interpretation and 'writing up'. Field notes can be seen as preparatory training which leads to 'writing up', a time when the intended audience of the story should be taken into consideration. Names of people and places should be concealed by the use of 'masking techniques', pseudonyms for names of people and places. Field notes mediate between the personae of the researcher and social worlds (Jackson, 1990: 72). During fieldwork, a difference between 'objective' reality and subjective experience is mirrored in the divided self of the 'professional' and the ordinary person.

Critiquing the 'ethical correctness' of fieldwork with field notes

Over the last three decades researchers have developed, refined and used criteria from a variety of disciplines to evaluate the credibility or authenticity of their findings. The concept of auditability was borrowed from accountancy (Lincoln and Guba, 1985: 283) and the concept of triangulation from sea navigation or land surveying (Patton, 1990: 187) or radio and radio broadcasting (Lincoln and Guba, 1985: 305). The auditor carefully 'examines both the process and content of the inquiry' (Lincoln and Guba, 1985: 283), using audit trail categories. Such categories include raw data, reduced data and analysed products (including 'write-ups' of field notes), the final report and notes of various categories, methodological, analytical, personal and reflexive (1985: 319–320). Contemporary scholars produce 'experimental texts'. Such texts have a variety of shapes and angles of approach and are without a fixed point that could be triangulated. Field notes can serve pragmatic ends by providing audit trail categories, enabling another researcher to trace the steps taken from proposal to 'writing up'. With such a pathway the analyst might be in a good position to evaluate 'ethically correct' research practice.

Students in the past have been advised to keep a diary on methods as well as a record of their own interpretations and those of members, which can be correlated to get a reading. Fieldworkers have kept field notes regarding researcher–researchee relationships, the effects of the researcher's presence on the nature of the data collected and descriptions of their own actions, interactions and subjective states. The diary is the preserve of personal notes, of 'feelings, statements about the research, the people I am talking to, myself doing the process, my doubts, my anxieties, my pleasures' (Richardson, 1994: 526). A trajectory of the interpretive researcher might be unearthed from a variety of notes (descriptive, methodological, analytical and personal). A number of cases exhibited in field notes might consolidate information about the researcher's presence on the nature of data collected.

The effects of the researcher's presence have been considered in relation to conducting interviews. The records provided by Baker, Yoels and Clair (1996: 188–189) suggest that a series of interviews carried out be physicians caused clients to become anxious and to display nervous laughter. Questions that reflected negatively on their self-worth, social/ mental competency or moral stature are linked with 'anxiety scenarios' or 'discomfort-laden' encounters. The records reveal the problematic nature of physicians probing to seek information from clients on drinking, smoking and sexual behaviours. Probing such matters can constitute physicians in the role of 'moral entrepreneurs', who are custodians and enforcers of mainstream societal modalities (1996: 192). A reading of the records reflects the researcher's presence on client response to power differentials and questions with negative connotations. Field note records provide evidence of precautions needed to ensure damage is not done to individuals and/or groups. Where links are made between people and activities in records, a glimpse of emotions is provided (embarrassment, anxiety, anger, shame, humiliation) that reflect possible risk of harm to subjects.

Participant-observation is a fieldwork technique with a number of components: observation, participation, interviewing and use of records. An examination of field notes might divulge a flaw in the use of participant-observation. Failure to use the full complement of methods with participant-observation might be deliberate, a way of avoiding interviewing on ethical and moral grounds. Some feminist scholars favour interviewee guided interviewing or phenomenological inter-viewing. Interviewing that allows women to take the lead gives them a voice in determining what they want to speak about and feel comfortable with. Alternatively, the decision not to probe and ask questions might be motivated on moral grounds by a researcher who ironically happens to be engaged in covert research. A fieldworker might refuse to use prompts like 'You mean?' 'Tell me more' or 'Do I take that to mean?' because probing is considered especially 'exploitative'. Informal consent, freely given, is no guarantee that interviewing will be ethical and moral (Wong, 1998).

Field notes of various types can become trail categories and provide evidence of a trail of deceit from proposal to 'writing up' that another researcher might trace. An auditor might capture contingencies or 'turning-point' events of a career pathway as 'way stations' on the way to analysis and interpretation. Field notes can exhibit problems that are without a satisfactory solution. Ethical dilemmas are characterized by 'good' but also contradictory ethical reasons, which present the researcher with a conflicting and incompatible course of action. The researcher may be unable to meet all standards involved (values, ethical allegiances, professional standards, personal beliefs and feelings). Some ideals and ideas may have to be neglected and the researcher compro-mised.

Scenarios depicted in field notes, where the fieldworker's own words provide reasons why decisions are made, could throw light upon researcher's predicaments in the field. Some scenarios might capture the fieldworker's values, ethical codes, professional allegiance and personal feelings that need to be reconciled during fieldwork. When confronted with dying women, Young felt uncomfortable with probing (Young and Lee, 1996). She was forced to reflect on her own moral values about what was 'good' and 'right' to do and her field note account indicates that she felt confused. The emotional-intuitive response to decision making on interviewing had to be worked out in the actual fieldwork situation. Only the rational and cognitive level of reasoning had been addressed explicitly in ethical codes. A decision was made by this author not to probe because doing so also made her feel uncomfortable. A decision was made on personal grounds not to use the full complement of options provided by participant-observation.

Conclusion

The ambivalences of ethnography are underscored by the desire to get close to the unknown and the other, yet maintain an appropriate distance for analysis. This tends to blur the sense in which fieldwork involves a feeling human being. A pure 'insider' account has been seen as running the risk of telling how it was without sufficiently questioning the vagaries of behaviour and fully comprehending the dynamics of the pressures at play within settings; therefore seeing behaviour as aberrant or without logic (Ram, 1996). The other desire to remain neutral, distanced and detached, to know the boundaries and the protocol of the modernist ethnographer and work strictly within them, assumes the researcher can be a 'dispassionate', objective and rational analytical machine, which we know is not possible in social research. 'Involvement' is a problem that is probably inherent in fieldwork and creates tensions to be experienced by researchers, since there is no common yardstick to measure competing claims of what is the 'right' thing to do.

The researcher may not have been in the field before, but approaches it only with a desire to record social process and learn, grow and change. In the struggle the researcher experiences the self in various layers of meaning, as words to express what is felt are recorded and not recorded in field notes and the text. The writing can be problematic for the analyst accustomed to sociological conceptualizations and language, and over-whelmed at times by fieldwork experiences that evoke in the self strong feelings which cannot yet be expressed in words. What is happening in the field, in anthropology, sociology and other disciplines (namely journalism), as part of the story behind the story, is that nobody seems able to translate the experience to writing because they are not used to talking about themselves in the first person (Wark, 1999).

The realm of emotions is yet to be accepted fully in ethnographic reports as data and this causes researchers to experience anxiety (Young and Lee, 1996). Trying to record one's personal investment, pleasures and fears experienced in the field can cause concern with duty, role, principles, values and the façade that disciplines maintain about self and emotions. The experiences of ethnographers, as they go about doing their work in the field, as a bundle of desires and prejudices, alternatively drawn towards and repelled by events in the field, are what doing fieldwork is about and what students would want to know (Wark, 1999).

Anthropology's failure to provide forums for discussing feelings and emotions is recognized in the literature (Behar, 1996; Jackson, 1995; Young and Lee, 1996). Traditionally, emotional matters have been communicated 'anecdotally during corridor talk' (Behar, 1996). When it comes to addressing emotionality we find few methods courses dealing with the topic. In courses where students are likely to explore field notes, 'one's defences are likely to be in place' (Behar, 1996). More emphasis in the past has been given to avoiding personal relations and emotional experiences. Even ethnographers of notable fame 'underscore the inter-action of their feelings' (Rosaldo, 1994). Berg (1988) believes emotions should be a central feature of reportage and not buried in a footnote or appendix. The absence in the text of the emotional dynamics of inter-personal relations hides from systematic analysis a piece of context necessary to interpret the findings (Berg, 1988).

Young and Lee (1996) recognize the importance of having a variety of forums for grappling with tensions created by the interplay of 'involve-ment', the 'comfort' of researchers with emotional issues and 'identify-ing' with subjects. Young and Lee (1996) draw their conclusions from having had the benefit of engaging in joint analysis of Young's field note data. Different theoretical approaches were brought to the analysis and issues were raised that probably would not have been discussed had only one researcher been involved. The usefulness of having a variety of forums to discuss the issues of 'involvement', 'comfort' and 'identifying' was thus realized. Young and Lee are not suggesting forums would solve the particular problems confronting fieldworkers in relation to 'emotion work'. Solving one problem could give rise to another.

A 'crisis of representation' in ethnography has identified new ways of writing that arouse the feelings of the audience. Authors of narratives, biographies and 'confessionals' have challenged the terms of reference and the writing styles that have been accepted as appropriate ethno-graphic reportage in 'ethnographic realism'. Ethnographers who write confessionals and deal with emotions might fail to meet the standards of traditional or modern ethnography, but the risks of charges of self-indulgence may be outweighed by the benefits that accrue to future researchers through informing of ways of correcting for the limitations of modern fieldwork.

CHAPTER 8

Textual 'impression management' of self and others

A t one time anthropology offered the opportunity to go into the field with little more than a willingness to learn, change and grow, but ethnography is no longer a 'simple look, listen and learn procedure'. The representation of culture in the text has become a prominent and problematic feature of contemporary ethnography (Van Maanen, 1995). The construction of an ethnographic report or account and, in particular, the mode of representation, the choice of literary genre and compositional practices featuring relationships, voice, intuition and the *unsayable*, are postmodern themes of ethnography currently assuming prominence in the other social sciences. They are creating concerns for ethnographers, subjects and other audiences who read ethnographies and other forms of qualitative research (Manning, 1995).

'Writing up' in anthropology and sociological ethnography has, by and large, been organized and dominated by a genre called 'ethnographic realism' (Clifford and Marcus, 1986; Van Maanen, 1988). Alternatives to academic realism have emerged (confessional ethnography, dramatic ethnography, critical ethnography and self- or auto-ethnography) while the ethnographic writings of classic theorists continue to instruct students of anthropology and sociology (Van Maanen, 1995). In the midst of change in conventions of fieldwork and constructing an ethnographic report or account, there are audiences (the readership), comprised of segments, which are receptive or otherwise to the conventional ethnographic form and style of text. A segment of the audience continues to look for 'the close study of culture as lived by particular people, in particular places, doing particular things at particular times' (1995: 23).

What is said about the social world is done in a particular place, for a particular reason, at a particular time and to a particular audience (Edmondson, 1995: 23). The interpretation presented in the text is influenced by the cognitive and emotional disposition of the readership. In other words, what an audience is assumed already to think and feel forms part of the process of constructing and shaping what is to be presented in the text. The unquestioned acceptance of the omniscient author of 'realist' texts during the 1950s and 1960s has undergone change. What is written nowadays in feminist literature presupposes a subject audience of women who are justified in anticipating the same courtesy be extended to them in print as was conveyed to their face by the researcher who is a friend (Hornstein, 1996). All members of the feminist academic audience may not applaud the idea of friendships intruding into print and neither would segments of the mainstream contingent assembled in sociology and anthropology.

In the past, anthropology and sociology have not been overly concerned with communicative contexts (dialogue, social relationships, voice, intuition, feelings), but all this has undergone change. Establishing validity and credibility in texts has monopolized debate within the social science over recent decades. Such issues have been surpassed in more recent times by a concern with ethics and morality, emotions and intuition and a demonstration of care. Partial self-censorship (Lee, 1993), and 'ethical proofreading' manuscripts (Johnson, 1982) have become a necessary part of the new ethnography. A more ethically conscious writer ensures that what is disclosed is not likely to breach privacy rights or present negative information that would devalue individuals and groups. The emergence of critical and collaborative research in social science, feminist scholarship, greater concern with the rights of the individual and the introduction of codes and guidelines in the universities and research institutions has impacted on the ethical consciousness of social scientists and moved ethical fieldwork forward from the 'ethnographic realism' of a past era (Punch, 1994).

Academic writers have framed their discussions in texts in ways they hope or believe audiences will understand and favourably accept. The composition and presentational style of texts is influenced by the potential receptivity of parties, with interests in the production. Some hope the receptivity of parties with interests in the production will unquestionably accept their authority to speak on behalf of the subjects studied. The prominent ethnographers of classical studies (Lévi-Strauss, Evans-Pritchard, Malinowski and Benedict) were not unduly worried about their authority, which they felt put them above their readers or people they wrote about (Fabian, 1991). They spoke from a position of security that was provided by the colonial power structure. The audience was accepting, not questioning what was said and how it was conveyed. Authority was grounded in having 'been there' and having witnessed events first-hand; reputation was validated with publications. A justifiable part of the process of trying to communicate to an audience is the part played in acknowledging the socio-political and interpersonal conditions of what can, in any particular circumstance, be said (Edmondson, 1995).

The main critics of 'ethnographic realism' have come from within the discipline of anthropology. The ethnographer critics 'are broadly sympathetic to ethnography, and themselves have considerable experience in the use of the ethnographic method', but they accuse each other of not being 'reflexive' enough and for failing to 'adopt a critical attitude' toward 'realist ethnographies' (Brewer, 1994: 232). In the debates between modernist and contemporary ethnographers the former seem to be holding their ground. They are clinging to the traditional modes of representing while the latter are more willing to experiment with texts. For various reader segments, particular ethnographic styles are more or less attractive (Van Maanen, 1995). Some of the contemporary and prominent sociologists command a following. New writers show allegiance and loyalty by incorporating recommended concepts (epiphanies) and theoretical orientations (critical interpretivism) into their writings. Journals have on their editorial boards a number of entrepreneurs of knowledge production, supported by an entourage of reviewers who make up the group of 'academic gatekeepers' that review articles submitted for publication and decide what gets into print.

Some favour 'realist, modernist tales about personal loss, recovery and the self writing it's way out of a painful past, sharing experiences so others can also move forward' (Denzin, 1997: 202). They retrace epiphanies that move the writer outward from a personal moment to a narrative description of the threat experience (1997: 208). New experimental texts privilege emotion and emotionality and the purpose of the text is to evoke emotional responses in the reader, thereby producing verisimilitude and a shared experience (1997: 210). Pathos has become a rhetorical device to engage the audience, to evoke emotions and perhaps achieve a vicarious experience, as the ultimate measure of the quality of qualitative inquiry.

A brief historical overview

The publication of the two postmodern texts, *Writing culture: the poetics and politics of ethnography* (Clifford and Marcus, 1986), *Anthropology as cultural critique* (Marcus and Fischer, 1986), and *Tales of the field* (Van Maanen, 1988), ushered in the 'crisis of representation'. A representational crisis that was set in motion was two-pronged, since it aroused anthropological speculation about traditional texts as well as feminist concern with 'writing culture'. The double crisis inspired feminist scholars to think about their own agenda, not only to speak from the position of other women, but to realize that research subjects are at grave risk of manipulation and betrayal by the ethnographer. Feminist sociologists and anthropologists seem in general more self-reflective about the ethical ambiguities of relationships in fieldwork, and with writing in ways that maintain the integrity of relationships formed in the field in the text.

Stacey (1988) is but one of a number of feminist ethnographers who has discussed ethical issues of fieldwork in detail. Her article 'Can there ever be a feminist ethnography?' conveys concern that the intimacy of feminist ethnography may make exploitative relationships between ethnographers and subjects more rather than less likely. Stacey (1988) points to the contradiction between the desire for collaboration on the final research report and of the research report being 'ultimately that of the researcher's, however modified or influenced by informants' as influential in the question being asked.

With 'ethnographic realism' the author disappears into the described world and fills the role of the third party scribe, who reports on observations and speaks for others with some authority from having 'been there'. The tone of the text is characteristic of science writing – the anonymity of the author, and authority resting on an unexplicated rendition of the researcher's experiences in the field. 'Realist tales' are not multivocal texts in the sense of presenting a perspective of first one way, then another, and then still another by drawing on various voices involved. What is produced is invariably a shared understanding, as interpreted by the ethnographer, with selected information about individuals and groups used as evidence to support interpretation. One reading is offered with the traditional realist tale. The researchers' experiences as they go about doing fieldwork are usually suppressed, traditionally. Ethnographers have produced accounts from which the self has been sanitized. 'To establish authority, it seems, requires only the briefest of appearances' (Okely, 1992: 5). The academic culture has traditionally devalued subjective experiences that do not contribute to analysis and interpretation.

Long-term immersion in the field was generally a total experience, one demanding all the fieldworker's resources, intellectual, physical, political, emotional and intuitive. Yet in the past, the pressure to be 'scientifically objective' has caused most qualitative researchers to compartmentalize the fieldwork experience, separate this from the personal experiences and dilemmas of fieldwork, as data to be used in the construction of the text (Okely, 1992: 8). The traditional idealized, 'scientific' presentation was at odds with first-person accounts. The person speaking in the first person 'I', who could have assumed a persona different from the impersonalized, authorative scholar, was not allowed to surface in the text; being non-representative could be equated with being on an ego trip. The first person account was not encouraged and a glimpse of the personal, silent identity and her or his experiences was relegated to field notes and 'headnotes'. Many contemporary ethnographers who speak in the first person to describe the trials and tribulations of the fieldworker in the course of research exhibit a conscious concern that they have risked damage to their professional identity, or have breached the conventions of a sociological audience on writing practice (see references to Lehnerer, 1996 and Young and Lee, 1996 in Chapter 7). In so doing they fear they may have rendered their entire work *unreadable* for a segment of the academic audience.

A segment of the academic audience that is modernist in persuasion anticipates ethnography will address the task of describing, analysing and interpreting how people in a particular place and time make sense of their lives. Hammersley (1995: 97) emphasizes that the whole point of research is to 'produce findings which are of general validity ... a researcher is expected, as far as possible, to operate as a representative of the research community'. The tradition is to try to 'eliminate the effects of one's own personal and social characteristics and circumstances where these may lead to bias' (Hammersley, 1995). The researcher's first loyalty is to colleagues and to 'established procedures and accepted knowledge'.

Another segment of the audience looks for general postmodern features and would undoubtedly favour a marked sensitivity to the dialogical underpinning of anthropological knowledge, 'transformed and obscured by the complex processes of writing ... and ... the differential power relationships that shape the ... modes of representing knowledge' (Marcus, 1998: 318). The concept of 'voice' has multiple dimensions: there is the voice of the author; the voices of subjects; the author's voice, when she or he is made the subject of the text (Hertz, 1996). Voice is seen as the product of complex sets of associations and experiences (Marcus, 1998). Whereas an account was once keyed into particular concepts, myths or symbols that tend to identify a people, as a contribution to anthropology, the alternative is to remake this exercise into a fully dialogic one (Marcus, 1998).

The ideal of the alternative contemporary approach features 'a polyphony of voices' rather than a single voice, to reduce bias and distortion (Fontana, 1994: 214). The feminist ethnographic perspective moves towards a 'dialogical' or 'polyvocal' approach, which simply means voices of the subjects should have equal or greater prominence than the voice of the ethnographer (Barrett, 1996: 29). An appreciation of the changes between 'ethnographic realism' and the alternative contemporary approach, of which a focus on 'voice' is apparent, includes also a 'remaking of the observer' (Marcus, 1998: 319).

Ethnographers, in questioning their own fieldwork, reporting styles and procedures, have drawn attention to the problematic nature of the author and ethnographic reportage procedures (Fontana, 1994: 220). Part of the contemporary problem with writing is to figure out how to present the author's self while simultaneously writing the respondent's accounts, and representing their selves (Hertz, 1996: 6). Captured in 'realist tales' are many omniscient qualities – the absence of the author from the text, minutely detailed descriptions and interviews and 'interpretive omniscience' (Emerson, Fretz and Shaw, 1995: 223). Quotes are sometimes made redundant, staged and edited to embellish the fieldworker's methodological observations and analytical categories. Voices are muted and silenced, depending on the part the author enables people to play in the social world they produce in texts.

Underlying the refocusing of ethnography, from the social and cultural structures to voice, is also a different approach taken towards the relationship of the observer to the observed and the playing out of power relations. A different approach to the relationship between the observer and observed is apprehended in voices. Feminist ethnographers reject the use of the omniscient third person author of the modern text and want previously unarticulated voices of women heard. They want the author made more accountable by being made more visible. In textual representation, the contemporary focus on voice is not built exclusively around the theme of power, but rather of ethics or the moral relationship of the observer to the observed, and ultimately 'the exploration of the critical purpose of contemporary ethnographic analysis' (Marcus, 1998: 328). Critical and collaborative approaches and feminist 'standpoint epistemology' explore the ethical and moral components of research that are related to power imbalances in a sexist and racist environment and ways to inhibit deception and betrayal of the research subjects. In feminist research, ethics and methods, like theory and action, must be intertwined.

To be consistent with feminist ideology researchers must choose methodologies that reflect feminist ethics, and when they do not they should point to areas that require change (Archibald and Crnkovich, 1995: 124). Identifying with others can sometime be problematic where there are differences in race and colour, and such matters are debated among feminists in terms of there being equality between interviewers and interviewees (Reinharz, 1992). The feminist ideal of equality and solidarity between researcher and researched underpins the emancipation of voices in the text. The focus in the experimental text that is accessed through language in context involves a direct engagement with processes of contestation and struggle arising from political circumstances (Marcus, 1998: 327). Feminists have attacked patriarchy and the conventional cannons of mainstream sociology that have marginalized and silenced women in the text.

Critical approaches that feature emancipatory and applied goals, spoken of by authors with reference to political forays with powers that be, have exposed conditions of ethnography (paradoxes, ambiguities and dilemmas) that make fieldworkers vulnerable, but the critique of fieldwork practices which expose their own ethics and morality has put some writers at risk. Readers seeing only the reflective operation as pure narcissism and the experience of the fieldworkers as self-indulgence have been critical. But by revealing the self as vulnerable, while risky, nevertheless provides a kind of ethical awareness that is valuable for future fieldworkers (Fabian, 1991).

Since the publication of the two important postmodernist texts *Writing culture*, (Clifford and Marcus, 1986) and *Anthropology as cultural critique* (Marcus and Fischer, 1986), and Van Maanen's book *Tales of the field* (1988), there has been much debate in the social sciences. The story behind the story is sometimes being told to foster more awareness among researchers about conditions of fieldwork (the paradoxes, ambiguities and dilemmas) that are potentially dangerous problematics in ethical and moral ways. A good deal of soul-searching and methodological self-consciousness is taking place in ethnography, which is reflected in contemporary texts and articles that have a moral or ethical message.

Interpretive, experimental, polyphonic and 'epiphanic' are different labels used to identify, both in anthropology (Marcus and Fischer, 1986) and sociology (Denzin, 1992a), new modes of doing contemporary ethnography (Fontana, 1994: 214). Some authors are writing 'experimental texts' or evocative representations ('narratives of self', ethnographic fictitional representations, poetic representations, ethnographic drama, mixed genres) in an evocative attempt to minimize what they consider the authorial bias present in 'realist tales'. Denzin (1992a) favours emancipatory, critical interpretivist interactionism as a framework that returns to the beginning, with *Writing culture* (Clifford and Marcus, 1986). An emphasis is on the 'epiphanic experiences' of the researcher that may be seen as a way of organizing materials and assisting the self to write its way out of the past and move forward in the twenty-first century.

Other ethnographers seek to promote 'highly polyphonic, highly impressionistic readings', for example, Richardson (1992) is known for her 'experimental representations'. Her struggles with 'alternative forms of representing the sociological' include criticism of sociology's concepts and methods, which has aroused criticism from more conventional ethnographers (Hammersley, 1995). Those who 'criticize conventional forms of ethnographic writing as philosophically and politically incorrect, as based on epistemological misconceptions and as reinforcing the socio-political status-quo' (the 'experimentalists' who attempt to right the wrongs of the world by the way they write) are said to blur the distinction between non-fiction and fiction genres and reality (1995: 89). Hammersley believes much 'textual radicalism' is fundamentally misconceived, epistemologically, and grounded on political pre-suppositions that are open to serious doubt (1995).

Despite recognition of the variety of audiences for whom texts and accounts that are comprehensible and persuasive are written, there is a sizeable segment in the academic audience that has not moved very far from the conventional format regarded as normative in parts of natural science and quantitative social research. For example, Hammersley believes an overarching and pre-eminent requirement in writing the wrongs of research 'is that the account lays itself open to rational assessment of its validity' (1995: 95). There is, 'an insistence on the importance of a clear voice on the part of the author, albeit one which does not pretend to infallibility or to cultural superiority' (1995: 95–96).

Narratives and the ethical ideal

Anthropologists have helped illuminate how a society uses devices to dramatize and underscore core cultural beliefs (rituals and myths)

(Mattingly, 1998: 14). Members make sense of their lives through narratives. Narratives may provide those who were previously voiceless to 'give voice' to their personal experiences in an emotionally charged rendering of personal experience.

Narratives provide one medium through which the authors might connect their fieldwork experience to an ethical or moral ideal. By convention, ethnographers have drawn on linguistic and cognitive traditions; aesthetic form has been subordinated to realism in modern ethnographic reports and accounts, and the author's voice has not been presented in an explicit way. Human interaction, social action, the description of what people do in their social world and what the social world does to them might be presented with narrative. The authors may infer or recount events that happened to them, that were not anticipated and not necessarily desired which subsequently changed their research agenda (see my reference to the epiphanies of Lehnerer (1996) and McGettigan (1997) in Chapter 7, pp. 161–165).

Narratives mean to be provocative, the trials and tribulations of fieldwork or epiphanic moments when the worldview was shattered and the possibility of an alternative paradigm emerges, reflect upon contemporary approaches. Narratives offer meaning through 'evocation, image and the mystery of the unsaid' (Mattingly, 1998: 8). An ethnographer might provide a narrative, written in the first person, to convey details of a dramatic event or perhaps recount a series of events in a particular way, ultimately to give the story its moral meaning and in this way attempt to 'right' the 'wrongs' of past ethnography. A personal account might incorporate a backward glance, with all the benefits of hindsight. The original experience, hidden in field notes or 'headnotes' and not interpreted in the midst of an incident, may be depicted in a text long after the event happened in the field. Narratives seduce the reader into the unfolding events, and provide a 'window on the psyche' (McGettigan's, 1997 account of the dramatic river crossing). Narratives may provide an 'inside view' of a people's customs, rites and ceremonies (Mattingly, 1998: 27).

Stories are to be distinguished from narratives, since narratives refer to the actual discourse that recounts events, from which a story might be constructed. The story may involve a sequence of actions and events, 'conceived as independent of their manifestations in discourse, or the discursive presentation of events' (Mattingly, 1998: 35). 'Little narratives' are common with contemporary ethnography, whereas 'grand narratives' of traditional society offer the possibility of a more complete picture (1998: 115).

Some 'new' writing features dramatic episodes and liminal experiences that capture abandonment of knowledge frameworks and role reversals which provide a moral reflection on the academy and its conventions (McGettigan, 1997). Unanticipated events and activities have human and emotional dimensions. They provoke a reflective and contemplative stance towards the social world of academe and one's place within it; and from that reflection can come a moral message for others. From the experience of the dramatic river crossing, McGettigan (1997) moved optimistically forward on a search beyond the horizon of critical inquiry, to redefine seemingly insurmountable difficulties with identity. The moral message seemed to be directing a focus away from the 'too big' critical issues of sociology, to privileging the welfare of people more in the pursuit of knowledge (1997: 380).

Narratives may touch on spirituality and moral tone. A spirit of 'goodness' may be expressed in contemporary texts that readers may anticipate as enjoyment and from which they are enriched. The reader's capacity to be moved and enriched may be a testimony to the text's aesthetic quality. Aesthetics is one of a number of criteria for assessing 'quality' of qualitative research (Garman, 1994). The text that is enriching, pleasing to anticipate and experience and touches the spirit may be deemed a quality piece of qualitative research. With ethnographies, stories and narratives of dramatic events like epiphanies, authors decide whose quotes to display. With the shift from data to theory and writing, decisions are made on whose voice is to move to centre stage and whose is to be lost in the small 'qualitative crowd'. Losing voice may become an ethical issue, as well as giving too much voice when the actor prefers not to be publicly identified.

An author might take the narrator role; a moral evaluation may itself provide a strong motivation toward self-presentation in the text (Ribbens, 1993: 85). Textual representation of the author in the role of 'learner', inducted and acclimatized to the culture under inquiry, may seem like an innocent strategy motivated by a value-neutral or objective postgraduate student (looking at the self under a microscope), when in fact the strategy may have been openly rationalized on moral grounds with an academic advisor when 'writing it up'.

A self-conscious reflexivity may include the researcher's interpretation of audience interpretation, derived from intuitive or empathic role taking. A researcher who has engaged in long-term immersion with group members, shared implicit understandings on a range of social phenomena – some secret, private and dubious – may confront the issue of disclosure with trepidation. They would not want the role of entrepreneur projected by an academic audience, nor have a potential subject audience feel their behaviour was held up to public scrutiny; better to draw attention to the self to achieve all-round favourable audience receptivity. The intention of avoiding moral evaluations does not necessarily imply a departure into some assumed value-neutrality or objectivity (Ribbens, 1993: 86).

'Double subjectivity'

Reflecting on the author's textual 'management of self' when 'writing it up', there is captured a 'double subjectivity'. The concept of 'double subjectivity' relates to 'a subjective view of one's own subjective view' (Ribbens, 1993: 84). In other words, there was recognition on the ethnographer's part (as researcher and human being working 'behind the scene') of a moral attitude that took into consideration the receptivity of the subject audience when deciding how to present sensitive material in the text. The moral attitude, which brought subjects to the negotiating table, subsequently became a source of the ethnographer's sociological scrutiny. With feminist research, moral ambiguity in respect of the relationships formed in the field and the moral obligation not to be seen as critical of the information that these relationships provided, is elaborated to a noticeable degree in recent years. With feminist women writing on women's lives there is recognition of the need for an author to realize the quandary that can arise when public moral judgements reflect on relationships. 'Double subjectivity' may arise when a journalist who has publicly accused a fellow journalist of betraying and exploiting a subject to get a good story is then publicly criticized by a subject on the basis of the same misdeed done to them.

'Confessional tales', confessional ethnography and an ethical ideal

Long-term fieldwork is conventional practice in anthropology. Long-term immersion in the field is generally a total intellectual, physical, emotional, political and intuitive experience (Rosaldo, 1994; Okely, 1992). The realist author experienced the trials and tribulations of fieldwork and the mini-melodramas and hardships that possibly evoked strong emotional and intuitive responses, but the descriptions of such events and episodes were usually relegated to a methodology appendix (Gumbrium and Holstein, 1997: 90). The convention of 'ethnographic realism' was to compartmentalize the fieldwork experience, whereas in more recent texts confessionals are a feature of the text (Behar, 1996) and confessional-like components are also found in chapters of books (Young and Lee, 1996) and in journal articles (Lehnerer, 1996).

The general theme of what fieldwork did to the fieldworker is a prominent feature of sociological confessionals (Van Maanen, 1988: 73). The cases mentioned above show how the fieldworker was made to feel vulnerable and confused or subsequently enlightened. The human qualities of the fieldworker (the personal biases, character flaws, oversights, failures, likes and dislikes, intuitive and emotional experiences) might be shown to influence the fieldworker's subsequent decision to adopt a new way of dealing with 'vulnerable writing' (Behar, 1996). Richardson (1992) speaks of her struggles with 'alternative forms of representing the sociological', and makes problematic sociology's concepts and methods by grounding them in lived experiences. She tells of how experimentation helped her to broaden her vision of the familiar sites and engage in a more adventurous approach toward new sites, as well as to intensify her feminist mission (1992: 136). Richardson's (1992) work has elements of the 'confessional tale' being self-revelatory (Van Maanen, 1988), but her work is perhaps to be seen more as a kind of 'personal sociology' that leads to a professional career in experimental texts (Gumbrium and Holstein, 1996: 94).

In contrast to the 'realist' account, where the author assumed the omniscient third-person position and spoke with some authority from a relatively invisible stance, the author of the confessional is moved to centre stage. Confessionals feature 'personalized author(ity)' (Van Maanen, 1988). The authorial presence in the text sometimes depicts the ethnographer as narrator not quite in control of the self, but eventually triumphing over the seemingly insurmountable difficulties with which fieldwork presents them. The theoretical, methodological and ethical preconceptions that the fieldworker takes to the field, and ethical codes and guidelines, are sometimes found to be inadequate models for fieldwork practice because feelings have not featured significantly in the traditional perspectives and models, or cannot be applied to the context-specific problems.

In Chapter 7, mention was made of how Young (Young and Lee, 1996) was unable to feel she had 'come home' with a reading of feminist writings; symbolic interactionism fared little better since the suggestion that 'involvement' and 'comfort' were markers to gauge 'right' relations with subjects was disproved by fieldwork experiences. Young was without allegiance to a particular methodological approach and confused. Wilkins (1993), on the other hand, was able to align her experiences with feminist writings and felt she had 'come home', while Lehnerer's (1996) fieldwork experience led her to a realization that a more 'existentialist' or 'subjective' approach was in order. Lehnerer's work contains elements of Van Maanen's (1988) confessional tale, but perhaps here too the definition of 'personal sociology' may be more apt.

Emotional reactions, new ways of seeing and doing things and unexpected occurrences are all conventional confessional materials that suggest how the fieldworker came to understand the various phenomena. In confessionals the fieldworker's point of view is presented in print. Lehnerer (1996) realized her experiences of 'becoming involved' should be the dissertation rather than the methods section. With epiphanies, the reader is provided with a means to learn about fieldworkers' disappointments, confusion and surprise, and gain a better understanding of what to expect in the field and from fieldwork.

Confessionals usually in some way support realist writing, but admit of some misgivings (Van Maanen, 1986). Both Lehnerer (1996) and Young (Young and Lee, 1996) exhibit a self-conscious vulnerability from having crossed the boundary into sensitive, emotional and personal issues, for which they could anticipate some adverse reaction toward professional identity; their work could be relegated to the margins of mainstream sociology. There is a consciousness that the personalized first-person account 'can leave the reader with the drama of the research experience but without the methodological substance' (Young and Lee, 1996: 102); and this could reflect poorly on the researcher. In anthropology and sociology it is not uncommon to find ethnographers being charged with self-indulgence and confessional self-absorption from having written about their own fieldwork experiences (Fabian, 1991; Okely, 1992); and that the authors exhibit in their writing a sensitivity towards an audience's negative interpretation of their accounts. The first personal account is knowingly but defiantly open to critique for being unduly self-indulgent, and not falsifiable or representative.

Notable scholars within mainstream ethnographic sociology (Denzin, 1997; Van Maanen, 1995) and anthropology (Marcus, 1998) recognize the value of confessional ethnography and other new experimental forms for ethical, moral and personal reasons. Van Maanen (1995: 9) says confessional ethnography 'conveys a good deal of the same sort of cultural information and speculation put forth in conventional realist works but in a more personalized and historically-situated fashion'. Marcus (1998: 327) acknowledges that the new experimental texts do not ignore 'objective conditions' (the play of interests and processes of coercion and contestation), but unlike realist texts the experimental ones are not built around power but rather around ethics. Among other criticalist issues there is a focus on the complex moral relationship of the observer and the observed that exposes the ethical concerns in any fieldwork (Marcus, 1998). One risk of writing about vulnerabilities is that of diverting critique to one's own ethics. Another risk is that readers, seeing personalized accounts as nothing more than narcissism, ignore the ethical implications of the conditions of knowledge production in ethnography. It is essential that such awareness be fostered in pursuing the traditional ends of 'ethnographic realism' in the late twentieth century (1998).

The story and the argument: criteria for assessment

The greater freedom to experiment with writing does not automatically guarantee a better product. The ethnographer still has to establish quality, but the criteria of assessment are different for postmodern texts. The distinction made about judgement is an important one in the current debate between modernists and postmodernists over experimental texts, since much writing takes the form of stories, narratives of the self, ethnographic fictional representations, ethnographic dramas and mixed genres (Richardson, 1994). Contemporary writers, while they seem to agree on only a few things, do share a belief that science cannot make claims about ultimate truth, and they have turned away from rational/technical explanations of knowledge claims. Their concerns are with rhetoric and philosophy and the need to address previously unheard voices and positions in human inquiry (Garman, 1994).

Postmodernists claim there are two modes of thought, the argument and the well-formed story, each of which provides distinctive ways of constructing reality and ordering research. Although complementary, the argument and the story are irreducible to one and the other. Any effort to reduce one mode to the other or to ignore one at the expense of the other fails to capture the rich diversity within ethnography and other forms of qualitative inquiry (Denzin, 1997). Each way of knowing differs radically in terms of criteria and procedures of assessment. A good story and a well-formed argument are different modes of thought requiring criteria of assessment that are drawn from different sources. Arguments convince one of their truths, story the likeness to reality; verification of stories is not by appeal to procedures for establishing formal empirical truth, but with establishing verisimilitude (1997: 10).

Verisimilitude connects with the natural world and draws on literary discourse of other texts (Denzin, 1997). It connotes having an appearance of truth, being like, probable or modelled on. Verisimilitude dispenses with the quest for validity and seeks to examine instead a text's ability to reproduce (simulate) and map the real (Denzin, 1997). Texts need to be produced that feel 'truthful' and 'real', the meaning of truths or verisimilitude is not in the text, but rather brought to the text by the reader. Verisimilitude, in its most naïve form, describes the text's relationship to 'reality' (Denzin, 1997). A text with high verisimilitude provides the opportunity for vicarious experience; the reader comes to know some things told as if she or he had experienced them and suspends disbelief (Denzin, 1997). A text does not have to be true to have high verisimilitude, only to be convincing. The text is always a site for political struggle over the 'real' and its meanings. Arguments are carried out between actors to establish truth and arguments are political. Verisimilitude is textual, linked with subjective experience, and amenable as criteria of assessment of the story in the text. The question asked of the text by postmodernists might be 'Does the work represent human experience with sufficient detail so that portrayals can be recognized as truly conceivable experience?'(Garman, 1994).

Postmodernist texts may validate themselves by providing a deepened, complex, thoroughly partial understanding of a topic. Strategies may include combining many dimensions and angles of approach. A multi-faceted approach to the text is characterized by Margery Wolf's *Thrice-told tale* (1992). She took the same event and told it as a fictional story, field notes and a social scientific story. Other ethnographers have written poetry, fiction, ethnographic accounts and field notes about one unit (a village), or they have intertwined autobiography, academic writing and survival stories (Richardson, 1994: 522–523).

Other criteria used by postmodernists to establish the 'quality' of writing include verité, integrity, rigour utility, vitality, aesthetics and ethics (Garman, 1994). Apart from endeavouring to ensure that a piece of work is structurally sound, rational, logical, appropriate and accords with a tradition or genre accepted by one's reference group, there are ethical matters to be addressed. Consideration needs to be given to who owns the words in the text; how ownership is to be attributed; and courtesy rights that link with proper textual 'impression management' of self and others. There is a need to exhibit evidence that privacy and dignity having been afforded to all research participants. One way of assessing the 'quality' of writing might be a consideration of the human and social good.

The ethics of relationships

The reader is drawn into the social world which the writer has created, to move among the characters. Sometimes the reader is forced to think of the writer or the writing 'as if a playwright were to run out on the stage, interrupting his characters, to remind us he has written all this' (Hornstein, 1996: 55). 'Who is to stop the writer from inventing their subjects out of their own needs?' 'What constrains the construction within certain bounds?' Data from interviews and records (including field notes) might be only 'the barest of tethers' to constrain imaginings about the inner life of subjects (Hornstein, 1996). To enable the subject to have a voice in the text (in a form the speaker can recognize and which does not conjure feelings of exploitation or abuse) is an ethical guideline rather than a writer's wish. A feminist ethical standpoint may force the writer to recognize relationships with subjects and to treat subjects in print in ways they would treat friends in the face-to-face situation (1996: 56).

An ethic of relationships in autobiographies, biographies and ethnographies commits the author's allegiance to a variety of audiences (peers and colleagues, gatekeepers and sponsors, subjects and the readership). The textual 'management of self' and others requires attention be given to the public's right to know and the researcher's right to protection. Every author has some sense of ethical need in order to satisfy an audience, and such awareness impacts on how the characters of the text will be presented. There is also a sense in which those who 'people' the social world that the author is busy creating themselves engage in the constitutive process, by virtue of being an audience of readers whose privacy rights could be infringed (Hornstein, 1996). Subjects can project themselves into the author's conscience, and pressure an author to get in touch with their own feelings, as a measure of what they might read in the book. When deciding on how to present the information, the guiding ethical principle of 'do no harm' might be combined with a more intuitive and moral frame that asks 'Does this feel right?' Conflicting loyalties and obligations owed to various audiences can exert a powerful moral force on the author, and heighten her or his awareness of the moral implications of textual 'impression management' of self and others.

In ethnography and other forms of qualitative inquiry, fieldwork puts people in contact with people in intimate ways. Direct access or co-presence establishes social relationships as context for interpretation. Unlike the impersonal mode of quantitative inquiry, qualitative field-work establishes relationships as a separate issue. These social relation-ships may have a claim on the author's loyalty and allegiance and run counter to and independent of the research enterprise (Ribbens, 1993). Friendships established in the field are a source of information and of great joy, but secrets shared with subjects can become entangled with data and transformed to information for uncensored public viewing. Friendships could inadvertently precipitate an invasion of privacy rights. An author may learn too much in the course of friendly interchange, and too much of the wrong information may find its way into print. Subjects and authors may differ in terms of definitions of what is 'ethical'. Friends could be portrayed in print different from how they were known in the field (depersonalized and theorized). They could be identified with activities that transfer by association a variety of negative aspersions and connotations. Ethnographic writing is about constructing a cultural or social world, 'peopled' by constructs which the author has created. The 'constructedness' may conceal identities of individuals and groups, but it may not.

The text could stand as a testimony of the author's betrayal of trust and friendship. The author could be exposed as a trickster, gaining people's trust and betraying them without any outward show of remorse. 'Treachery' and 'deception' are words that could be used by subjects who believe privacy rights have been betrayed. Fieldwork practice is characterized by ambiguities and dilemmas and probing is one of the 'tricks of the trade' ethnographers commonly use to extract more information from subjects than they may want to give, or would want disclosed as uncensored information to a wider public (Bernard, 1994). While the ethics of probing acknowledges that collecting and distributing information is the researcher's responsibility, students may not always adequately anticipate what this means in terms of disclosure and publication. Subjects themselves do not always agree with the researcher's acceptance of what is assumed 'ethical' (Harrison and Lyon, 1993: 107).

Authors need to be accountable to the relationships they write about and reflect in print the same degree of care and concern expressed in the field with friends (Hornstein, 1996). At the minimum, the author should not say things in print that they would not say to the people themselves. A feminist ethical standpoint forces the writer to recognize relationships with subjects, and not treat subjects in ways they would not treat their friends. At minimum authors should not say things in print they would be ashamed to say to their faces. Hornstein is not suggesting the writer omit material because subjects would find it embarrassing, or because it would elicit a denial (1996: 56). Instead she acknowledges the need to balance the subject's right to privacy with the reader's right to know. Taking a feminist ethical stand may not prevent subjects from experiencing negative feelings, but it would help the author live with herself after the book was done.

Hornstein (1996) agrees there is a great deal to be learned from moments when the analyst feels estranged from subjects, a point made in the last chapter with a focus upon epiphanies and degradation ceremonies. The author may be abruptly snapped out of a world of fantasy and forced to think about the self and relationships with others. Thus they may gain new insight to ways of writing the self and others into the text. Estrangement can lead to deeper understanding of relationships with subjects (wanting to be *with*, rather than *looking at*). My degradation ceremony was a source of enlightenment. I was forced to confront the revelation that the subjects did not define me as *one of them* for reasons not entirely clear to this day, but probably linked with past ways I acted (with too much enthusiasm to get data), that inadvertently breached implicit understandings and offended group members during early fieldwork in one store. The ambiguity of relationship in the research context may resonate around the researcher wanting a 'real' relationship with subjects in the field, but perhaps being satisfied with an impersonal relationship in print that releases them from normative constraints of friendship (trust, care and support).

By highlighting ethical ambiguities of the research process and censoring material, the author as reviewer may make rehearsals a central part of the production process, before readers have a chance to judge the text's merit. The rehearsal may feature partial self-censorship, for the management of a professional and moral identity.

Biographies, autobiographies and ethics

With a single biography or autobiography the author is not exonerated from the same sorts of ethical responsibilities with other forms of writing that have plagued feminist scholars. Like the writer of ethnographies, biographers and autobiographers need to be reflexively self-aware as the producer of a 'reality' in the text (Harrison and Lyon, 1993: 106). The biographer or autobiographer is not a self in isolation. Rarely in the text is the author the only person to whom the information refers; there are institutions, groups and relationships linked with key figures in anthropological and sociological writings. Subjects may be identified in interactions and situations in autobiographies, biographies and narratives in similar fashion to being grounded in field notes in descriptive and background information. Subjects may be revealed through work roles linking them with the author in co-operative, co-ordinated assembly-line-like work processes and mentor–learner relations.

There is a variety of issues to contend with in sociological autobiographies, apart from the problem with identifying others. There is a need to make the writing sociologically relevant (not merely personal) and to avoid claims of self-indulgence from too much inward-looking activity. The decision to write the self into the text with a personalized account, a case study, life history, trajectory, moral career and the like, singles out the author. While invariably such devices to organize materials produce a wealth of descriptive background information, other people may be identified in fieldwork settings and establishments. The audience may deduce the identity of people or groups from roles, relations with the author and the general overall texture of a setting. A detailed description of a person's life history or a case study can produce sufficient descriptive material to lead to a deductive disclosure (Lee, 1993: 186).

Acknowledgements and references

Introductions to books can reveal loyalties and allegiance between colleagues rather than with participants, or establish a change in relationships. The textual 'presentation of self' by another person in the introduction of a text may unfold as a programme to announce, show, express or propose an unknown identity to a discipline or academic audience for social placement (Stone, 1962). The spokesperson may not only announce the author for placement in structural terms (achievement standards, title, credentials, past experience), but also provide a track record of where she has come from and where she proposes to travel in the book. The textual 'presentation of self' by a spokesperson with high profile and good reputation may launch a relatively unknown author onto the publishing scene and short-circuit the otherwise lengthy procedure of establishing a name for oneself.

The foreword may provide an opportunity to give an account of how professional relations developed between the spokesperson and the author, and identify where and how they met. The spokesperson may provide readers with a glimpse of the human being behind the name (marital status and family details) and draw attention to ties of friendship which they want others to know about. An integrating function may be served by introducing the author to a readership in the foreword. Announcing an identity for social placement is a historically and politically contingent activity that leaves little doubt where allegiances and loyalties lie. Acknowledgements in the text have been seen as a strategy to protect relationships and an expression of the meaning of a relationship. Ben-Ari says that 'acknowledgements ... bring together meta messages about the value of the ties binding author and acknowledged about commitment to these ties in time to come' (1995: 139).

Many people write alone, yet belong to a team that is constituted by people drawn from a variety of disciplines, each with a different role to play, depending on credentials and workplace experience. One person may design the study, another collect the data and a third analyse and help 'write it up' with the principal researcher. In health research, beyond the solitary writer there are often a number of people working collaboratively, and sometimes individuals jointly write the report or article for publication. Those who have worked 'behind the scenes' need to be acknowledged in the report or book. Someone who has actually engaged in analysis of materials and written part of the report is usually acknowledged as a co-author (Kellehear, 1993: 29). The message to heed is: 'If you are part of a group or team, ensure that you know your role and the credit which will be accorded to your work. These matters should *never* be left unclear' (Kellehear, 1993: 29). The issue of public recognition of merit through co-authorship should be negotiated at the beginning of any research collaboration.

With publication, the issue of who sponsored the research is important, since the power relationship between sponsors and the researcher exists whatever the topic of research, and may be felt most at the time the researcher wants to publish the results and make material accessible to a wider audience (Minichiello et al., 1997). It is when research takes an unexpected turn, 'or the researcher comes up with embarrassing findings, or the analysis and explanation made by the researcher is not in keeping with the interests of the sponsors . . . that the exercise of power is most likely' (1997: 212). When the researcher wants to publish they could be made most vulnerable in sponsored research; ownership of the data or report could become an issue (1997: 212–213).

Before going on to some practical and ethical issues with disclosure it is worthwhile mentioning that some people consider dissemination to a wider audience as the 'public's right to know' and with notions of the 'common good'. Furthermore, research that is not applied has been given dubious ethical or moral status. Atkinson (1993: 69) pondered in the postscript over failure to find a mainstream publisher for her book produced from research with disabled people. She worried over whether a book that was not published widely was representative of 'a universally good outcome for her project'. One gets the impression she felt her work fell short of the moral ideal, that she was disillusioned and disappointed with her research experience.

Disclosure: some practical and ethical problems

Most fieldworkers create textual materials through social interaction with participants in the field site and from records kept by organizations. Field notes contain data that are descriptive and personal, which when organized into categories and concepts are transformed to information.

Such information within a text is defined as knowledge. As previously mentioned, and commented upon by Akeroyd (1991: 101), there is nothing inherently sensitive, harmful or damaging in data themselves; 'the possibilities of damage arise from their use(s) and the context(s) in which they are transformed into information' (Sieghart, 1982: 103). Data could fall into the wrong hands and be used for purposes other than the researcher intended and would not want (Fabian, 1991).

When uncensored information is disseminated to a wider audience people could be harmed. The guiding principle is to safeguard participants from harm or embarrassment due to disclosure of confidential or personal information learned from research (Akeroyd, 1991: 97; Finnegan, 1992: 226; Lee, 1993: 185). The notion of harm has perhaps been emphasized more in medical research than in ethnography and other kinds of qualitative research. Compared to biomedical experimentation, the harms of fieldwork are more difficult to measure, since the matter of physical damage is not usually an issue, although it could be. Harms in social research are more a matter of 'wrongdoing'. 'Wronging', as opposed to harming, is about causing embarrassment, anger and shame over what is said in print (Cassell, 1982: 10). While data are relatively safe in field notes, harms may come with disclosure and publication and often does (Lee, 1993). The researcher is responsible for the data they collect and for what is done with them. Social researchers need to consider fully what specific precautions are needed to protect privacy rights, safeguard materials and eliminate risk of threat to self from disclosure and dissemination. The use of pseudonyms to disguise individuals, groups and research sites is common, and mandatory practice in the social sciences to protect the privacy of individuals (Lee, 1993: 185).

A number of scholars (Ellen, 1984; Finnegan, 1992; Kidder and Judd, 1986; Peace, 1993) have addressed the variety of parties with interests and responsibilities in a research enterprise (sponsors, donors, gatekeepers, colleagues, participants, academic and lay audiences) that constitute the power and professional structure of the research enterprise. While sponsors, gatekeepers and subjects feature prominently in the early phases of fieldwork, to both facilitate and inhibit access, other interests and interested parties may come to the fore with disclosure and publication. Scholarly academics and publishers may exert a powerful moral pressure on the writer to conform to professional standards. The subjects and lay audience may have far less weight, but this may be influenced by theoretical orientation. In action and participatory research, researchers sometimes edit manuscripts with the people on whom the research is done. The subject could become a co-author and have a much more substantial input to the production of the text than might be anticipated for the subject in interpretivist research.

Part of interpreting data collected in the field is 'interpreting an audience's interpretations of the ethnographer's representation' (Hunt and Benford, 1997: 116). This may mean interpreting the participating audience's position on disclosing information to a wider audience made up mainly of members from the academic audience. Privacy rights may be involved. The ethnographer may be entrusted with a considerable amount of information over a lengthy period of time that subjects consider confidential, yet the professional norms of a discipline may require publishing information about behaviour, irrespective of it having been derived from friendships (Hansen, 1976: 131). With disclosure the rights of various parties may be sacrificed because of the demands of powerful others who offer better spin-offs. The ethnographer's own values, ideals, ethical codes and allegiances may be compromised in the negotiation process.

Disclosing the 'interpersonal dimension of privacy' (how social interaction and information are managed in the 'back region') may be a source of ethical and moral dilemma for the ethnographer. Ethical dilemmas do not always reveal themselves clearly in actual research, especially where researchers are not attuned to ethical issues; it can take some time adequately to anticipate the ethical consequences of fieldwork (Sieber, 1996: 15). An ethical dilemma can arise where an ethnographer is sympathetic toward the interests of subjects and this comes into conflict with obligations owed to academic gatekeepers who are working on behalf of the discipline and the university (see Chapter 7).

Stacey (1988: 23) describes how she was party to private information given her by one woman about a relationship she had with another, and how she was placed in an ethically awkward situation with regard to relations with both women, each of whom competed for her allegiance. An ethical dilemma arose from a 'conflict of interests'. 'Should the private information constitute data or should it remain outside the research agenda?' Disclosure can alter friendships and damage the ethnographer's perception of self and the fieldwork. Stacey (1988) was left to question whether there could ever be a feminist ethnography after her fieldwork experience. All parties to the research enterprise may not be equal when it comes to 'writing up', and exploitation could be a consequence of fieldwork when the author assumes the upper hand and speaks for the other.

In principle there is probably nothing immoral about advancing knowledge. Ethical and moral issues arise from the way information was gathered, the way it is portrayed and the purpose to which it is put. Intrusion into the lives of others, in order to get or upgrade qualifications or advance a career, without so much as attempting to discover whether subjects share the ideal of advancing knowledge or prefer their affairs to remain unknown, is likely to meet with strong opposition (Finnegan, 1992). The first aim of advancing knowledge has a number of consequential questions, not always adequately anticipated at the outset of research. Obligations owed to various parties with interests in the enterprise and their own agendas may or may not prove problematic (1992). Finnegan (1992) says that conflicting obligations are never totally unavoidable, but can be somewhat mitigated if anticipated and made more explicit in initial applications and contracts (1992: 218). I tend to agree with Fabian (1991), who says ethical and moral dilemmas are inherent characteristics of the fieldwork that puts people in close contact with people. They invariably emerge *ex post factum* and do not always admit of a solution. According to Hammersley and Atkinson (1995: 72), given the way in which research problems may change over the course of fieldwork, the fact that demands likely to be made on people in the setting cannot be adequately anticipated, and that policy and the polit-ical consequences are often a matter for little more than speculation at the outset, establishing a research bargain right from the start with all those involved is neither possible, nor desirable.

Various parties have differing interests and expectations: participants to privacy and protection from harm; the wider community to the 'right to know'; the profession to original and unbiased knowledge; the student to credentials and career opportunities; the academic audience to origi-nal and unbiased knowledge. The relative weight in importance given to each party's rights is a matter of negotiation with the various parties involved and outcomes cannot always be predicted. Research findings tend to be controlled by researchers, or by those who control researchers (gatekeepers). The author may fix an interpretation of the text as 'the version' and neglect competing views of reality. Whose view should prevail and why, is a moral issue that impinges on the control of the author. Those who remain powerless to establish in print what per-spective they want and what information will be disseminated for a wider public viewing are usually the subjects of the research (Brechin, 1993: 73).

Self-censorship

Authors ask questions such as 'Do we really endanger anyone when we describe secret knowledge or name persons in processes we analyse. Does the fact that our writings may be used by the powers that be make much or any difference in the way these powers carry out their designs?' (Fabian, 1991: 190). 'What are my responsibilities to people I write about?' 'For whom do I write?' 'What should be disclosed?' 'Should individuals be identified, and if so, then what if anything should be done to avoid harming them?'

The act of handing over a report or dissertation to academic gate-keepers, who are entrusted to move the work on to markers and library officials, may constitute an epiphany of considerable import to identity conceptualization and reformulation. In the immediacy of the handover process, the researcher could experience intense introspection, a reflex-ivity that draws on a conglomerate of values, ideals, principles and feelings. Featured may be the fundamental ethical principles of non-malfeasance ('above all, do no harm') and an intuitive response to an assumed audience interpretation of the author's representation that sparks questions like 'Would I like this done to me?' and 'How would I feel if this was me that was being written about?' In retrospect, my advice is that if it does not feel right there is a problem and if in doubt, leave out.

Self-censorship, a central anticipatory issue with social research, takes a number of forms. At one extreme the author may decide on not publishing at all, but more often the ethnographer engages in partial self-censorship (Lee, 1993). Materials might be disclosed or published in a restricted form (a dissertation but not a book, an article in a scholarly journal with a restricted readership, but not with the popular press, where sensationalizing events may be common practice). The ethnographer, social scientist or author may choose to omit specific information that might identify participants in a published article or report (Lee, 1993). Researchers may deliberately conceal aspects of a research that went wrong, or attempt to protect research participants by hiding information which could be used against them (French, 1993: 121).

Where participants are observed experiencing difficulties with role performance, the researcher may be put in a dilemma over whether to disclose information that would negatively impact on the competency of the actor and harm her or his career opportunities. Superiors with a duty of care may rule someone incompetent on the strength of a researcher's report. Information may be concealed to safeguard employment (French, 1993). An ethical dilemma of this nature reflects on allegiances and loyalties at work, which demand some measure of partial self-censorship. Some feminists believe researchers have a duty to advocate for their female research participants rather than reveal damaging information about them. Where partial self-censorship occurs there is a risk of contaminating the information: 'If information which is likely to offend is omitted, then rather bland results may be produced' (French, 1993: 121).

Ethnographers who partially censor their own work to avoid negative repercussions falling on themselves and/or subjects may delay publication or seek to have a closure put on aspects of the work for a period of time. The researcher might be embarrassed by the thought of subjects' responses to methods used, or fear reprisal over the information divulged. An 'ethic of openness' of knowledge might at some times have to be reconciled with the ethnographer's right to protection. Ethnographers who study sensitive topics and situations, or use sensitive methods, often carry 'guilty knowledge' they would not want others to know. Gaining an understanding of social phenomena often entails being socialized into a group and participating in activities that one could never adequately anticipate at the outset of fieldwork. The author may deliberately decide, on moral grounds, to present the self in the text in the role of 'learner', and analyse induction and acclimatization with use of the concept 'moral career'; but in doing so one needs to be mindful of avoiding being cast in the role of 'moral entrepreneur'. By directing attention to the self, the author assumes responsibility for activities, but some people may identify themselves by virtue of ties of friendship with the author, or through their role as mentor and be embarrassed at having been identified in this role.

With partial self-censorship one needs to be careful that the materials do not suffer some distortion and bias or loss of interest through tinkering with them. Where description and analysis are missing from a research article, academic gatekeepers with power to refuse articles for publishing may ask: 'Where are the people? Where is the evidence? What about rigour?' A failure to support theory with evidence could mean the difference between being accepted or rejected for publication. I decided not to include details on grounds that so doing might identify partici-pants, but vital supporting material was noticeably missing and helpful critics said as much. After a couple of rejections I decided not to publish at all.

Goffman's (1959, 1961a, 1961b) reportage failed to link social practices with theory. This may have had little to do with ethics and morality and there is little to suggest he engaged in partial self-censorship, but this does not seem to have hindered his publishing capacity. While students must attend to both matters, such oversights by Goffman do not detract from the value of using his work in an ethical discussion. Goffman presents readers with concepts without telling them how or what contributed to his knowledge. He imposes concepts on phenomena rather than drawing from what people actually do (Fine and Martin, 1995). His phenomenologically oriented critics say he fails to show how the actor acquires information or utilizes information already processed, and that the whole analytical process needs to go back a step (Cicourel, 1970).

In Goffman's work *Asylums* (1961a), there is a lack of perspective on how the patients view their world, or at least how they report their experience in a mental institution (Fine and Martin 1995: 170). Goffman's experience as a covert researcher at St Elizabeth's Hospital provided categories that are assumed for the inmates, in similar fashion to actors in the world of the shops, where those who filled a status, a position, a social place, are provided with 'a pattern of appropriate conduct, coher-ent, embellished, and well-articulated' (1959: 81). A self virtually awaits an actor who takes up a role: 'a judge is supposed to be deliberate and sober; a pilot in a cockpit to be cool' (Goffman, 1961b: 88). In *Asylums* (1961a) Goffman's ethnography is grounded in theoretical concepts of social organization and interaction, 'total institution', 'moral career', 'secondary adjustments' (Fine and Martin, 1995: 171).

Goffman frees himself of particulars in the situation and avoids identifying designated people with identifiable activities. The reader is left wondering how he came to know such things, but also acknowl-edging how the 'guilty knowledge' he accumulated was concealed by not disclosing personal particulars. The textual 'presentation of self' and others in Goffman's work avoids some of the tricky problems with disclosure, where identifying actual people with 'sensitive' activities or an institution can be offensive. Whether he intended to do this or not on ethical grounds is not at issue here. While Goffman's superb writing has been commented upon (Fine and Martin, 1995), so too has the lack of evidence to support theory. A phemenologically-oriented segment of the academic readership, anticipating finding evidence of a people's sub-jective perceptions, thoughts and feelings, may understandably be less than impressed by the mystifying aspects of his reportage.

It is definitely worthwhile being sensitive to the possible ethical overtones of differing theoretical orientations and perspectives, for they are likely to affect the types of methods, treatment of collaborators, the final interpretation and publication (Finnegan, 1992: 219). Symbolic interactionists like Goffman have a history of studying sensitive topics and regions, and some have used dubious methods (Ditton, 1977a). Many carry 'guilty knowledge' from having been socialized into the subculture they have studied. Getting feedback from participants has not been part of the interactionist tradition as it is with participatory or action research, where subjects may have input into what they want left out of the text or project. When the ethnographer's concern entails addressing micro processes of human interaction to generate 'shared understanding' or a 'definition of the situation', and includes the inter-personal dimension of privacy (how social interaction and information are managed in the 'back region'), then ethical problems and dilemmas may arise (Hansen, 1976).

The need to provide explicit fieldwork references to elaborate the author's inference procedures might be a weakness that restricts publica-tion opportunities. One needs to take care not to provide descriptive statements that are prematurely coded, interpreted by the author and subsumed under categories without telling the reader how all this was recognized and accomplished (de Laine, 1997: 85). Goffman emerged from 'behind the scenes' relatively uncontaminated by the vision he presented of the inmates in the asylum, but critical readers have a problem with his seeming lack of interest in describing the processes that underpin the concepts commented upon. What you need to do, when correcting for this, is to be careful that the evidence you provide to support interpretations does not identify individuals and groups in negative ways which might embarrass and anger them.

When workers say 'You don't tell your friends where you get your things' or 'I like to shop early, you don't want others seeing what you've got', it is quite obvious that, as members of small work parties, they do not want personalized information about shopping practices divulged to 'outsiders'. Such 'secret' matters belong in the 'back region' and to allies who can be trusted to maintain confidentiality. Women with whom I worked the various shifts were concerned that 'outsiders' were not party to 'insider' information. They joked about this with co-workers, drawing the boundary between themselves and those who moved in social circles beyond the store. Because close friends moved in social circles beyond the store, and members outside were unlikely to interact with those inside, it was improbable that information would trickle from one social circle to another and spoil the identity which women had established and were keen to maintain.

A researcher who is obligated by professional rules of a discipline to reveal 'back region' information to a 'front region' audience knowing that a 'back region' group would not want that information made public, is faced with an ethical or moral dilemma with disclosure. What does a researcher do, who is informed by symbolic interactionism to promote shared understanding derived from observation of individuals and their activities, when there is an assumption that most of the information gained from fieldwork experience, which is needed to support theory, the subjects of the observed social world would not want divulged to others?

For the study of sensitive topics and regions it may be more prudent to select a sociological perspective that does not require description of individuals' activities and identify others in quite the same way as a micro-sociological study. Anthropological fieldworkers are usually more interested in groups and collections of people rather than individuals, although an individual may become the focal concern of an extended case study or extended case. The unit of analysis used to build or refine a theory may be a person, a group, an organization or a behavioural pattern. A 'collective case study' in sociology (Stake, 1994) or an 'extended case study' in anthropology (Van Velsen, 1967) may be used to organize material in order to elaborate a theory. A number of cases may be strung together to enable the reader to trace the key figure's movement through a variety of circumstances, and within a number of social networks. A characteristic of case studies is that much of the relevant information available is assembled in the text, and this material may identify people who do not want to be identified.

Describing particular cases to make a general point about private or unflattering behaviour may make people feel they have been singled out (Lee, 1993: 190). Individuals or groups identified through the case study method may have good reason to believe they have been devalued. Goffman (1961a) avoided this problem by not 'peopling' the social world of the asylum with characters who had identifying markers or could be linked with the author by virtue of role activities and relationships they jointly shared. For this he was criticized, but not on ethical and moral grounds. The ambiguity with writing people into the text is evident with Goffman's work. The author has a moral choice of developing a 'real' caring relationship with subjects in the text, or an impersonal relationship. The implications are a difference in moral as opposed to technical procedures.

A good segment of the academic audience continues to look in texts for evidence of how culture is lived by particular people, in a particular place, doing particular things (Van Maanen, 1995: 23). A sensitivity toward both the subject's and the observer's perspectives is required, and context is needed to 'clarify' the perspective of the subjects or the observer. Information on work processes may provide the reader with insight to the moral order of a workplace, its coping strategies and the kinds of relationships valued by members. The participation of others (subjects) in patterned practices within a 'moral community' may identify people for an audience, even where those who 'people' the social world of the text are social constructs. People who are identified through roles performed in organizations may feel they have been 'wronged'. Self-censorship needs to be brought to case studies, life histories, trajectories, degradation ceremonies and epiphanies that rupture routines, and lives and provoke radical redefinitions of self to avoid possible breaches of privacy, and protection from harm. There is more than one way of organizing the same material for presentation in the text, and theoretical orientations provide guidance. Rather than using the case-study method, where sensitive issues are involved, it may be better to make general statements first, and then go on to discuss specific instances. This strategy is considered less threatening than singling out a person or group for discussion (Lee, 1993).

The ethnographer needs to take care against trivializing workplace conditions and workplace roles since this can cause subjects to be distressed; and in turn the writer could be dismayed. Data become potentially harmful when reported in ways that increase subjects' previously not so apparent controversial character. Treating activities in a sensationalist way can encourage a negative image of social research and have political consequences (Lee, 1993: 198). A critique of the liberal tendency that some academics have towards ethics may be interpreted as a personal attack, and could turn back on the researcher in most unexpected ways. Among the various parties with interests and expectations of research are one's colleagues and peers (other fieldworkers and authors). There is evidence of a case where peers have not supported each other, or of the profession having ironical ethical and moral consequences.

As previously mentioned, Hornstein (1996: 63) refers to a case where a journalist accused fellow journalists in the The New Yorker of being 'confidence men, preying on people's vanity, ignorance or loneliness, gaining their trust and betraying them without remorse'. Underlying the angry outburst was resentment toward a colleague who had befriended a man accused of murdering his wife and children in the process of writing a book on the case. When the book was published a supportive relationship between the author and the accused was betrayed through the author's interpretation of his guilt. Subsequently the author's innocence was made questionable when a complaint by a former subject, who felt she had crossed the boundary, was filed against her. He claimed she attributed statements to him in print that he never said. The subject appeared to do what the journalist had done (making one's political alignment public). Hornstein, believes that feminists should take a moral issue on relationships, however partisan and unpostmodern this sounds, 'because failing to distinguish between research and exploitation opens our subjects to abuse' (Hornstein, 1996: 64).

The distance of emotion and time

A matter of integrity is at issue; scholars should not be less accountable to women when they write about them. Researchers must juggle with the interests and agendas of the two major audiences (the academic and member audiences) during fieldwork and 'writing it up'. Because they write for an academic audience, removed from the lay audience, there can be distancing in emotion and towards relationships. Once fieldwork ends the distance in social and emotional terms may help the author feel less vulnerable and become careless with writing. Distance in emotion and time may complicate a writer's capacity to persevere on a pathway through competing loyalties (Hornstein, 1996: 61). On the other hand, a writer's capacity to persevere without being unduly stressed by ethical ambiguities of relationships and to cut a path through the 'thicket of loyalties' may be facilitated by distance in emotion. Having no personal contact with the subject/s (as with a biographer and a deceased subject) may mean authors worry less about protecting them and their rights to proper acknowledgement. The distance created in social and emotional terms may create a potential to say things one might not otherwise say to subjects if they were alive, personally known, or in regular social contact with the ethnographer/author. One may feel safe in legal terms to say derogatory things with regard to people who are dead, but those who are alive and personally attached to the deceased may exert a moral pressure on the researcher to exercise partial self-censorship.

Those who analyse and interpret data collected by someone else may be distanced in emotion and time, but should they print information that reflects negatively on reputations of a subject or group and this impacts on community acceptance, it is doubtful whether the analyst and data collector would avoid some form of retribution. Some researchers, in a desire to avoid ethical implication of research, suggest use of quantitative records, and other unobtrusive methods in health research (Kellehear, 1993, 1996). Writers would want their findings to have as wide an audience as possible. They have a responsibility to elite academic audiences and the public at large who 'have a right to know'.

Ethical proofreading

Johnson (1982: 87) offers guidelines for 'ethical proofreading' of manuscripts. The researcher is advised to assume that the identities of individuals and the location of the study will be uncovered. 'Assumed' rather than 'actual' outcomes are the base upon which to work to avoid 'wronging' other people and groups. What is to be reported should be evaluated in an explicit manner (Lee, 1993: 192). The feminist notion of 'identifying' with subjects, as a standard for establishing equality in social relationships, is appropriate to the area of sociological and ethnographic reportage.

Ethical proofreading covers 'member checks' (Lincoln and Guba, 1985), having research participants discuss findings with the researcher, and provide feedback with a view to refining the writing of manuscripts and making them more ethically sound (Johnson, 1982: 88). There are clearly responsibilities to subjects to explain findings, methods and limitations, and not suppress 'factual' evidence. Providing access to drafts, discussing them with subjects and jointly refining the manuscript may sound fairly straightforward to accomplish. But what does the ethnographer do when the subjects say 'I don't like that' or 'That's not what I meant, or remember'. Interpretations between social scientists and lay people vary. Individuals can be offended by abstract, depersonalizing treatment guided by heavy sociological theories. Bloor (1997: 37–50) addresses modernist techniques of validation and the pitfalls with 'member checks'. The distance in time between collecting and interpreting can make a difference. Factual details and interpretations may be contentious and elucidate rights that have not been voiced previously. For many varied and obvious reasons, 'member checks' for some researchers are not a choice (very obviously the covert researcher falls into this category).

I suspect most ethnographers go on to extract themselves from the fieldwork setting in which they were immersed, but not before experiencing some negative ethical or moral consequences from participant-observation. Most settings of ethnographic interest are complex and stratified, with differing and shifting allegiances and loyalties that set up a 'conflict of interests'. During fieldwork, the researcher is faced with a complexity of choices and subject to a number of situational constraints. The external and internal constraints continue to exert a pressure on the researcher when fieldwork ends and 'writing it up' begins in earnest. At the beginning of fieldwork the problem was how to get the material; at the end it is what to do with it and, furthermore, what might someone else do with it should information fall into their hands.

Researchers have to be careful with their materials. Staff members who process notes and manuscripts are provided with access to other people's lives and have obligations to maintain privacy. Personal information may be accessed on the Internet and field notes and manuscripts can be lost if not properly taken care of. There may be information that implicates subjects in ways which reflect poorly on reputation. The ethnographer may be held responsible for defamatory information when materials are disseminated to others to advance political agendas and implicate subjects. People interpret social phenomena differently and meaning changes with the passing of time and place. Irrespective of the topic or issue, what is appropriate at one time for a segment of the academic audience or wider community may not be the same at another place. The neophyte ethnographer who is about to embark on fieldwork for the first time cannot hope to anticipate adequately all the possible ethical and moral possibilities to avoid, which can leave a mark on the moral career of the identity.

Conclusion

Fieldwork is inherently problematic by virtue of the conditions that make knowledge production possible (paradoxes, ambiguities, dilemmas), where personal relations and social interaction are the context for unearthing meaning, in modes that are very different from positivistic-oriented, quantitative research (Fabian, 1991). The ethnographer is not always the autonomous self-directing actor, in control of the situation, but can be required to mediate between the two main audiences (academic and subject) and be in a quandary over what to do. A focus on ethical dilemmas fosters insight into the inherently problematic nature of fieldwork. Naming key informants and other participants, acknowledging sources and helpful others, using discretion and decency, are the ethical and moral considerations that researchers must confront when 'writing it up'.

Fieldwork has been shown to be problematic, in ethical and moral terms, when the ethnographer crosses the boundary between private and public places, conventional and sensitive topics, overt and covert methods, professional and friendship roles. So too with 'writing it up', there are boundaries one must not cross. Broadly speaking the area between field notes and text is ethically and morally problematic. There is nothing inherently dangerous or harmful with data, but when the ethnographer transforms data to knowledge and discloses it to a wider public, harmful possibilities are created. The purpose to which information is put and the context(s) elaborated upon by others may not be what the researcher intended or desired. The researcher may acquire information in a context of friendship and use that information data for reasons other than the subject/s intended or wanted. The researcher may be under pressure from sponsors or gatekeepers to disclose information that will implicate subjects in professional incompetence, or make them vulnerable to political oppression and exploitation.

Power relationships between the researcher, sponsors and/or gatekeepers may often be felt most with disclosure and publication. Should the researcher come up with embarrassing findings, or the analysis and explanation made by the researcher not be in keeping with the interests of sponsors, the exercise of their power might be most strongly felt. Authors are urged to remember they owe friends the same courtesy rights that apply in social interaction and are advised not to say anything in print which they would not say to their face (Hornstein, 1996).

The distance of emotion and time works in favour of being careless with writing, and making the author vulnerable to discrepancies. Subjects may be depersonalized by not having their voice heard in the text, or by having been given too much voice. It is not easy to lose people in a small 'qualitative crowd' and over-exposure may come with singling people out in case studies, life histories, trajectories, dramatic incidents, and so on. People may be offended by having been identified in print with activities, roles, institutions, suburbs and life style. The degree of sensitivity of the topic is a measure of what lengths the ethnographer may need to go to with self-censorship and ethical proofreading of manuscripts.

With disclosure and publication decisions have to be negotiated that draw on values, principles, ethical codes and guidelines, professional standards, personal reasoning, feeling and intuition. A new ethic or new moral imperative to inform contemporary fieldwork practice and textual representation is not well codified yet. Moral values, principles, intuition and feelings could feature prominently with the textual management of others, and professional codes and guidelines used to ensure that privacy rights are not breached and subjects are protected from harm from reportage.

With textual representation a consideration of the audience's interpretation of the writer's perspective may have to be based on 'assumed' rather than 'actual' response and may apply in some circumstances for partial self-censorship. The researcher must guard against risk of distortion, bias and loss of publication opportunities, while at the same time ensure that personalized accounts and confessionals which find their way into print do not expose them as tricksters, frauds or simply self-indulgent. Some researchers have rationalized the risk of telling the 'story behind the story' against rectifying the wrongs of 'ethnographic realism'. There is conscious and defiant awareness that conventions are challenged with the use of first person accounts, confessionals, personalized sociology and dramatic ethnography. Those who travel this pathway may lay themselves open to critique, but they do so in an attempt to write themselves out of some of the wrongs of past ethnographic realism and the silence that has surrounded the ethics and morality of fieldwork for too long.

CHAPTER 9

Conclusion

In 'realist' texts the author once flourished behind descriptive narrative. Good faith surrounded the ethnographic account and the narrator 'passed' relatively uncontaminated through a presumed neutral stance of not being personally involved in political goals or moral judgements and actions. Since the mid-1980s however, there has been considerable critique aimed at the third person omniscient author, whose own experience in the field is rendered invisible but who operates 'behind the scenes' in processes of inclusion and exclusion, deciding whose voice will and will not be heard. Some researchers do not want their shared experiences deleted from texts or reduced to ethnographic writing; nor do they see why the crisis of ethnography should be reduced to the 'crisis of representation', to writing practice and communication to a readership. They see a need to consider the social context in which researchers work and become politically and ethically involved (Fabian, 1991). Fieldwork implies that the researcher was physically present in the field, used sponsor's money and travel possibilities and relied on such assets in their initiatives; negotiations occurred at every step within the research process between parties with vested interests, hidden agendas and unequal power, that importantly involve obligations to others (Fabian, 1991).

Negotiations over choice of 'problem', roles, methods, field sites, presentational form occur throughout the research process and involve different parties who can exert a powerful moral pressure on the researcher to perform in certain ways. Qualitative researchers who write of themselves in texts are sometimes linked by roles to others in shared activities and in relationships of various kinds (power, intimate and social). Sometimes self is presented in the process of socialization, only reluctantly at first, but gradually granted intragroup responsibilities and access to the workplace experiences of others (conflicts, hopes, aspirations, and so on), and eventually called upon to make a commitment to one group in preference to another and to 'takes sides'. Researchers may manage to avoid 'taking sides' and effectively get around problematic and controversial issues without making their opinions known, but find they have inadvertently been placed in an ethical dilemma by virtue of materials being used by others for purposes other than they intended or desired. One may anticipate to some extent the potential for ethical and moral problems to arise in some areas of fieldwork, but there will always be ethical problems in various phases of fieldwork that cannot be anticipated or planned for. Solutions are needed which are suited to the situation.

In the sociological and anthropological literature there is evidence of ethical and moral dilemmas being part of the taken-for-granted under-standing of social science research. The very 'conditions of possibility' of producing ethnographic knowledge in interactive, communicative and dialogical rather than impersonal, objective positivistic ways, in critical anthropology, is qualified by the existence of impasses, paradoxes and dilemmas (Fabian, 1991). There is no way of knowing in advance the kinds of consequences likely to create dilemma in critical anthropology (Fabian, 1991). Unanticipated or inadequately anticipated consequences of qualitative inquiry that become ethical and moral dilemmas are experienced as negative, often because of the potential to damage people with whom the researcher has formed ties of friendship, as well as disrupting the goals the researcher has set for the self (Fabian, 1991). Dilemmas are not necessarily about the researcher's personal integrity or the discipline's professional standing or repute. Dilemmas can arise in critical anthropology and other forms of qualitative research purely from unintended misrepresentations that reflect the social and political posi-tions of researchers in other societies and/or because the researcher cannot guarantee information she or he has gathered can be saved from misuse of hegemonic interests (Fabian, 1991). More grass-roots accounts would advance an understanding of the location of self within power hierarchies in the field and highlight structural constraints in the field (Fabian, 1991). Such accounts can reflect upon the lived experience of the researcher caught in a web of social relationships which they have contributed to creating that trap them and make problematic the man-agement of *anonymity* and *confidentiality* (Hansen, 1976).

These perplexities may be dismissed by researchers with the same sort of disregard with which they reject 'confessionals' as self-indulgent accounts that enable the researcher to make the self the subject of the story. With dismissal, however, the impasses, paradoxes and dilemmas of fieldwork are not confronted for what they are, and an understanding of the ethical and moral dangers and pitfalls of fieldwork is not advanced. The risk of rejection is considered by some scholars well worth taking since information on the complex moral relationships of the observer and observed can expose the kinds of contradictions embedded in doing fieldwork and writing that make the researcher vulnerable. A kind of ethical awareness of the distinctive grounds from which knowledge is constructed through fieldwork is essential to pursuing an end to the traditional ethnographic realism of a past era. This is what the remaking of the observer and observed in moral terms in ethnography stands for (Marcus, 1998: 328).

Ethical problems unknown to past generations or unnoticed by them as well as new problems are emerging in fieldwork today. The 'moral' agenda of contemporary fieldwork is scattered with issues that field-workers of the past hardly even touched or did not touch at all, perhaps for reasons connected to the fact that moral and ethical issues of the human experience were neglected. The traditional researcher stance as social 'scientist' was characterized by moral and value neutrality. Whereas moral and ethical issues were not a significant part of social science research, the new researcher is a moralist who articulates moral and ethical issues as part of the human experience of *being* a researcher.

A number of external forces have been linked with the development of ethical consciousness in social research, the rise of feminism and feminist scholarship, a heightened consciousness of human rights more generally, the emergence of critical and participatory approaches and the spread of ethics committees within universities, academic departments and dis-ciplines and research units in the wider community (Punch, 1994). During the first half of the twentieth century, in anthropology and sociology it was not unusual for traditional and urban ethnographers to intrude into other people's lives and explore their ideas and beliefs without consent, but the free use of other people's ideas without consent has been put to rest with acceptance of the need to make explicit one's research goals and seek permission to do fieldwork in cultures or subcultures other than one's own (Barrett, 1996).

The choice of either quantitative or qualitative research, and within these parameters interpretivist or constructivist and criticalist approa-ches, has a bearing on the type of role/s the researcher performs in the field; the type of relations developed with research participants (collabo-rative and participatory or otherwise); the methods used to explore sensitive regions; methods of analysis, interpretation and ways results are published. Different theoretical orientations have variously been criticized for downplaying human creativity, ignoring (or alternatively exaggerating) power relations and overstressing tradition. These criti-cisms are not solely grounded on intellectual foundations, but involve, importantly, the researcher's moral attitudes and personal values (Finne-gan, 1992: 219). The moral issues arising from relationships of various types, notably power relations and intimate relations that rest on a base of shared experience, caring and nurturance, were not a feature of quantitative research. The whole issue of face-to-face contact in qual-itative research, which puts the researcher in contact with people in intimate ways, generates all the same problems that beset intimate human intercourse in everyday life (personal likes and dislikes, animos-ities, jealousies, resentments, conflicts of interest).

In quantitative research, distance was expected between the researcher and participants for instrumental and rationalized reasons; data had to be protected from contamination and findings were not to be distorted. The presented researcher was the dispassionate rational analyst. Feelings and emotions are not rational and thus not 'scientific' and not recognized as part of the 'analytic psyche'. Qualitative fieldwork, especially long-term immersion in the field, is now recognized as a total human experience, demanding all the researcher's resources: intellectual, physical, emotional, political and intuitive (Okely, 1992). With the rise of critical approaches, fieldwork came to be seen as a political activity. Those who depersonalized and treated subjects as objects, scientific specimens or exhibits were criticized for depersonalizing and using individuals as resource for research ends. Grand theory and all-encompassing models have been rejected by some feminist scholars on the grounds that they were exploiting and oppressing people. Research should be collaborative, useful to research participants and provide a means of empowerment.

Many researchers, both of interpretivist and critical persuasion, identify links between ethical problems and dilemmas with dual roles of friend and researcher and the formation of close or intimate relationships, which create problems with the management of *anonymity* and *confidentiality* (Hansen, 1976; Lincoln, 1995). Betrayal of trust is recognized as a potential outcome of multiple roles. Stacey (1988) claims fieldwork is potentially treacherous because of intrusion and intervention into a system of relationships that the researcher is freer to leave. Fieldwork ethics is not limited to dual roles of researcher and friend as conditions of possibility of 'conflicts of interest' and ethical and moral dilemma. With textual representation, it is not the interpretation of those who have been placed in collaborative, reciprocal relationships of friendship in the field that is given primary recognition, but rather the author who is in charge of the selective process, who determines whose voice will be heard and whose will not (Stacey, 1988: 23).

Marja-Liisa Swantz (1996) more recently makes questionable the nature of relationships in her participatory research project by reflecting on the genuine involvement of the studied people and the potential of the researcher purposely creating an intercommunication situation to camouflage the existing power differentiation.

The interpretivist approach of symbolic interactionism has been linked to ethical and moral dilemmas by virtue of the researcher's central concern with explaining the micro-processes of human interaction to which the role of friend is harnessed to provide access to back regions and sensitive sites (Hansen, 1976: 132). The rule governing any scientific enterprise, that 'the scientist's analyses and conclusions must be adequately documented by reference to the concrete data on which they are based' (1976: 132), means that information gathered in back regions and during informal relations with friends may be translated into data for an uncensored wider public viewing. A back-stage vantage point may facilitate the collection of information about violation of traditional or ideal rules of behaviour and other human weaknesses. Disclosure could be defined as betrayal of implicit obligations of *anonymity* and *confidentiality*. Loyalty to friends may be sacrificed to the promotion of the research goal, as an outcome of an ethical dilemma.

New trends

Nowadays, researchers are moving closer than they have ever been with respondents, and this closeness demands greater sensitivity, authenticity and discretion than in previous moments in social science (Lincoln, 1995). The more intimate or passionate research being promoted by some of the foremost exponents of qualitative research would suggest that boundaries to the teaching and supervision of research might have to change to meet the different ethical and moral demands of fieldwork. The new ethnography that takes the researcher into the field to study sensitive fieldwork sites requires maturity, high self-awareness and high personal authenticity, a powerful sense of confidentiality and an understanding of how identities and information must be safeguarded. Lincoln (1998) considers the demands may be too great on students who are simply too young to handle the rigours of fieldwork. Lincoln has assumed more responsibility in decision making with regard to students in preparation for fieldwork. She admits to asserting her gatekeeper role by not approving dissertation proposals where immaturity might be thought adversely to influence researcher reputation in a situation and hinder opportunities for future research.

The likelihood of more rather than less sensitive research occurring in the future might be gauged with the emergence of topical subjects that paradoxically have taboo status and reflect upon current social problems of changing western societies (AIDS, homosexuality, lesbianism, euthanasia, marital breakdown, home violence, child custody, sexual harassment, and so on). The fact that ethnography is now accepted as a favoured methodology in other than the originating disciplines of anthropology and sociology is a matter of consideration here. More researchers may be drawn into back regions of establishments and to the private terrain of everyday life where violation of traditional and ideal rules might be revealed, along with disagreements, hostilities and conflicts of interest. Researchers may be expected to participate in tasks that are not anticipated and which are mildly illicit, and/or observe activities that make problematic an uncensored wider public viewing. The increasing number of taboo topics or sensitive problems available for study suggests the need for thinking hard about the types of relationships you would want to form with subjects and the roles you would want to activate in the name of research.

Choice of 'problem' and role are dilemmas of fieldwork at the best of times and the field is a situation fraught with numerous choices and ethical implications (Partridge, 1979). There is not one choice of role to be made but several sequential choices that through time may become a complex of allegiances and commitments and which may raise a number of ethical questions and dilemmas. To whom should the details of a sensitive project be explained? To what extent should the researcher participate in the illegal or unofficial activity? Listening to disclosures of violence in the home, child abuse and sexual harassment, while providing positive rewards to respondents from having had the opportunity to be involved in a worthwhile project, can create ethical problems for the researcher by virtue of the emotions evoked with questioning that could require the professional service of a therapist. Further to this, there is the matter of research goals to consider; providing counselling could interfere with the research agenda. Overlapping and dual roles present researchers with a range of complex but unavoidable ethical and practical dilemmas that may reflect negatively on professional responsibility and render one's fieldwork questionable.

Traditionally, fieldwork has sought to provide a role for the ethnographer that is accessible to the 'native's point of view' of the culture, while maintaining a certain distance from that culture (Berg, 1988: 214). Feelings were not part of a self-commentary or the traditional academic culture in anthropology, but remained implicit or latent, lived and not talked about. A 'method' section was the traditional place to describe procedures, the formation of relationships with people who participated in the study and any ethical problems and dilemmas the researcher may have confronted in the field. Nowadays, the story behind the story ironically can become the central feature of a dissertation, to provide insight about the struggles – emotional and intellectual – that went on 'behind the scenes'. A piece of the framework necessary to interpret the experience of the personally involved, politically committed and ethical and morally oriented researcher may thus be provided (Lehnerer, 1996).

The 'feminist communitarian ethical model' that values the connectedness of people and celebrates personal expressiveness, emotionality and empathy is being promoted to take researchers into the twenty-first century (Denzin, 1997: 276–277). For some, the challenge of qualitative fieldwork is seriously to engage in emotion-charged research, defined as 'existential sociology' or 'emotionalism' (Gumbrium and Holstein, 1997: 58). This form of fieldwork shows the lived experience of the fieldworker, as he or she goes about their work in the field, as multi-layered. It reflects doubt on the pervasive problem in conventional sociological analysis to separate the subjective from the rational actor model and treat emotion and cognition separately, as if each can be activated by choice. The necessary and inevitable tension between thinking and feeling is confronted when controversies in the field touch on the problem of self-identity, relationships and frameworks of knowledge that have perpetuated distorted perceptions in academe (McGettigan, 1997). Fieldwork controversies demand the union of intellect and passion and the organi-zation of the connections between self, other and the world, and reflec-tion on what is right to do and good to be as a researcher (Schwandt, 1995: 133–134). In the traditional mode, to observe sociologically meant to cede experiencing to the members of the setting and to exhibit that which was observed with words. The wholly detached objective rational analyst is debunked with recognition that the duality which has been perpetuated of a 'real' dispassionate objective analyst, in some way separated from the feeling human being, is only the 'presented' and not the observer that is experienced in the field.

In feminist research, taking a moral stance reflects a partisan approach that is justified on the grounds of need to distinguish between research that can be exploitative, and puts subjects at risk of abuse, and research that reflects integrity, sharing and accountability for relationships formed in the field. Some feminist scholars do not seem to have addressed or made their allegiances clear in terms of relationships that are recognized in print. An 'ethic of relationship', when carried over to the text, directs authors not to say in print anything they would not say to people themselves. An ethical standard that forces writers to recognize their relationships with subjects in print is an ethical guide rather than a writer's wish (Hornstein, 1996). To enable subjects to have a voice in the text, in a form the speaker can recognize and which does not conjure up feelings of exploitation and abuse, is an ethical guideline that would help authors to live with themselves once the book is done. There is no suggestion that material be omitted on the basis that subjects would find it damaging or because it would elicit a denial. There is a need to balance the subjects' rights to privacy with the rights of the readers to know, and the writer's need (Hornstein, 1996). On the other hand, however, there is a need to be accountable for the relationships that are written about and to reflect in one's writing an alignment with propriety rules governing interpersonal relations in the face-to-face situation.

The new experimental texts capture the 'messiness' of fieldwork. Some attempt to tell the story behind the story is made at times. Secondary analysis provides a mechanism for extending the contexts in which the researcher is able to use and interpret qualitative research data (Thorne, 1998: 548). Where researchers conduct a secondary interpretation of their field notes or existing database, perhaps in order to tell their own stories or to develop themes that emerged with primary analysis but were not fully analysed, methodological, intellectual and ethical problems may be created. The second take on materials for a different purpose to that originally established with subjects raises the possibility of new ethical issues that resolve around the rationalized and impersonal ethical princi-ples encapsulated within formal codes (confidentiality, informed consent, privacy, protection from harm).

Secondary analysis done by someone who is not the primary researcher has a potential to violate confidentiality by virtue of the second researcher not knowing what the subjects considered sensitive. The extent to which all research will be published might be adversely influenced by the emotional distance from subjects and the passage of time that has elapsed since data collection. To some extent, close social relationships may safeguard subjects by assisting the researcher to calculate any risks inherent with divulging sensitive information (Thorne, 1998: 550). With a second take on materials one is made more aware of the need to have 'a process of consent' that would account for the ever-changing field (Wax, 1982). Where consent is not forthcoming, the secondary researcher is at risk of breaching confidentiality rules. Subjects may have consented to share their ideas and beliefs about social phenomenon for an identified purpose, but a radical departure from that shared purpose could violate the conditions under which consent was obtained (Thorne, 1998: 551). Representation of a particular phenomenon or group may carry significant ethical overtones that compound the ethical problems of confidentiality, privacy and consent.

Technological advancement creates different ethical issues with storage and privacy rights. Many social scientists might use computers without being fully aware of either legal or technological hazards (Akeroyd, 1991: 99). Data themselves are not necessarily sensitive, damaging or potentially harmful: 'the possibilities for damage arise from their use(s) and the context(s) in which they are transformed into information' (Akeroyd, 1991: 101). Field notes and data files may need to be organized in terms relative to what is considered confidential and/or private (Akeroyd, 1991). The researcher may be responsible for information that may come into the wrong hands or be used for purposes other than originally intended or wished, and this has relevance for email.

Lincoln predicts an emergent ethical problem in qualitative research where revelations made in case studies relate to individuals who work in close proximity with each other (1995: 45–46). Achieving trust in order to collect authentic data, and negotiating decision making in a context of differential power imbalances, poses ethical problems (1995: 46). The problem of voice in case studies creates ethical problems because there are inclusion and exclusion processes that mean some voices will be heard and others left out, and some people are making choices and exerting power over others.

Most concerns with ethics revolve around questions of consent, privacy, confidentiality and harm. In the past, formal codes addressed the questions of consent, privacy, confidentiality and harm and the right of the individual to withdraw data about the self. The stated priorities of ethics committees 'can give the false impression that ethics is about "what we do to others" rather than the wider moral and social responsibilities of simply *being a researcher*' (Kellehear, 1993: 14). The traditional ethical principles are now being seen as inadequate when used alone to inform ways of handling ethical dilemmas of fieldwork that are situational, personal and value related. The 'grey areas' of research are made even more sensitive when research is qualitative and not quantitative (Lincoln, 1995: 45). Rather than submit solely to formal codes, many fieldworkers prefer to address ethical dilemmas situationally, perhaps justifying individual choices in the belief that ethical and moral dilemmas are an inescapable and thus inevitable part of fieldwork (Hertz, 1996: 4).

The 'new activism' suggests a new ethic, a new moral imperative for research but, as Lincoln points out, the new moral imperatives are not well codified yet (1995: 47). Passionate engrossment is being called for in some sectors of the academic audience, but different researchers have different 'moral boiling points', which could be problematic (Lincoln, 1995). Fieldworkers continue conducting studies informed by criteria of formal codes and guidelines, believing that while they are within such parameters they are engaged in ethical fieldwork, but their behaviour could be perceived as morally objectionable. Ethical codes cannot adequately deal with the 'grey areas' of qualitative field research, and these 'grey areas' seem to be increasing. The space for debate, made available with the departure of topics like validity, reliability and the quantitative/ qualitative duality, has been filled with ethics. The battleground for debate on the issue of ethics is set with extension and reconfiguration of what is considered ethics in field research.

References

Adler, P.A. and Adler, P. (1987). *Membership roles in field research*. Newbury Park, CA: Sage.

Adler, P.A. and Adler, P. (1994). Observational techniques. In N.K. Denzin and Y.S. Lincoln (eds). *Handbook of qualitative research*. Thousand Oaks, CA: Sage. pp. 377–392.

Akeroyd, A.V. (1991). Personal information and qualitative research data: some practical and ethical problems arising from data protection legislation. In N.G. Fielding and R.M. Lee (eds). *Using computers in qualitative research*. London: Sage. pp. 89–106.

Altheide, D.L. and Johnson, J.M. (1997). Ethnography and justice. In G. Miller and R. Dingwall (eds). *Context & method in qualitative research*. Thousand Oaks, CA: Sage.

Alty, A. and Rodham, K. (1998). The ouch! factor: problems in conducting sensitive research. *Qualitative Health Research*, 8 (2): 275–282.

Appell, G.N. (1978). *Ethical dilemmas in anthropological inquiry: a case book*. Waltham, MA: Crossroads Press.

Archibald, L. and Crnkovich, M. (1995). Intimate outsiders: feminist research in a cross-cultural environment. In S. Burt and L. Code (eds). *Changing methods: feminist transforming practice*. Peterborough, Ontario: Broadview Press. pp.105–135.

Ashworth, P.D. (1995). The meaning of 'participation' in participant-observation. *Qualitative Health Research*, 5 (3): 366–367.

Atkinson, D. (1993). Relating. In P. Shakespeare, D. Atkinson and S. French (eds). *Reflecting on research practice: issues in health and social welfare*. Buckingham: Open University Press. pp. 58–69.

Atkinson, P. (1997). Narrative turnover or blind alley? *Qualitative Health Research*, 7 (3): 325–344.

Atkinson, P. and Hammersley, M. (1994). Ethnography and participant observation. In N.K. Denzin and Y.S. Lincoln (eds). *Handbook of qualitative research*. Thousand Oaks, CA: Sage. pp. 248–261.

Bailey, F.G. (ed.) (1971). *Gifts and poison: the politics of reputation*. New York: Schocken Books.

Baker, P.S., Yoels, W.C. and Clair, J.M. (1996). Emotional expression during medical encounters: social dis-ease and the medical gaze. In V. James and J. Gabe (eds). *Health and the sociology of emotions*. Oxford: Blackwell. pp. 173–199.

Barrett, R.A. (1991). *Culture and conduct: an excursion in anthropology*, 2nd edn. Belmont, CA: Wadsworth.

Barrett, S.R. (1996). *Anthropology: a student's guide to theory and method*. Toronto: University of Toronto Press.

Becker, H. (1963). *Outsiders*. New York: Free Press.

Becker, H.S. (1967). Whose side are you on? *Social Problems*, 14 (3): 239–247.

Behar, R. (1995). Introduction: out of exile. In R. Behar and D.A. Gordon. *Women writing culture*. Berkeley, CA: University of California Press. pp. 1–29.

Behar, R. (1996). *The vulnerable observer: anthropology that breaks your heart*. Boston, MA: Beacon Press.

Behar, R. and Gordon, D.A. (eds) (1995). *Women writing culture*. Berkeley and Los Angeles, CA: University of California Press.

Ben-Ari, E. (1995). On acknowledgements in ethnographies. In J. Van Maanen (ed). *Representation in ethnography*. Thousand Oaks, CA: Sage. pp. 130–164.

Berg, D.N. (1988). Anxiety in research relationships. In D.N. Berg and K.K. Smith (eds). *The self in social inquiry: researching methods*. Newbury Park, CA: Sage. pp. 213–228.

Bernard, H.R. (1994). *Research methods in anthropology: qualitative and quantitative approaches*. Newbury Park, CA: Sage.

Biaggio, M. and Greene, B. (1995). Overlapping/dual relationships. In E.J. Rave and C.C. Larsen (eds). *Ethical decision making in therapy: feminist perspectives*. New York: Guilford Press. pp. 88–123.

Bloor, M. (1997). Techniques of validation in qualitative research: a critical commentary. In G. Miller and R. Dingwall (eds). *Context & method in qualitative research*. Thousand Oaks, CA: Sage. pp. 37–50.

Blumer, H. (1969). *Symbolic interactionism: perspective and method*. New York: Prentice Hall.

Bochner, A.P. (1997). It's about time: narrative and the divided self. *Qualitative Inquiry*, 3 (4): 418–438.

Brannen, J. (1988). Research note: the study of sensitive subjects. *Sociological Review*, 36 (3): 552–563.

Brechin, A. (1993). Sharing. In P. Shakespeare, D. Atkinson and S. French (eds). *Reflecting on research practice: issues in health and social welfare*. Buckingham: Open University Press.

Brewer, J.D. (1994). The ethnographic critique of ethnography: sectarianism in the RUC. *Sociology*, 28 (1): 231–244.

Burns, T. (1992). *Erving Goffman*. London: Routledge.

Cassell, J. (1982). Harms, benefits, wrongs, and rights in fieldwork. In J.E. Sieber (ed). *The ethics of social research: fieldwork, regulation and publication*. New York: Springer Verlag. pp. 7–31.

Chrisman, N.J. (1976). Secret societies and the ethics of urban fieldwork. In M.A. Rynkiewich and J.P. Spradley (eds). *Ethics and anthropology: dilemmas in field-work*. New York: Wiley. pp. 136–147.

Cicourel, A.V. (1970). Basic and normative rules in the negotiation of status and role. In H.P. Dreitzal (ed.). *Recent sociology no. 2: patterns of communicative behaviour*. New York: Macmillan. pp. 4–45.

Clifford, J. and Marcus, G.E. (eds) (1986). *Writing culture: the poetics and politics of ethnography*. Berkeley, CA: University of California Press.

Codd, N. (1971). Reputation and social structure in a Spanish Pyrenean village. In F.G. Bailey (ed.). *Gifts and poison: the politics of reputation*. New York: Schocken.

Coffey, A. (1996). The power of accounts: authority and authorship in ethnography. *Qualitative Studies in Education*, 9 (1): 61–74.

Coffey, A. and Atkinson, P. (1996). *Making sense of qualitative data: complementary research strategies*. Thousand Oaks, CA: Sage.

Crick, M. (1993). Introduction. In M. Crick and B. Geddes (eds). *Research methods in the field: ten anthropological accounts*. Geelong: Deakin University Press. pp. 3–8.

Daly, J. and McDonald, I. (1996). Introduction: ethics, responsibility and health research. In J. Daley (ed.). *Ethical intersections: health research, methods and researcher responsibility*. Sydney: Allen and Unwin.

de Laine, M. (1997). *Ethnography: theory and applications in health research*. Sydney: Maclennan and Petty.

Denzin, N. K. (1968). On the ethics of disguised observation. *Social Problems*, 15: 502–50.

Denzin, N.K. (1992a). *Symbolic interactionism and cultural studies: the politics of interpretation*. Cambridge, MA: Blackwell.

Denzin, N.K. (1992b). Whose Cornerville is it, anyway? *Journal of Contemporary Ethnography*, 21 (1): 120–132.

Denzin, N.K. (1996). Sociology at the end of the century. *Sociological Quarterly*, 37 (4): 743–752.

Denzin, N.K. (1997). *Interpretive ethnography: ethnographic practices for the 21st century*. Thousand Oaks, CA: Sage.

Denzin, N.K. and Lincoln, Y.S. (1994). *Handbook of qualitative research*. Thousand Oaks, CA: Sage.

Devault, M.L. (1990). Talking and listening from women's standpoint: feminist strategies for interviewing and analysis. *Social Problems*, 37 (1): 96–116.

Ditton, J. (1974). The fiddling salesman: connivance and corruption. *New Society*, 30: 535–537.

Ditton, J. (1977a). *Part-time crime*. London: Macmillan.

Ditton, J. (1977b). Alibis and aliases: some notes on the 'motives' of fiddling bread salesman. *Sociology*, 11: 232–255.

Edmondson, R. (1995). Rhetoric and truthfulness: reporting in the social sciences. In R.H. Brown (ed.). *Postmodern representations: truth, power, and mimesis in the human sciences and public culture*. Chicago: University of Illinois Press. pp. 20–37.

Eipper, C. (1998). Anthropology and cultural studies: difference, ethnography and theory. In A. Peace (ed.). *Australian Journal of Anthropology*. Special issue 10: (3), 310–326.

Ellen, R.F. (1984). *Ethnographic research: a guide to general conduct*. London: Academic Press.

Emerson, R.M., Fretz, R.I. and Shaw, L.L. (1995). *Writing ethnographic fieldnotes*. Chicago: University of Chicago Press.

Fabian, J. (1991). Dilemmas in critical anthropology. In L. Nencel and P. Pels (eds). *Constructing knowledge: authority and critique in social science*. London: Sage. pp. 180–202.

Fine, G.A. and Martin, D.D. (1995). Humour in ethnographic writing: sarcasm, satire, and irony as voices in Erving Goffman's *Asylums*. In J. Van Maanen (ed.). *Representation in ethnography*. Thousand Oaks, CA: Sage.

Finnegan, R. (1992). *Oral traditions and the verbal arts: a guide to research practices*. London: Routledge.

Foddy, W. (1993). *Constructing questions for interviews and questionnaires: theory and practice in social research*. Cambridge: Cambridge University Press.

Fontana, A. (1994). Ethnographic trends in the postmodern era. In D.R. Dickens and A. Fontana (eds). *Postmodernism and social inquiry*. London: UCL Press. pp. 203–223.

Fontana, A. and Frey, J.H. (1994). Interviewing: the art of science. In N.K. Denzin and Y.S. Lincoln (eds). *Handbook of qualitative research*. Thousand Oaks, CA: Sage.

Fordham, G. (1993). Participant observation and language learning. In M. Crick and B. Geddes (eds). *Research methods in the field: ten anthropological accounts*. Geelong: Deakin University Press. pp. 9–36.

Frankenburg, R. (1957). *Village on the border*. London: Cohen and West.

French, S. (1993). Telling. In P. Shakespeare, D. Atkinson and S. French (eds). *Reflecting on research practice: issues in health and social welfare*. Buckingham: Open University Press. pp. 119–130.

Gagnon and Simon, W. (1973). *Sexual conduct: the social sources of human sexuality*. Chicago: Aldine.

Ganguly-Scrase, R. (1993). The self as research instrument. In M. Crick and B. Geddes (eds). *Research methods in the field: ten anthropological accounts*. Geelong: Deakin University Press. pp. 37–58.

Garfinkel, H. (1956). Conditions of successful degradation ceremonies. *American Journal of Sociology*, 61: 420–424.

Garman, N. (1994). Qualitative inquiry: meaning and menace for educational researchers. In J.S. Smyth (ed.). *Conference proceedings for the mini-conference, qualitative approaches in educational research*. Flinders University, South Australia. pp. 3–11.

Gergen, K.J. (1994). *Realities and relationships: soundings in social construction*. Cambridge. MA: Harvard University Press.

Glassner, B. and Loughlin, J. (1987). *Drug and adolescent worlds: burnouts to straights*. New York: St. Martin's Press.

Glucksmann, M. (1994). The work of knowledge and the knowledge of women's work. In M. Maynard and J. Purvis. *Researching women's lives from a feminist perspective*. London: Taylor & Francis. pp. 149–165.

Goffman, E. (1959). *The presentation of self in everyday life*. Harmondsworth: Penguin.

Goffman, E. (1961a). *Asylums: essays on the social situation of mental patients and other inmates*. Harmondsworth: Penguin.

Goffman, E. (1961b). *Encounters*. Harmondsworth: Penguin.

Goffman, E. (1963). *Behaviour in public places*. New York: Free Press.

Goffman, E. (1967). *Interaction ritual*. New York: Doubleday.

Goffman, E. (1969a). *Where the action is: three essays*. Harmondsworth: Penguin.

Goffman, E. (1969b). *Strategic interaction*. Oxford: Blackwell.

Gold, R.L. (1958). Roles in sociological field observations. *Social Forces*, 36: 217–223.

Gumbrium, J.F. and Holstein, J.A. (1997). *The new language of qualitative method.* New York: Oxford University Press.

Hall, J.R. (1999). *Cultures of inquiry: from epistemology to discourse in sociohistorical research.* Cambridge: Cambridge University Press.

Hammersley, M. (1990). *Reading ethnographic research: a critical guide.* London: Longman.

Hammersley, M. (1995). *The politics of social research.* London: Sage.

Hammersley, M. and Atkinson, P. (1995). *Ethnography: principles in practice.* 2nd edn. London: Routledge.

Hansen, J.F. (1976). The anthropologist in the field: scientist, friend and voyeur. In M.A. Rynkiewich and J.P. Spradley (eds). *Ethics and anthropology: dilemmas in fieldwork.* New York: Wiley.

Harrison, B. and Lyon, E.S. (1993). A note on ethical issues in the use of autobiography in sociological research. *Sociology,* 27 (1): 101–109.

Hastrup, K. (1992). Writing ethnography: state of the art. In J. Okely and H. Callaway (eds). *Anthropology and autobiography.* London: Routledge. pp. 116–133.

Hertz, R. (ed.) (1996). Introduction: ethics, reflexivity and voice. *Qualitative Sociology,* 19 (1): 3–9.

Hill, M., Glaser, K. and Harden, J. (1995). A feminist model for ethical decision making. In E.J. Rave and C.C. Larsen (eds). *Ethical decision making in therapy: feminist perspectives.* New York: Guilford Press. pp. 18–37.

Holland, J. and Ramazanoglu (1994). Coming to conclusions: power and inter-pretation in researching young women's sexuality. In M. Maynard and J. Purvis (eds). *Researching women's lives from a feminist perspective.* London: Taylor & Francis. pp. 125–148.

Hornstein, G.A. (1996). The ethics of ambiguity: feminists writing women's lives. In C.E. Franz and A.J. Stewart (eds). *Women creating lives: identities, resilience and resistance.* Boulder: Westview. pp. 51–68.

Hoschild, A. (1979). Emotion talk, feeling rules, and social structure. *American Journal of Sociology,* 85 (3): 551–575.

Hoschild, A. (1983). *The managed heart: commercialization of human feeling.* Berkeley, CA: University of California Press.

Humphreys, L. (1970). *Tearoom trade: impersonal sex in public places.* Chicago: Aldine.

Humphreys, L. (1975). *Tearoom trade: impersonal sex in public places* (enlarged edition). New York: Aldine.

Hunt, S.A. (1984). The development of rapport through the negotiation of gender in field work among police. *Human Organization,* 43, (4): 283–294.

Hunt, S.A. and Benford, R.D. (1997). Dramaturgy and methodology. In G. Miller and R. Dingwall (eds). *Context and method in qualitative research.* London: Sage. pp. 106–118.

Jackson, B. (1987). *Fieldwork.* Chicago: University of Illinois Press.

Jackson, J.E. (1990). 'I am a fieldnote': fieldnotes as a symbol of professional identity. In R. Sanjek (ed.). *Fieldnotes: the makings of anthropology.* New York: Cornell University Press. pp. 3–34.

Jackson, J.E. (1995). 'Déjà entendu': the liminal qualities of anthropological fieldnotes. In J. Van Maanen (ed.). *Representation in ethnography.* Thousand Oaks, CA: Sage. pp. 36–78.

Jacob, E. (1987). Qualitative research traditions: a review. *Review of Educational Research*, 57 (1): 1–50.

Johnson, C.G. (1982). Risks in the publication of fieldwork. In J.E. Sieber (ed.). *The ethics of social research: fieldwork, regulation and publication*. New York: Springer-Verlag.

Johnson, J. M. (1975). *Doing field research*. New York: Free Press.

Jordon, S. and Yeomans, D. (1995). Critical ethnography: problems in contemporary theory and practice. *British Journal of Education*, 19 (3): 389–408.

Kellehear, A. (1993). *The unobtrusive researcher: a guide to methods*. Sydney: Allen and Unwin.

Kellehear, A. (1996). Unobtrusive methods in delicate situations. In J. Daley (ed.). *Ethical intersections: health research, methods and researcher responsibility*. St Leonards: Allen and Unwin. pp. 97–105.

Kelly, L., Burton, S. and Regan, L. (1994). Researching women's lives or studying women's oppression? Reflections on what constitutes feminist research. In M. Maynard and J. Purvis (eds). *Researching women's lives from a feminist perspective*. London: Taylor & Francis. pp. 27–48.

Kelly, L., Regan, L. and Burton, S. (1992). Defending the indefensible? Quantitative methods in feminist research. In H. Hinds, A. Phoenix and J. Stacey (eds). *Working out: new directions for women's studies*. London: Falmer Press. pp. 149–160.

Kidder, L.H. and Judd, C.M. (1986). *Research methods in social relations* (5th edn). New York: CBS Publishing.

Kleinman, S. (1991). Field-workers' feelings. What we feel, who we are, how we analyze. In W.B. Shaffir and R. B. Stebbins (eds). *Experiencing fieldwork: an inside view of qualitative research*. Newbury Park, CA: Sage. pp. 184–195.

Kleinman, S., Copp, M.A. and Henderson, K. A. (1997). Qualitatively different: teaching fieldwork to graduate students. *Journal of Contemporary Ethnography*, 25 (4): 469–499.

Lee, R.M. (1993). *Doing research on sensitive topics*. London: Sage.

Lehnerer, M. (1996). Caring, information control, and emotionality: fieldwork trade-offs. *Qualitative Inquiry*, 2 (3): 337–350.

Liberman, K. (1999). From walkabout to meditation: craft and ethics in field inquiry. *Qualitative Inquiry*, 5 (1): 47–63.

Lincoln, Y.S. (1995). The sixth moment: emerging problems in qualitative research. *Studies in Symbolic Interactionism*, 19: 37–55.

Lincoln, Y.S. (1998). The ethics of teaching qualitative research. *Qualitative Inquiry*, 4 (3): 315–327.

Lincoln, Y.S. and Guba, E.G. (1986). *Naturalistic inquiry*. Thousand Oaks, CA: Sage.

Lipson, J.G. (1989). The use of self in ethnographic research. In J.M. Morse (ed.). *Qualitative nursing research: a contemporary dialogue*. Rockville, MD: Aspen. pp. 61–75.

Lofland, J. and Lofland, L.H. (1995). *Analyzing social settings: a guide to qualitative observation and analysis*. 3rd edn. Belmont, CA: Wadsworth.

Lupton, D. (1998). *The emotional self*. Thousand Oaks, CA: Sage.

Lutz, C. (1995). The gender of theory. In R. Behar and D.A. Gordon (eds). *Women writing culture*. Berkeley, CA: University of California Press. pp. 249–286.

Lyman, S.M. and Scott, M.B. (1975). *The drama of social reality*. New York: Oxford University Press.

McGettigan, T. (1997). Uncorrected insight: metaphor and transcendence 'after truth' in qualitative inquiry. *Qualitative Inquiry*, 3 (3): 366–383.

Malinowski, B. (1922). *Argonauts of the Western Pacific*. London: Routledge.

Manning, P.K. (1995). The challenges of postmodernism. In J. Van Maanen (ed.). *Representation in ethnography*. Thousand Oaks, CA: Sage. pp. 245–272.

Marcus, G. (1998). Past, present and emergent identities: requirements for ethnographies of late twentieth-century modernity worldwide. In S. Lash and J. Friedman (eds). *Modernity & identity*. Oxford: Blackwell. pp. 309–330.

Marcus, G.E. and Fischer, M.M.J. (1986). *Anthropology as cultural critique: an experimental moment in the human science*. Chicago: Chicago University Press.

Mars, G. (1974). Dock pilferage. In P. Rock and M. McIntosh (eds). *Deviance and social control*. London: Tavistock.

Mattingly, C. (1998). *Healing dramas and clinical plots: the narrative structure of experience*. Cambridge: Cambridge University Press.

Matza, D. and Sykes, G. (1957). Techniques of neutralization: a theory of delinquency. *American Sociological Review*, 22: 664–670.

Mead, G.H. (1934). *Self and society*. Chicago: University of Chicago Press.

Mies, M. (1983). Towards a methodology for feminist research. In G. Bowles and R.D. Klein (eds). *Theories of women's studies*. London: Routledge & Kegan Paul. pp. 117–139.

Minichiello, V., Aroni, R., Timewell, E. and Alexander, L. (1997). *In-depth interviewing*. 2nd edn. Melbourne: Longman Cheshire.

Mitchell, R.G. Jr. (1983). *Mountain experience: the psychology of adventure*. Chicago: University of Chicago Press.

Mitchell, R.G. Jr. (1991). Secrecy and disclosure in fieldwork. In W.B. Shaffir and R.A.Stebbins (eds). *Experiencing fieldwork: an inside view of qualitative research*. Newbury Park, CA: Sage.

Morse, J.M. (1994). 'Emerging from the data': the cognitive processes of analysis in qualitative inquiry. In J.M. Morse (ed.). *Critical issues in qualitative research methods*. Thousand Oaks, CA: Sage. pp. 23–43.

Noddings, N. (1984). *Caring*. Berkeley: University of California Press.

Oakley, A. (1981). Interviewing women: a contradiction in terms? In H. Roberts (ed.). *Doing feminist research*. London: Routledge and Kegan Paul, pp. 30–62.

Okely, J. (1992). Anthropology and autobiography: participatory experience and embodied knowledge. In J. Okely and H. Callaway (eds). *Anthropology and autobiography*. New York: Routledge. pp.1–28.

Okun, B.F., Fried, J. and Okun, M.L. (1999). *Understanding diversity: a learning-as-practice primer*. Pacific Grove, CA: Brooks/Cole.

Partridge, W. (1979). Epilogue: ethical dilemmas. In S.T. Kimball and W.L. Partridge (eds). *The craft of community study: fieldwork dialogues*. Gainsville: University Press of Florida, pp. 239–248.

Patai, D. (1991). U.S. academics and third world moment: is ethical research possible? In S.B. Gluck and D. Patai (eds). *Women's words: the feminist practice of oral history*. New York: Routledge. pp. 137–153.

Patton, M.Q. (1990). *Qualitative evaluation and research methods*. 2nd edn. Newbury Park: Sage.

Peace, S. (1993). Negotiating. In P. Shakespeare, D. Atkinson and S. French (eds). *Reflecting on research practice: issues in health and social welfare*. Buckingham: Open University Press. pp. 25–35.

Phoenix. A. (1994). Practising feminist research: the intersection of gender and 'race' in the research process. In M. Maynard and J. Purvis (eds). *Researching women's lives from a feminist perspective*. London: Taylor and Francis. pp. 49–71.

Prideaux, D. (1994). Joining the club: action research and the problem of facilitation. In J.S. Smyth (ed.). *Conference proceedings for the mini-conference, qualitative approaches in educational research*. Flinders University, South Australia. pp. 68–76.

Punch, M. (1986). *The politics and ethics of fieldwork*. Newbury Park, CA: Sage.

Punch, M. (1994). Politics and ethics in qualitative research. In N.K. Denzin and Y.S. Lincoln (eds). *Handbook of qualitative research*. Thousand Oaks, CA: Sage. pp. 83–97.

Ram, M. (1996). Ethnography, ethnicity and work: unpacking the West Midlands clothing industry. In E.S. Lyon and J. Busfield (eds). *Methodological imaginations*. London: Macmillan.

Ramsay, K. (1996). Emotional labour and qualitative research: how I learned not to laugh or cry in the field. In E.S. Lyon and J. Busfield (eds). *Methodological imaginations*. London: Macmillan. pp. 131–146.

Reinharz, S. (1992). *Feminist methods in social research*. New York: Oxford University Press.

Ribbens, J. (1993). Facts or fictions? Aspects of the use of autobiographical writing in undergraduate sociology. *Sociology*, 27 (1): 81–92.

Richardson, L. (1990). Narrative and sociology. *Journal of Contemporary Ethnography*, 19: 116–135.

Richardson, L. (1992). The consequences of poetic representation: writing the other, rewriting the self. In C. Ellis and M.G. Flaherty (eds). *Investigating subjectivity: research on lived experience*. Newbury Park, CA: Sage. pp. 125–137.

Richardson, L. (1994). Writing: a method of inquiry. In N.K. Denzin and Y.S. Lincoln (eds). *Handbook of qualitative research*. Thousand Oaks, CA: Sage. pp. 516–529.

Rosaldo, R. (1994). Subjectivity in social analysis. In S. Seidman (ed.). *The postmodern turn: new perspectives on social theory*. Cambridge: Cambridge University Press. pp. 171–183.

Rynkiewich, M.A. (1976). The underdevelopment of anthropological ethics. In M.A. Rynkiewich and J.P. Spradley (eds). *Ethics and anthropology: dilemmas in fieldwork*. New York: Wiley. pp. 47–60.

Saks, M.J. and Melton, G.B. (1996). Conclusion/Is it possible to legislate morality? Encouraging psychological research contributions to the problem of research ethics. In B.H. Stanley, J.E. Sieber and G.B. Melton (eds). *Research ethics: a psychological approach*. Lincoln: University of Nebraska Press. pp. 225–253.

Schmied, V. (1995). A fine-line: ethical issues in nursing research. Abstract submitted to Research for Practice: Making a Difference International Nursing Conference, Newcastle, Australia, 6–8 July.

Schwandt, T.A. (1995). Thoughts on the moral career of the interpretive inquirer. *Studies in Symbolic Interaction*, 19: 131–140.

Scott, M.B. and Lyman, S.M. (1968). 'Accounts'. *American Sociological Review*, 33: 46–62.

Shakespeare, P. (1993). Performing. In P. Shakespeare, D. Atkinson and S. French (eds). *Reflecting on research practice: issues in health and social welfare*. Buckingham: Open University Press. pp. 95–105.

Sieber, J.E. (1982). *The ethics of social research: fieldwork, regulation, and publication*. New York: Springer-Verlag.

Sieber, J.E. (1996). Introduction/empirical study of ethical issues in psychological research. In B.H. Stanley, J. E. Sieber and G.B. Melton (eds). *Research ethics: a psychological approach*. Lincoln: University of Nebraska Press. pp.1–33.

Sieghart, P. (1982). The data protection debate. In P. Sieghart (ed.). *Microchips with everything*. London: Comedia Publishing Group.

Simon, W. and Gagnon, J.H. (1986). Sexual scripts: permanence and change. *Archives of Sexual Behavior*, 15 (2): 97–120.

Skeggs, B. (1994). Situating the production of feminist ethnography. In M. Maynard and J. Purvis (eds). *Researching women's lives from a feminist perspective*. London: Taylor and Francis. pp. 72–92.

Smith, C.R. (1975). Bereavement: the contribution of phenomenological and existential analysis to a greater understanding of the problem. *British Journal of Social Work*, 5 (1): 75–92.

Spradley, J.P. (1980). *Participant observation*. New York: Holt, Rinehart and Winston.

Stacey, J. (1988). Can there be a feminist ethnography? *Women's Studies International Forum*, 11 (1): 21–27.

Stake, R.E. (1994). Case studies. In N.K. Denzin and Y.S. Lincoln (eds). *Handbook of qualitative research*. Thousand Oaks, CA: Sage. pp. 236–247.

Stanley, L. and Wise, S. (1983). *Breaking out: feminist consciousness and feminist research*. London: Routledge and Kegan Paul.

Stone, G.P. (1962). Appearance and self. In A.M. Rose (ed.). *Human behavior and social processes: an interactionist approach*. London: Routledge and Kegan Paul.

Strauss, A. and Corbin, J. (1990). *Basics of qualitative research: grounded theory procedures and techniques*. Newbury Park, CA: Sage.

Swantz, M. (1996). A personal position paper on participatory research: personal quest for living knowledge. *Qualitative Inquiry*, 2 (1): 120–136.

Taylor, S.J. (1991). Leaving the field: research, relationships, and responsibilities. In W.B. Shaffir and R.A. Stebbins (eds). *Experiencing fieldwork: an inside view of qualitative research*. Newbury Park, CA: Sage. pp. 238–247.

Tesch, R. (1990). *Qualitative research: analysis types and software tools*. Hampshire: Falmer Press.

Thorne, B. (1980). 'You still takin' notes?' Fieldwork and problems of informed consent. *Social Problems*, 27 (3): 284–297.

Thorne, S. (1998). Ethical and representational issues in qualitative secondary analysis. *Qualitative Health Research*, 8 (4): 547–555.

Tourigny, S.C. (1994). Integrating ethics with symbolic interaction: the case of oncology. *Qualitative Health Research*, 4 (2): 163–185.

Turner, V.W. (1969). *The ritual process*. Harmonsdworth: Penguin.

Van Gennep, A. (1960). M.B. Vizedom and G.L. Caffee (trans.). *The rites of passage*. London: Routledge and Kegan Paul.

Van Maanen, J. (1988). *Tales of the field: on writing ethnography*. Chicago: University of Chicago Press.

Van Maanen, J. (1995). An end to innocence: the ethnography of ethnography. In J. Van Maanen (ed.). *Representation in ethnography*. Thousand Oaks, CA: Sage.

Van Velsen, J. (1967). The extended-case method and situational analysis. In A.L. Epstein (ed.). *The craft of anthropology.* London: Tavistock. pp. 129–149.

Wark, M. (1999). Objectivity on the campaign trail. *The Australian,* 27 October: 34.

Wax, M.L. (1977). On fieldworkers and those exposed to fieldwork: federal regulations and moral issues. *Human Organization,* 36: 321–329.

Wax, M.L. (1980). Paradoxes of 'consent' to the practice of fieldwork. *Social Problems,* 27 (3): 272–283.

Wax, M.L. (1982). Research reciprocity rather than informed consent in fieldwork. In J.E. Sieber (ed.). *The ethics of social research: fieldwork, regulation and publication.* New York: Springer-Verlag.

Whyte, W.F. (1955). *Street corner society: the social structure of an Italian slum.* Chicago: University of Chicago Press.

Wiley, J. (1990). The dramatisation of emotions in practice and theory: emotion work and emotion roles in a therapeutic community. *Sociology of Health and Illness,* 12 (2): 127–150.

Wilkins, R. (1993). Taking it personally: a note on emotion and autobiography. *Sociology,* 27 (1): 93–100.

Williams, A. (1990). Reading feminism in fieldnotes. In L. Stanley (ed.). *Feminist praxis: research, theory and epistemology in feminist sociology.* London: Routledge. pp. 253–261.

Wolcott, H.F. (1995). *The art of fieldwork.* Walnut Creek, CA: Alta Mira Press.

Wolf, D.L. (ed.) (1996). Situating feminist dilemmas in fieldwork. In D.L. Wolf (ed.). *Feminist dilemmas in fieldwork.* Colorado: Westview Press. pp. 1–55.

Wolf, M. (1992). *A thrice-told tale: feminism, postmodernism, and ethnographic responsibility.* Stanford, CA: Stanford University Press.

Wong, L. Mun (1998). The ethics of rapport: institutional safeguards, resistance, and betrayal. *Qualitative Inquiry,* 4 (2): 178–199.

Woods, P. (1990). Educational ethnography in Britain. In R.R. Sherman and R.B. Webb (eds). *Qualitative research in education: focus and methods.* Brighton: Falmer Press.

Woods, P. (1992). Symbolic interactionism: theory and method. In M.D. LeCompte, W.L. Milroy and J. Preissle (eds). *The Handbook of qualitative research in education.* New York: Academic Press. pp. 338–403.

Young, E.H. and Lee, R. (1996). Fieldworker feelings as data: 'emotion work' and 'feeling rules' in first person accounts of sociological fieldwork. In V. James and J. Gabe (eds). *Health and the sociology of emotions,* Oxford: Blackwell. pp. 97–113.

Index

field notes, 11, 12, 146–76
   and construction of social reality,
      148–51
   liminal quality of, 165–72
Fine, G.A., 199, 200
Finnegan, R., 195, 196–7, 200, 209
first-person accounts, 180
Fischer, M.M.J., 12, 179, 182, 183
Foddy, W., 80, 159
Fontana, A., 85, 181
Fordham, G., 99
French, S., 123, 198
Fretz, R.I., 166, 181
Frey, J.H., 85
Fried, J., 40, 43, 48, 56, 59
friendship or friend-like relations, 9,
      29, 30, 50, 53, 54, 109, 112, 113–16,
      134, 138–9, 145, 191
front regions, 69
'fronts' creation of, 49

Garfinkel, H., 6, 33, 100, 156
gatekeepers, 2, 123–7
   academic, 127–32
gender, 98, 99
Gergen, K.J., 152
Glaser, K., 3, 17, 121, 136, 144
Glassner, B., 41
Glucksmann, M., 139
Goffman, E., 32, 34, 36, 38, 46, 47–8,
      96, 126–7, 152, 158–9, 199–200,
      201
   on back regions and front regions,
      8, 69
   concept of moral career, 5, 18–19,
      21, 35, 72, 172
   on moral and instrumental
      demands, 7
   on self-identity, 22
'going native', 9, 25, 54, 105–6, 108–9,
      140, 141
Gold, R.L., 104–5
Gordon, D.A., 123
Greene, B., 131, 132, 134, 135
grounded theory, 103
Guba, E.G., 9, 105, 173
'guilty knowledge', 8, 22, 52, 67,
      199–200
Gumbrium, J.F., 11, 186, 187, 212

Hall, J.R., 159
Hammersley, M., 102, 105, 106, 124–5,
      126, 180–1, 197
Hansen, J.F., 9, 29, 30, 68, 115, 196, 210
Harden, J., 3, 17, 121, 136, 144
harming, 195, 214
Harrison, B., 170, 191, 192
Hastrup, K., 65
Hertz, R., 181, 215
Hill, M., 3, 17, 121, 136, 144
Holstein, J.A., 11, 186, 187, 212
Hornstein, G.A., 13, 190, 191–2, 202–3
Hoschild, A., 12, 152, 153
human rights, 1
Humphreys, L., 68, 84, 85, 95, 97
Hunt, S.A., 7, 10, 34, 41, 42, 48, 49, 62,
      63, 140, 167, 195

impression management, 6, 7, 34, 38,
      48–9, 60, 63, 127, 158
   textual, 177–206
indeterminancy repertoire, 88
informed consent see under consent
inner 'I', 61–2
instrumental demands, 7
interests
   conflict of, 9, 11, 29, 30, 97, 109, 113,
      121, 196, 210
   variety of parties with, 195
interpersonal scripts, 43–4, 45–6
interviewing
   effect of researcher's presence
      during, 173
   interviewee-guided, 138, 174
   structured, 115
intimacy, paradox of, 53

Jackson, B., 103
Jackson, J.E., 11, 12, 150, 165, 166,
      168–9, 170, 171, 172
Johnson, C.G., 130, 203–4
Johnson, J.M., 107, 109, 154, 166, 168
Judd, C.M., 121

Kellehear, A., 4, 133, 144, 194, 214
Kelly, L., 109, 110
Kidder, L.H., 121

leaving the field, 141–2
Lee, R., 12, 112, 117, 153–4, 157, 175,
      176, 188, 204